CHANGING
Children's
BEHAVIOR

by changing the
PEOPLE, PLACES, and ACTIVITIES
in their lives

Also from Boys Town Press

Teaching Social Skills to Youth

No Room for Bullies: From the Classroom to Cyberspace

Common Sense Parenting

Common Sense Parenting of Toddlers and Preschoolers

Who's Raising Your Child? Battling the Marketers for Your Child's Heart and Soul

Fathers, Come Home

Good Night, Sweet Dreams, I Love You: Now Get into Bed and Go to Sleep!

Tools for Teaching Social Skills in School

Parenting to Build Character in Your Teen

Practical Tools for Foster Parents

Angry Kids, Frustrated Parents

Safe and Effective Secondary Schools

The Well-Managed Classroom

Treating Youth with DSM-IV Disorders: The Role of Social Skill Instruction

Unmasking Sexual Con Games

Skills for Families, Skills for Life

For a free Boys Town Press catalog, call 1-800-282-6657, or visit www.boystownpress.org

CHANGING
Children's
BEHAVIOR

by changing the
PEOPLE, PLACES, and ACTIVITIES
in their lives

by
RICHARD L. MUNGER, Ph.D.

BOYS
TOWN
PRESS

BOYS TOWN, NEBRASKA

Changing Children's Behavior by Changing
the People, Places, and Activities in Their Lives

Published by the Boys Town Press
Boys Town, Nebraska 68010

Boys Town Press is the publishing division
of Girls and Boys Town, the original Father
Flanagan's Boys' Home.

Publisher's Cataloging in Publication

Munger, Richard L., 1951-
     Changing children's behavior by changing the people, places,
     and activities in their lives / Richard L. Munger. -- 1st ed. -- Boys
     Town, NE : Boys Town Press, 2005.

          p. ; cm.

     Includes index.
     ISBN: 1-889322-68-7
     ISBN-13: 978-1-889322-68-1

          1. Child development. 2. Problem children--Behavior
     modification. 3. Behavior disorders in children--Prevention.
     4. School environment. 5. Ecopsychiatry. I. Title.

RJ506.P63 M86 2005
618.92/89--dc22   0508

10 9 8 7 6 5 4 3 2 1

To Bun

Table of Contents

ACKNOWLEDGMENTS   vii

PREFACE   ix

CHAPTER 1   Children's Environments and Their Pathways   1

CHAPTER 2   Patterns of Time Use in Childhood   11

CHAPTER 3   The Importance of "Flow" in Children's Lives   25

CHAPTER 4   Home Setting   37

CHAPTER 5   Neighborhood Setting   49

CHAPTER 6   School, Co-Curricular, and   59
             Service-Learning Settings

CHAPTER 7   After-School Settings   77

CHAPTER 8   Electronic Setting   87

CHAPTER 9   Friends Setting   107

CHAPTER 10   Faith Setting   121

CHAPTER 11   Work Setting   137

CHAPTER 12   Recreational and Leisure Settings   149

CHAPTER 13   Sports Settings   167

CHAPTER 14   Creating a Lifetime of Enthusiasm for Sports   187

CHAPTER 15   Promoting a Lifestyle of   199
             Vigorous Physical Activity

CHAPTER 16   Examining Children's Lifestyle Profiles   209

CHAPTER 17   Professionals' Involvement in   231
             Arranging Lifestyle Activities

CHAPTER 18   Finding the Balanced Lifestyle   243

ATOGAKI   A Japanese-Style Afterword   253

APPENDIX   Creating Environmental Opportunities   267
             for Children

ABOUT THE AUTHOR   281

INDEX   283

Acknowledgments

ALTHOUGH I NEVER KNEW ROGER BARKER, THE LATE University of Kansas Professor of Psychology, this book is about his ideas. It did not escape my notice that this book will be published in proximity to the hundredth anniversary of Roger Barker's birth. Environmental psychologist Robert Bechtel argues that over the course of history the three great revolutions in thinking were the Copernican, the Darwinian, and the ecological-environmental paradigm. Roger Barker was the first to scientifically demonstrate the inextricable nature of environment and behavior. We have only begun to mine the contributions Roger Barker has made to the understanding of human behavior. Future generations will be challenged to apply his work for the betterment of children and families in our society.

During my 30-year career in public community mental health, I have been privileged to study with or work alongside of some of the most capable professionals in the field. These persons have left their mark not only on the field of children's mental health, but also on me and, thereby, in this book: Al Cain, Saul Cooper, and Allen Menlo at the University of Michigan; Jerome Hanley at the South Carolina Department of Mental Health; Lenore Behar at the North Carolina Division of Mental Health; Scott Henggeler at the Medical University of South Carolina; and Naleen Andrade at the University of Hawaii. These individuals embody mental health professionals as keepers of hope, honoring clients' struggles while appreciating their goodness and potential.

I also would like to acknowledge the University of Michigan's Educational Psychology Program. In the era in which I attended the program, I was fortunate to benefit from its comprehensive perspective of studying childhood. While most psychology programs narrow the study of children into niches, such as pediatric, clinical, school, and developmental psychology, Michigan's program encouraged the need to understand children across all of the domains of their lives. At Michigan, too, I had the good fortune to study under the tutelage of Bill Morse – a more compassionate and brilliant teacher I do not know.

I would like to thank the librarians at the Mountain Area Health Education Center in Asheville, North Carolina, for assistance in obtaining the voluminous literature I reviewed for this book, as well as consultation regarding technical documentation.

I am grateful to Julie Corey and Reverend Howard Hanger for permission to reproduce in this book the touching vignettes about their children.

Special thanks to Tom Bensman for his splendid editorial assistance on the book. The subject of this book is much less clearly articulated in the literature than traditional approaches to working with children. Therefore, much of my responsibility is one of translation. My task is to bridge the gaps between our familiar view of childhood and unfamiliar conceptions about children. This is Tom's fifth book with me and he has been a godsend in helping me to translate unfamiliar concepts in a way that can be of practical use to people.

Thanks, too, to Barbara Lonnborg at Boys Town Press for the final editorial recommendations which brought the book to fruition.

And finally, my heartfelt appreciation to the many parents and children who sat with me over the years, facing the challenges of growing up and living together as families. Their bravery will always inspire me!

Preface

THIS BOOK IS ABOUT THE PATHWAYS OF CHILDHOOD. Children confront many possible paths throughout life, and each path presents a unique mix of people, places, and activities. Do I play a musical instrument or play basketball? Do I hang out with this crowd or with my neighbor friends? Do I go to a large public high school or a small, religiously affiliated school? Each choice shapes a child's life both by bringing the advantages – and disadvantages – of the option that is chosen and by eliminating the disadvantages – and advantages – of the options not chosen. When a decision is made, one path or the other, the possibilities for particular consequences are often set. Leaving this journey to chance may result in good things, but it also may result in a child descending a spiral pathway away from growth and success.

Parents, teachers, and professional counselors can be guiding forces in helping children find particular pathways that will improve their chances of arriving at desirable places. This guidance can take the form of encouragement or indirect manipulation. The assumption here is that knowledge about optional pathways in a child's life, *lifestyles*, if you will, can guide those that are helping children learn to be successful human beings. In this book, we will explore the pathways whereby children become motivated, compassionate, competent adults.

The environments that children inhabit every day have been studied by researchers; the family, school, work and relationships with friends have been the topic of numerous investigations. But the challenge of this volume is to fit together *all* of the environments of childhood to help us understand and improve the quality of a child's life. Also, most of the writings about children's environments have not been written for a general audience, and when they have, it has been on narrower topics such as the effects of the media or the effects of "over-scheduling" children with activities. Furthermore, scholarly presentations about children's environments, such as the seminal work of Mihaly Csikszentmihalyi and Reed Larson, have not widely penetrated the curricula of graduate professional schools. So the challenge of this book is to integrate all of the life spaces of childhood, and to present the concepts in a way that is informative to both parents and professionals.

I believe passionately that adults can make an extraordinary difference in the lives of children when armed with relatively simple knowledge about children's environments. My assumption is that the more parents know and understand, the more flexible they can be in their decision making. For professional counselors, the hope is that they can build on the viewpoints described in this book to develop more effective approaches for helping children and families.

In the case of children who have significant behavioral problems, lifestyle change calls for professionally oriented interventions that increase the child's involvement in positive environments. Environmental interventions may be the sole focus of professional intervention; in other situations, environmental interventions may supplement other psychologically oriented strategies. The environmental interventions described in this book are typically not the only interventions made with children. My discussion somewhat artificially removes them from their full context. In most situations, an environmental modification is used as part of a broader intervention plan. Indeed, much can be achieved through environmental change alone, but often traditional individual change techniques (e.g., cognitive behavior modification, family therapy) are also needed.[1]

This book is organized into 18 chapters. Chapter 1 presents the concept of "behavior settings," which are the places where children spend time, and typically interact with other children and adults. You will discover that children's behaviors settings are often more important factors in shaping children's behavior than are their personalities. These behavior settings can greatly influence how easy or difficult it is to help children develop the competencies for successful adulthood. Chapter 2 explores a fundamental principle behind the methods in this book: How children spend their waking hours defines the kind of developmental experiences they will have. We will pay special attention to how children can spend time in environments and activities conductive to healthy development. The concept of "flow" in the lives of children is introduced in Chapter 3. Flow is a state of pleasure derived from achievement in an activity. As much as we can, we should structure children's activities to foster the experience of flow, because flow activities cause youth to come alive in ways that rarely happen in other activities. Chapters 4 through 13 discuss each of the 10 major environments in which children spend their time:

- Home Setting
- Neighborhood Setting
- School, Co-Curricular, and Service-Learning Settings
- After-School Settings
- Electronic Setting
- Friends Setting
- Faith Setting
- Work Setting
- Recreational and Leisure Settings
- Sports Settings

All of these are real settings – actual physical places – except two: the electronic environment and friends. I have elevated these two "developmental factors" to the status of settings because each exerts a powerful influence in particular environments. Sports, which can overlap with the recreational and leisure settings, also have been given their own chapter because of their prominence and often unique power in children's lives. After a discussion of each environment, I've included a "quiz" at the end of the chapter to help parents make the concepts practical in terms of their own child and family situation.

Because sports have generated so much controversy about their potential negative effects on youth, I have devoted Chapter 14 to addressing those controversies, and I offer some thoughts on how to ensure that sports participation is a positive experience. As I wrote about sports, I became more and more convinced of the critical importance of physical activity in children's lives. Then, as I attempted to integrate information about exercise into the sports chapter, I concluded that it deserved its own chapter. So, while physical activity is not technically an environment – it is associated with recreational pursuits – I devote Chapter 15 to the important role of exercise and physical education in healthy lifestyles.

Using the results of the Chapters 4 through 13 quizzes, Chapter 16 helps you develop a profile of a child's environmental strengths and weaknesses, with a summary of action steps you can take to help change the child's environments for the better.

For youths who come to the attention of professional counselors because of behavior problems, likewise, there is an important place for assessing children's lifestyles. In Chapter 17, we'll look specifically at professionals' involvement in arranging lifestyle activities. Some people argue that the hectic lifestyles of families are caused by *too many* activities, so in Chapter 18 I conclude with some advice on how to find a balanced lifestyle.

The Atogaki at the end of the book is a Japanese-style "Afterword" that freely admits that the ideas presented in this book are not the final word on the subject. I summarize the main points of the book, present criticisms of some ideas, and attempt to address the criticisms.

One thing is guaranteed: as you read this book, your perception of children's environments will change forever. You will come to see children's environments as one of the most powerful tools for transforming children's lives available today.

A Note on Language and Format

I am in total sympathy with the view that women feel put down by the use of "he" in reference to a person in general. However, I find a "himself-herself" in the middle of a sentence to be disruptive. Until someone comes up with a set of gender-neutral pronouns, there is no good solution to the problem. Therefore, I have chosen to deal with the problem by making general references in female terms in some instances, and in male terms in others, randomly alternating throughout the book.

I have used the terms *youths* and *children* throughout the book to refer to children and adolescents in general. When the content is relevant to a particular developmental period, such as elementary-age children or teenagers, I use those specific terms. For the most part, the span of childhood covered by this book is school-age children, typically ages 5 to 18. When the discussion pertains to younger children, ages birth to 5, I note it. Some find the terms "kids" and "youngsters" to be disrespectful, although I personally find their use to be affectionate. Except in quotations, I have eliminated them.

I use the word *parent* throughout the book to indicate the child's primary caretaker. The term covers biological parents, stepparents, foster parents, adoptive parents, grandparents, guardians, and all such adults with primary care-taking responsibility.

To help the reader navigate this book more easily, I've highlighted in bold type key concepts, salient quotations, illustrative vignettes, and important research findings. In the chapters that address the 10 "environments," I've included a "Summing Up" section at the end of each chapter. This brief section reviews main points, with an emphasis on action steps for parents and others to consider. In all cases, I've attempted to keep the chapters short, crisp and to the point. There is an immense amount of knowledge about children's environments. Any effort to cover, or even just briefly review, all the available information would inevitably overwhelm the reader. I have tried to present the most practical, salient issues, while accepting the fact that virtually all knowledge in this area of study is tentative and conditional. The ideas herein are "good" and "true" only to the extent that they are useful to the reader.

Finally, I chose to footnote references in the book as opposed to using scholarly citations. The intended audience is broader than just professionals, and I find footnotes to be less scholarly and more user-friendly, allowing the reader to locate the source of information easily. The liberal use of footnotes reflects the fact that this is more a work of synthesis than one of creation.

---

[1] Kemp, S., Whittaker, J., & Tracy, E. (1997). *Person-environment practice: The social ecology of interpersonal helping.* New York: Aldine De Gruyter.

CHAPTER 1

Children's Environments and Their Pathways

I N 1947, ROGER BARKER HAD A WILD IDEA. BARKER was a professor of psychology at the University of Kansas. He convinced the small town of Oskaloosa, Kansas (population 762) to serve as a field station for the study of the psychological habitats of children. The novel idea was to record the minute-by-minute lives of many of the approximately 100 children living in Oskaloosa. With help from graduate students and the cooperation of the local residents, he documented the daily lives of the children, recording everything they did. He followed them from their homes into the schools and community and observed all of their activities. This might sound rather strange, having an adult hovering around writing about everything a child does. Weren't the children's natural behaviors inhibited by this constant presence? Of course they were initially, but the observers refused to interact with the children, and after a while, with instruction, the children learned to ignore the observers.[1]

Barker's observations were thorough and detailed. Activities often blurred together so Barker used two observers. He called this method of recording children's behavior *collecting a specimen record*. It is similar to a doctor collecting specimens from a person or animal. However, in this case, they were specimens of behavior, and they were collected

1

from the natural environment. Barker published the first book-length specimen record as *One Boy's Day* in 1951. Over the years, he collected about 20 specimen records, each one detailing the minute-to-minute activities of a child over a period of several days.

After looking at the data, Barker came to a rather surprising conclusion: the children's settings were more important factors in determining their behavior than their personalities. So, Barker discontinued his observation of individual children because he found the "behavior setting" to be a more promising focus of observation.

As he and his observers watched children live minute-to-minute in neighborhoods, on playing fields, in churches, at schools, and other places, Barker realized that individuals in particular settings exhibit fairly predictable behavior patterns. When a child enters one of Barker's "behavior settings" – a classroom, a gymnasium, a playground – everything in that environment presses behavior in the direction of conforming to behavior that is typical for that particular environment. As Barker put it, "When in church, people behave church." The fancy term for this is the *principle of progressive conformity*.[2]

For someone sitting in a church pew, spiritual reflection is easy. That same person sitting in the baseball stands finds reflection more difficult, but yelling loudly is made easy. Each place offers opportunities for specific behaviors, while placing limits on others. The physical location, including the people we are with, affects our immediate behavior, as well as longer-term development if we sit in that pew a lot.

In this book, we will be mapping out the behavior settings of childhood and adolescence. My goal is to describe the major developmental contexts that make up children's lives. "Context is the water in which we fish swim."[3] Take, for example, these two behavior contexts: a child slumped in front of the TV watching cartoons, and the same child building a volcano model at a Saturday science event at the local nature center. Both are developmental contexts. Is one developmentally better than the other? We will try to answer that question in this book.

Taking a Look Back

How do children grow to become motivated, compassionate, competent adults? Let's think about that for a minute. In your mind's eye, take a trip back into your childhood. Think of a period of time about which you still carry vivid memories, perhaps when you were around 9 or 10, or when you were a teenager, around 14 or 15. Begin by identifying your life-spaces – the principal areas or contexts where you carried out your life. Typically, these include your home, the neighborhood, and your school. There also may be other areas, such as church life, or your parent's place of work, or even your own place of work. Revisit each of these life spaces to reacquaint yourself with your pre-adult life.

Now that you have revisited the general *geography* of your child-hood, think about a specific place that made you feel competent and good about yourself. Try to focus on just one place. What was it about that special place that made it so positive for you? Did you learn something there? Were you challenged? Were you free from stress there? Try to recapture the feeling of that supportive place.

Now shift your mind's eye to a place from your childhood that was not so positive for you. Pick just one and think back. What was it about the place that made you feel uncomfortable or not good about yourself? Did you experience failure there? Did the place lack supportive people? Were you stressed? Having reacquainted yourself with your own childhood experiences, what conclusions can you draw about the environments in which children grow up?

Children learn to be healthy, fully functioning human beings by interacting meaningfully with diverse people in their everyday environments. There are many examples of developmentally healthy environments. Families where all the family members sit down to eat dinner and share the activities of the day. Neighborhoods where a child shovels snow from a neighbor's driveway for extra money and builds a tree fort with friends on a vacant lot. Schools where a child learns among diverse peers and is encouraged to "hustle" by a coach in after-school volleyball. Communities where a child works on a building project for the Boys Club and takes music lessons from a retired musician. Church groups in which teenagers eat Sunday dinner with a friendly group of peers who discuss their frustration about teachers at school. Communities where a child can participate in a hospital volunteer program or get a job at a local ice cream parlor and learn that certain social graces come first, even when someone is discourteous to you. These are all developmentally healthy environments of childhood.

> So how do youths become psychologically vigorous adults, who are honest, take responsibility for their actions, and learn from their mistakes? These are some of the characteristics of a successful adult and children will succeed only if we "give" them opportunities to develop these capacities. These types of traits are not transmitted to children only by instruction but rather are also learned during their participation in developmentally healthy activities in supportive environments. This is how children learn to function well. They take advantage of the competence-building opportunities in their everyday environments.

What Is a Supportive Environment?

Wild animals in captivity live and flourish best when their environments approximate the natural surroundings from which they come. For instance, animals that live naturally on the plains are more healthy and contented when they are not confined to cages, but are placed in open areas where they can roam at will – in other words, where their environment supports, even encourages their natural, healthy behavior. Animals that live in caves or dens need a place of solitude where they can feel protected. The most successful zookeepers structure the optimal environments for meeting the innate needs of those in their care. In this respect, parents and professional counselors who use environmental strategies for children share similar goals and methods.

Let's clarify a little terminology here. When professional counselors talk about the *environment* of children and adolescents, they usually are referring to the effects of the child's immediate caregivers and close friends (e.g., "This child lives in an abusive environment"). However, in this book we are using the term quite differently. University of

North Carolina professor Mark Fraser notes that the environments of childhood can be thought of as consisting of interrelated and often nested parts.[4] Children usually live in a family. A family lives in a neighborhood. As they grow up, children become involved with school, and later perhaps with a job in the community. Each context involves a set of activities and resources, including people, within a specific social and physical space. Children develop their personhood in these environments through interactions with parents, brothers and sisters, friends, teachers, coaches, ministers, neighbors, and a variety of others who, sometimes for better and sometimes for worse, affect their lives. This "person-in-environment" perspective, as Fraser calls it, is at the heart of what we're talking about here.

The approach to child psychology presented in this book is based on the belief that it is usually easier and more effective to change the environment of a child than it is to alter the child's personality, because the environment is a known, visible quantity and producing concrete changes is fairly straightforward. The acclaimed psychologist Mary Pipher puts it this way:

"A good rule of thumb is that life is more important than therapy. Friends, family, work, school, vacations, and ball games are more important than therapy, because the goal of good therapy is to get them into healthy, normal activity."[5]

So, along with exploring the various environments of childhood, we'll also be identifying *environmental modifications* that can help optimize children's healthy growth and development. Moving to a new neighborhood, or attending a different school can change dramatically a child's experiences and the course of the child's life. Implementing such major environmental changes in a child's life can be a little frightening, however, especially since it is so hard to be sure in advance what effects your choices will have. But this is where Roger Barker's findings can bring reassurance – the "right" environment will generally bring about desired effects.

A behavior setting (or environment) – that is, a place where activities occur – exerts an *environmental press*, which is the combined influence of various forces working in a particular setting to shape the behavior of individuals in that setting. According to psychologist James Garbarino, environmental press arises from circumstances confronting and surrounding the individual – circumstances that generate psychosocial momentum tending to guide the individual in a particular direction.[6] Most people understand the concept of peer pressure. Well, here we're talking about environmental pressure. Helping a troubled youth, then, can involve linking the child with an environmental network of behavior settings that facilitate specific, desired behavior changes.

Pathways to Success or Failure

In the early 1960s, Americans huddled around television sets to watch the first space flights return to earth. Reporter Walter Cronkite described the tense moments of re-entry, when the space capsule had to penetrate the earth's atmosphere at the precise trajectory or, if its path veered only slightly, face fiery destruction. The critical path, or trajectory, meant a course with the proper angle for the crucial dynamics of flight to unfold – a corridor of safety.

Just as a space capsule must maneuver through the invisible forces of space, children must navigate through their life spaces. They, too, are on trajectories, or pathways – some that offer safe passage to positive opportunities, and others that lead to failure and negative outcomes. Finding the proper trajectories for children to follow through their life spaces might be just as important as it is with a space capsule. The case study below, which contrasts the lives of two young adolescents, depicts how the elements of particular settings, as a result of their positions in the environment, influence behaviors.

Anthony is 13 years old and lives with two brothers and his single mother in a two-bedroom apartment. His mother has physically abused him in the past, and Anthony was once placed in a foster home for nine months. His mother has only one friend, a neighbor with whom she is very close, but the relationship limits her involvement with others. She works the 3 p.m. to 11 p.m. shift at a local hospital, which means that Anthony is usually unsupervised after school and has little opportunity for activities outside his neighborhood.

Unsuccessful in sports in a large, competitive junior high school, Anthony has befriended several neighborhood boys who spend their after-school hours "hanging out." As a result, Anthony has begun to skip school and experiment with drugs. Excessive TV viewing prevents Anthony from extending his friendship network. Anthony has recently been reported to local juvenile justice authorities for breaking into a neighbor's house.

Another youth, Tony, appears to live in an environment similar to Anthony's: he also is 13 years old and lives with two brothers and his single mother in a two-bedroom apartment. His mother also has physically abused him in the past and he also was placed in a foster home for a few months. Tony's environmental circumstances, however, place him on a different trajectory. Tony has a pet to care for after school. A neighbor, who breeds dogs, acts as a mentor and friend to him. His school is small and needs every student to participate in activities in order to have sufficient manpower for sports teams and other groups. Therefore, Tony is involved in school plays, the band, and the soccer team. The school also encourages involvement in community activities and – with the help of funding from a local church that Tony's family attends on Sundays – got Tony enrolled in a Tae Kwon Do class. The class has helped Tony with unresolved angry feelings he harbored because of his mother's physical abuse. Tony and his mother and brothers participate in a family softball club sponsored by the hospital – which offers flexible work hours for his mother, enabling her to be at home most evenings and to broaden her friendship network.

There are two very different outcomes for Anthony and Tony. While their life circumstances are similar, Anthony's environmental circumstances have put him on a negative pathway, while Tony's environmental factors put him on a more positive trajectory. As you can see, then, relatively small events and alterations may push children down one path rather than another, shape their inclinations, and ultimately, determine the quality of their life experiences. Anthony's and Tony's lives are examples of environmental distinctions that alter the developmental paths of children. One of the goals of this book is to show parents how to help children engage in positive environmental trajectories.

Childhood and adolescence are times when many developmental trajectories become established. It is important that the environments that children spend their time in are structured in ways that optimize the youths' chances to learn the skills that will help them become healthy, successful adults.[7] Effective environments for children promote the development of competence and provide opportunities for beneficial relationships.[8] According to Claremont Graduate University psychologist Mihaly Csikszentmihalyi, "the first step in improving the quality of life consists in engineering daily activities so that one gets the most rewarding experiences from them."[9]

The processes leading to particular outcomes for children and adolescents are not completely predictable, and specific outcomes are rarely linked to a single cause. Instead, the pathways leading to an end point of failure – or to successful transition into adulthood – involve many factors in the environment interacting with the psychological and physiological characteristics of the individual.[10]

Further, just looking at the environmental effects alone on child and adolescent behavior is not a simple task. Some effects are directly attributable to the environment, while others influence youths indirectly. Let's take the faith environment as an example. Research indicates that youth who participate in religious activities get intoxicated less often. The influence of religion is direct and fairly straightforward. With indirect effects, the influence is more difficult to demonstrate. For instance, here is an illustrative fictional study from the National Study of Youth and Religion: Religious service attendance is found to lack any *direct* effect on reckless driving in late adolescence. However, other research suggests that parental religiosity affects a number of variables, suggesting that the influence of religion on reckless driving is not absent, but rather indirect. For example, religion influences the extent of parental monitoring, as well as a teenager's choice of friends, and then these in turn affect the likelihood of reckless driving. Therefore, religion has an *indirect* effect on reckless driving via its influence on friendships and parenting practices.[11] The multi-layered contexts of children's lives makes the understanding of environmental influence a great challenge!

In this chapter, I have emphasized that the life courses of children may be explained in large measure by circumstances within their environments. The next chapter presents a fundamental principle behind the ideas in this book: how we use time in our lives deeply affects how our lives turn out, or – as is often said – we are what we do. How children spend their waking hours in various environments defines their circumstances and the kind of developmental experiences they will have. I will pay special attention to how children can spend time in environments and activities that promote healthy development.

---

[1] Bechtel, R. (1996). *Environment & behavior: An introduction.* Thousand Oaks, CA: Sage.

[2] Garbarino, J. (1992). *Children and families in the social environment* (2nd ed.). New York: Aldine De Gruyter.

[3] Trickett, E. (1966). A future for community psychology: The contexts of diversity and the diversity of contexts. *American Journal of Community Psychology, 24*, 209-229. p. 226.

[4] Fraser, M. (1997). *Risk and resilience in childhood: An ecological perspective.* Washington, D.C.: NASW Press.

[5] Pipher, M. (1997). *The shelter of each other: Rebuilding our families.* New York: Ballantine, 1997. p. 130.

[6] Garbarino, J. (1992). *Children and families in the social environment* (2nd ed.). Hawthorne, NY: Aldine De Gruyter.

[7] Institute of Medicine (1998). *Protecting youth at work: Health, safety, and development of working children and adolescents in the United States.* Washington, DC: National Academy Press.

[8] Kemp, S., Whittaker, J., & Tracy, E. (1997). *Person-environment practice: The social ecology of interpersonal helping.* New York: Aldine De Gruyter.

[9] Csikszentmihalyi, M. (1997). *Finding flow: The psychology of engagement with everyday life.* New York: Basic Books. p. 39-40.

[10] Burt, M., Resnick, G., & Novick, E. (1998). *Building supportive communities for at-risk adolescents: It takes more than services.* Washington, D.C.: American Psychological Association.

[11] Regnerus, M., Smith, C., & Fritsch, M. (2003). *Religion in the lives of American adolescents: A review of the literature.* Chapel Hill, NC: National Study of Youth and Religion.

CHAPTER 2

Patterns of Time Use in Childhood

O BVIOUSLY, HOW WE USE OUR TIME IS IMPORTANT in our lives, and particularly so in childhood, when habits are being formed. Time-use patterns become habits, and these habits become the stuff of daily experience. How do your children spend their time? Do they invest it in activities that they are passionate about or squander it in empty pursuits? Every decision has implications for the quality of a child's life. How youths spend their waking hours defines the kinds of developmental experiences they will have. According to the largest survey of adolescents ever conducted, the *National Longitudinal Study of Adolescent Health,* how young people spend their free time is a critical factor in reducing risky behaviors.[1]

Time can be viewed as a scarce resource that should not be wasted or as a plentiful asset. Children who have been socialized to see time as a precious resource have learned about the nature of time through subtle patterns of family interactions or by direct statements about the best ways to spend time. In this chapter, we will look at how children invest the limited time that they have. (Take a look at "How Precious Is Time?" on page 12, for an inspiring insight about time.

There are approximately 16 waking hours each day that are available to youth, or 112 hours a week. Each child must choose how

How Precious Is Time?[2]

Imagine there is a bank that credits your account each morning with $86,400. It carries over no balance from day to day. Every evening it deletes whatever part of the balance you failed to use during the day. What would you do? Draw out every cent, of course!!!

Each of us has such a bank. Its name is TIME. Every morning, it credits you with 86,400 seconds. Every night it writes it off, as failed to invest to good purpose. It carries over no balance. It allows no overdraft. Each day it opens a new account for you. Each night it burns the remains of the day.

If you fail to use the day's deposits, the loss is yours. There is no going back. There is no drawing against the "tomorrow." You must live in the present on today's deposits. Invest it so as to get from it the utmost in health, happiness and success! The clock is running. Make the most of today.

To realize the value of ONE YEAR, ask a student who failed a grade. To realize the value of ONE MONTH, ask a mother who gave birth prematurely. To realize the value of ONE WEEK, ask the editor of a newspaper. To realize the value of ONE HOUR, ask the lovers who are waiting to meet. To realize the value of ONE MINUTE, ask a person who missed a train. To realize the value of ONE SECOND, ask a person who just avoided an accident. To realize the value of ONE MILLISECOND, ask the person who won a silver medal in the Olympics.

Treasure every moment that you have! And treasure it more because you shared it with someone special, special enough to spend your time with. And remember that time waits for no one. Yesterday is history. Today is a gift. That's why it's called the present!!

to fill approximately one-quarter of these hours, that is, time not devoted to school, chores, eating, or health maintenance activities, that can be used at his discretion. A child who spends most of his discretionary time watching television will develop different habits of action than a child who spends more time with neighbor friends or practicing a musical instrument.

In today's society, many children's free-time schedules are filled with developmentally "empty" activities, such as watching TV or hanging out with friends. Educator Reginald Clark compares such activities to a poor diet, and the results can be similar too.[3] "Twinkies-chips-and-candy"-type activities do not promote healthy psychosocial development. For adolescents, who have lived less than one-fifth of their lifetime, time appears to be a free resource with little consequence for making unwise choices about how it is spent. Parents and teachers must convey a strong message to youth that the balanced use of time is essential.

What is a balanced time-diet? Consider the following classification that Professor James Bruno at the UCLA Graduate School of Education has developed around the four principle ways that people use time:[4]

Achievement-directed time. This is time spent acquiring information skills and life experience in order to later sell one's time (that is, to make a living). Examples of these types of activities include studying, doing chores, learning a trade, or acquiring some other marketable skill. Achievement-directed time is used to achieve outer world goals such as money, status, power, position, and in the case of children, grades.

People-directed time. This is time spent acquiring the information, life experience, and skills needed to develop and maintain healthy friendships and social relationships. Conversing with someone, reading about another culture, sharing something with someone, and helping others are examples of this type of activity.

Self-directed time. This time is spent fulfilling a person's need for personal development. Hobbies, special interests such as playing a musical instrument, religious experience, and sports can be the focus of self-directed time.

Entertainment-directed time. This is time spent on activities with the sole objective of being entertained. This use of time is often passive and relaxation-driven. Watching TV or a movie is a classic example.

It is possible to take part in more than one time-directed activity at once. For example, when "surfing" the Internet, a teenager also might be intermittently working on the next day's homework. A teenager watching TV while riding an exercise bike is spending both self-directed and entertainment-directed time. Keeping a diary of how a child "invests" her time can help identify potentially dangerous imbalances in time use. The use of time by at-risk youths is particularly important because the misuse of time can result in a cycle of failure. A general characteristic of at-risk youths is that they tend to have a great deal of free time, while high-achieving youths seem to be almost always starved for time. The challenge for parents and teachers is not simply to fill children's time, but to provide a balance of activities that are important for healthy development.

A useful barometer of a child's time use is recreation. Bart Giamatti, the late Commissioner of Baseball, said, "We can learn more about the conditions and values of a society by contemplating how it chooses to play, to use its free time, to take its leisure, than by examining how it goes about its work."[5] It is during children's leisure time, spent away from required school and family activities, that they are free to do whatever they choose. When children have free time, they usually choose activities that reflect what is of most value to them. Therefore, by looking at what a child chooses to do at these times, we can know what he considers to be most important.[6]

Bart Giamatti tracks the origin of the word "recreation" to the description of activities when a person "re-creates," that is, changes some aspect of self. Through recreation, a person changes himself, either spiritually, mentally or physically.[7] Structured leisure activities, such as sports, hobbies, and participation in clubs, account for a relatively small amount of a teenager's time, but it is these activities in which the elements of many personal attributes come together.[8] "Initiative" is an example of a key personal attribute. In the next chapter we will look at how youth activities can help a child develop initiative.

Talented Children or Passionate Children?

Seventh-grader Maggie — a fictitious name, like those of other youths highlighted in this book — is a standout in music, science, and soccer, where she's mastered the art of "heading" the ball. Her dream of playing on the national soccer team someday seems reasonable.

Eighth-grader Melinda is a math whiz whose instincts for calculation came in handy in a recent science competition. She also took first place in a state choir competition and plays softball for her school.

Both Maggie and Melinda are goal-oriented and are excited by new challenges. They stand out compared to most youths their age. While they excel in school, music and athletics, they did not inherit all of these abilities. Perhaps the inborn ability to comprehend information and remember it may give these teenagers an advantage over their peers, but high-achieving youths generally share one particular characteristic: passion for what they do, whether it be their schoolwork, an artistic activity, or a sports activity. According to Mihaly Csikszentmihalyi, all youths have strengths or talents, but passion is the ingredient that is necessary for them to germinate and develop. There are many talented youths, but the talent often is not accompanied by passion.[9]

According to Maggie's mother, "She's pushed herself as much as anything; we always try to support her, but a good bit comes from within." Melinda is equally self-motivated and finds that success in one activity can lead to success in another. Far from coasting through on talent alone, both these youths have worked hard to get where they are. "It takes hard work. It takes studying," says Melinda. "There are a lot of kids who are really smart who don't put enough effort into it."

Csikszentmihalyi and his colleagues studied a group of 200 talented teenagers to learn how they invest their time.[10] Why do some teenagers use and develop their talents while others don't? All too often during adolescence, youths with natural abilities lose interest and energy to develop their talents and pursue challenging careers. Csikszentmihalyi found that when trying to understand how these two groups of youth differ – the talented group of teenagers versus those who are less talented – one of the most important things to know was how the two groups spend their time.

The lifestyles of talented youths reveal that they typically make the kinds of choices that lead to the development of maximum potential. Talented youths may have some innate advantages, but like everyone else, they only have 24 hours to work with. But they use their time differently. Talented youths are involved in more solitary activities. They also are more disciplined in performing the particular activities related to their talent. Interestingly, Csikszentmihalyi found that talented youths do not study more than typical students – both groups spend about 11–12 percent of their time doing homework and studying.

The groups differ in their leisure activities, however. Typical teenagers spend the preponderance of their time socializing (e.g., going to parties, going out with friends, and talking to friends). Talented students spend more time engaging in some type of artistic activity that requires skilled performance. In fact, a talented teenager usually spends 20 to 35 hours a week in various achievement-directed or self-directed activities. Talented youth are generally involved in more-structured leisure activities, compared to the average teenager who spends more time in informal social interactions. Csikszentmihalyi notes:

> **"When talented students were free, they tended to be involved in activities related to art and hobbies more often than average students. These hobbies included working on computers, collecting stamps, singing, drawing, and so on. To enjoy these activities requires skill and knowledge. Ability and interest in such areas as math, music, and art might have allowed these students to develop the kind of expertise needed to enjoy structured leisure activities. Students in the average group may either not have seen the challenges in these activities or lack the skills and knowledge to pursue them, and thus were less often involved in leisure requiring complex and disciplined behavior."[11]**

His studies also have shown that engaging in activities that result in the "flow" experience (pleasure derived from achievement) is important to high-achieving students. During these activities, teenagers lose awareness of everything except the activity itself. Because of this depth of involvement, the activity is not only enjoyable but becomes intrinsically rewarding. In the next chapter, we'll take a closer look at the concept of flow as it relates to the activities of all youth.

Measuring Children's Use of Time

Children's and adolescents' lives consist of their hour-to-hour activities. Therefore, to understand their lives, it is necessary to measure children's use of time in various settings, and to describe and evaluate these activities as they travel through typical days. In order to evaluate a child's experience of time, it is not necessary to follow children around like Roger Barker did. Using a simple time diary, like the one on pages 18–19, will do. If a child is old enough, he may complete the diary himself. Otherwise, the parent may complete it by using observation and by asking the child about his activities.

Make copies of the time diary and have your child keep track of his use of time for one week. Take a look at the results and try to categorize the different activities. For example, Csikszentmihalyi found that a child's use of time generally falls into 13 activity categories:

- Doing classwork
- Doing homework
- Performing personal maintenance activities (e.g., eating, grooming)
- Doing household maintenance chores
- Talking with friends
- Participating in media activities
- Playing sports
- Participating in community activities
- Working
- Sleeping
- Participating in hobby activities

Time Diary

Day of Week: _____ Date: _____

Note: 1) where you are, 2) who you are with, and 3) the activity that you are involved in. If there are multiple activities during the hour, note them on the same line.

Morning

6:00   _____

7:00   _____

8:00   _____

9:00   _____

10:00 _____

11:00 _____

Afternoon

12:00 _____

1:00   _____

2:00   _____

3:00   _____

4:00 _____

5:00 _____

Evening

6:00 _____

7:00 _____

8:00 _____

9:00 _____

10:00 _____

11:00 _____

Night

12:00 _____

1:00 _____

2:00 _____

3:00 _____

4:00 _____

5:00 _____

- Participating in extracurricular activities at school
- Participating in church/synagogue services and activities

Studying How Americans Use Their Time

Once a decade, beginning in 1965, researchers John Robinson and Geoffrey Godbey have had a sample of Americans keep minute-to-minute diaries of how they spend a single 24-hour period. These researchers have published the results of these "time diary" studies in a volume entitled, *Time for Life: The Surprising Ways Americans Use Their Time*.[12] The data is revealing about the structure of daily life in America and how it has been changing.

The most striking finding is the trend toward Americans having much more free time. For example, since 1965 there has been a gain of two hours a week in free-time activities, especially recreation. Television, however, remains the focus of up to 50 percent of free-time activity. Most of the added "leisure" gained over the last 30 years has been spent on the couch in front of the TV. Television-viewing now occupies 40 percent of the free time of the average American adult. The respondents in the time-diary studies, however, seem not to enjoy watching television as much as many alternatives. (We'll take a closer look at this finding in the next chapter.) So why do Americans spend so much time watching TV if it results in lower levels of pleasure? According to Robinson and Godbey, television is convenient, undemanding, free or inexpensive, and possibly even addictive!

But American children are not just watching TV. Children's time-use patterns reflect commitments to many areas of involvement. Time devoted to one activity is best understood when looked at in the context of time spent in other areas. The point is that how children and teenagers organize their time across multiple areas of involvement is important to get a valid picture. For example, a child may spend an excessive number of hours in front of the television and playing computer games, but a daily after-school program may expose the same child to healthy recreational pursuits.

Implications of Children's Time Use

The school curriculum is the dominant socialization process whereby children learn the skills which are necessary to function well as adults. Similarly, the "hidden curriculum" of growing up lies in how youths are living their daily lives, that is, their day-to-day activities: what they spend their time doing, where they spend it, and who they spend it with. Patterns of habit are established as a result of these activities. These habits can become so ingrained that they end up forming something akin to a personality trait. These habits of living are often developed early in life and can be difficult to alter.[13]

How our adolescents spend their time is a frequent topic of discussion today. For example, critics ask whether the typical school year of 180 days puts our youth at a disadvantage relative to other countries. Japanese teenagers, for example, spend Saturday attending school, going to martial arts classes, and then spend time with their families in the evening. On the other hand, on a typical weekend, American adolescents watch TV, engage in leisure, or work at jobs, with the evenings often spent partying with friends.[14]

One study found that American teenagers spend much more time without an adult monitoring their activities than did their counterparts a few generations ago. It is conjectured that this may explain in part the steep rise in problem behaviors among teenagers in the past two decades.[15]

In East Asian countries like Japan and Korea, the school day is longer and parents more closely monitor their children's other activities. These youths have much less unstructured time than do American youths. East Asian parents limit their adolescents' participation in activities away from home. Youth also are not allowed to stay out late. In many communities, stores close early and there are fewer nighttime activities. Fewer teenagers are employed. Typically, the evening meal occurs later so families may eat together. Sunday is often reserved for family activities. Compared with American youth, there are fewer activities like Scout meetings and soccer games to compete with family time.[16]

The basic concern, then, is that many children and teenagers are not spending time that is consistent with healthy development into adulthood. So what might we do to better organize youths' time? We need to increase opportunities for youths' constructive use of time. In succeeding chapters, we will look at how we can expand the amount of time that children and adolescents spend engaged in activities conducive to healthy development.

In this chapter we have looked at how childhood is a critical period for establishing healthy time-use patterns. Knowledge of how children and teenagers spend their time is valuable to efforts to improve their lives. Beginning in Chapter 4, the behavior settings in which children and teenagers spend their time will be discussed. These behavior settings are not quite "destiny" when it comes to raising children, but there is no question that they do influence how easy or difficult it is to help children develop the competencies for successful adulthood. Before moving on to specific behavior settings, however, in the next chapter we'll take a closer look at the concept of "flow" and its importance in the lives of children.

---

[1] Carpenter, S. (2001, January). Teens' risky behavior is about more than race and family resources. *Monitor on Psychology, 32,* 22-23.

[2] www.goodthink.com/86400.html; accessed 9-17-01

[3] Clark, R, (1988). *Critical factors in why disadvantaged students succeed or fail in school.* New York: Academy for Educational Development.

[4] Bruno, J. (1996). Time perceptions and time allocation preferences among adolescent boys and girls. *Adolescence, 31,* 109-126.

[5] Giamatti, B. (1989). *Take time for paradise: Americans and their games.* New York: Summit Books. p. 13.

[6] Jeziorski, R. (1994). *The importance of school sports in American education and socialization.* Lanham, MD: University Press of America.

[7] *Ibid.*

[8] Larson, R. (2000). Toward a psychology of positive youth development. *American Psychologist, 55*, 170-183.

[9] Csikszentmihalyi, M., Rathunde, K., & Whalen, S. (1993). *Talented teenagers: The roots of success and failure.* New York: Cambridge University Press.

[10] *Ibid.*

[11] *Ibid*, p. 87-88.

[12] Robinson, J., & Godbey, G. (1999). *Time for life: The surprising ways Americans use their time* (2nd ed.). University Park, PA: The Pennsylvania State University Press.

[13] Csikszentmihalyi, M., Rathunde, K., & Whalen, S. (1993).

[14] Crouter, A., & Larson, R. (Eds.). (Winter, 1998). Special Issue. Temporal rhythms in adolescence: Clocks, calendars, and the coordination of daily life. *New directions for child and adolescent development, 82.* San Francisco: Jossey-Bass. p. 2.

[15] Felson, M. (1994). *Crime and everyday life.* Newbury Park, CA: Pine Forge Press.

[16] Crouter, A., Larson, R. (Eds.). (Winter, 1998). p. 83-84.

CHAPTER 3

The Importance of "Flow" in Children's Lives

AS DESCRIBED IN THE PREVIOUS CHAPTER, MIHALY Csikszentmihalyi's studies of time use have shown that some of the success of talented youths is related to their ability to experience flow (pleasure derived from achievement) from activities.[1] Flow is so enjoyable that it becomes, in Csikszentmihalyi's words, "autoletic," that is, done for its own sake without external motivation. Common flow activities are music, sports, and challenging games. These activities give a child feedback on his success. A child must use her skill to overcome a challenge. During flow, the challenge is manageable. If the challenges are overwhelming, anxiety can occur; however, if the activity offers little challenge, boredom may result. When challenges are in balance with adequately developed skills, flow may be possible. Harvard psychologist Dan Kindlon has nicely described the experience:

> "This state of absorption goes by many names: being in the zone, engagement, flow. It doesn't matter what the activity is as long as it takes skill and concentration — tennis, composing music, reading to a child. People in the zone say that they lose themselves completely in what they're doing."[2]

Csikszentmihalyi has studied what youths do every day by using the Experience Sampling Method (ESM).[3] The technique is simple:

youths carry an electronic pager and a booklet of self-report forms. Every day for a week, at randomly chosen times, the youths are paged. They immediately stop what they're doing and complete the self-report booklet. The booklet asks where the youth is, what he is doing, what he feels like, and who is present.

From the results of his ESM study, Csikszentmihalyi was able to calculate the percentage of time each activity results in flow experience, relaxation, apathy, and anxiety.[4] For example, teenagers experience flow 13 percent of the time when they are watching television, 34 percent of the time when involved in hobbies, and 44 percent of the time when playing sports and games.[5] Therefore, hobbies are two-and-a-half-times more likely to produce flow than TV. Sports activities are three times more likely to produce flow than TV. It is noteworthy that teenagers spend at least four times more time watching TV than doing hobbies and sports. These ratios remain true for adults. Why do we spend so much more time engaged in activities which produce less satisfaction? Relaxing has its place, but it is a question of balance. Researchers call this a dosage effect. Low-yield activities become a problem when they occupy too much of a child's free time. When excessive passive activities become a habit, they intrude on a child's life space, leaving little time and few opportunities for flow experiences.

Activities that can lead to flow experiences are called "flow activities." While such activities do not always lead to flow, they are more likely to cause flow to occur. Why do youths not engage in more flow activities? Teenagers openly confess that biking, playing soccer, or playing the flute are more enjoyable than "cruising Main Street" or watching TV. The key is this: To prepare for the soccer match takes time and effort. You have to dress in special clothes, make arrangements to get to the field, etc. Further, it requires many practice sessions before playing soccer – or playing the flute – begins to be fun. In a nutshell, flow-producing activities require initial commitment and discipline before they begin to be pleasurable. It requires what Csikszentmihalyi calls "activation energy" to enjoy complex activities. In other words, if a youth does not have the discipline to overcome obstacles to the engagement of an activity, he will default to an activity that is easier to engage, even though it is less pleasurable.[6]

Usually when a complex task is accomplished, the flow experience results. Looking back at the activity, we are happy. Of course, it is quite possible to be happy without experiencing flow. The pleasure that comes from flow is due to achievement, and it leads to increasing competence. For example, during a difficult soccer match, a youth may feel exhausted and defeated. But the match is hard fought and the youth contributed to the team valiantly. There is recognition of the many hours of practice. A good effort can result in flow.

Csikszentmihalyi puts it this way: "Only after the task is completed do we have the leisure to look back on what has happened, and then we are flooded with gratitude for the excellence of that experience – then, in retrospect, we are happy."[7]

To get a better sense of the daily activities that inhibit and enhance flow, let's look at the weekends of several teenagers.

Sandra is 14 years old. She is extremely talented in art, especially drawing. Her art teachers feel she could be a professional artist some day. However, while Sandra does well in art classes, she does not engage in artistic activities outside of schoolwork. Although the family has a spare room that her mother converted into a mini-studio for Sandra's artwork, Sandra uses the room infrequently. She was interested in basketball but did not try out for the middle school team because she felt the other girls were so much better. She has not enrolled in any extracurricular activities; she rides the bus home from school every day and is there alone from about 3:45 until 6:30, when her mother arrives. She often takes a nap and watches television during this time. Sometimes she hangs out with a friend who lives nearby, but most of her friends live farther away. Sometimes she draws for fun at home, but she takes no special instruction or art classes in the community. Her evenings are spent talking on the telephone to friends and watching television, accounting for at least five hours of her time use on school nights. On weekends, Sandra often sleeps until 10 or 11. She watches television, listens to music and talks on the phone. Usually she goes to the mall or a movie with a friend. Sometimes she and a friend will do something special, such as go to the roller-skating rink. Her mother is not involved in any community activities, nor does she engage in physical activities; neither does Sandra. Sandra has few responsibilities around the home. While Sandra is intellectually quite capable, she puts forth only the minimum effort at school and enjoys only her art class. The family does not attend church. Occasionally, Sandra baby-sits her younger sister and enjoys spending time with her.

Leah – age 14 – soon to be 15 – has worked two days a week for the past two summers helping physically-challenged children learn to ride horses. She is a junior volunteer at the local hospital, where she has developed work experience in neo-natal care. She's also been a volunteer at the public library, re-shelving books, and her church service projects have included cleaning up neighborhoods and Christmas caroling at homes for the elderly. Leah is very talented with music and chose the piano as her primary instrument. She practices religiously for an hour and a half every weekday after school, or in the evening if she has another activity. Her mother insists that she do homework every night, whether or not she has any assigned. Her television watching and phone use is limited to one-half hour a night. She usually foregoes television in favor of chatting with friends on the telephone. She's allowed to use the family computer whenever she wants and has created her own Web page. Leah doesn't like sports, but prefers to read for a leisure activity. She goes walking with her mother every night before bedtime. Most of her friends she sees at school or at church, but she usually plans an activity with a neighbor girlfriend on Saturday nights, typically a movie.

Andrea Smith and her two daughters spend Saturday mornings at a park participating in a cross-training workout session. While some adolescent girls spend Saturday mornings arguing with their mothers about whether they can take the Visa card to the mall, Janice and Kim Smith are stretching, power-walking, and doing calisthenics with their mother. Twelve-year-old Janice reflects, "It's really pretty out here. I like to ride my bicycle and I've gotten a lot stronger since doing these workouts." Kim, a 16-year-old sophomore, observes that "some Saturday mornings it's pretty hard to get up and get going, but my mom gets me out of bed, and once I'm up, I'm happy. They push you to do more. I always have a lot of energy afterward." Kim's experience teaches us an important concept:

A child can perform at a higher level — and overcome obstacles to engaging in flow activities — by being provided support by a skilled adult. This process is called *scaffolding*. The process works the same way as scaffolding at a construction site. There, workers erect a scaffold around a non-self-supporting structure. An example with children is the scaffolding typically used by a teacher to give support to the learner. The process enables a child to act confidently at the outer edges of his capabilities. Scaffolding may be the key ingredient for a child to develop the *activation energy* needed to engage in an activity. Some youths will overcome barriers on their own; others may need adults to build scaffolding to help them participate in activities that lead to flow.

Parents often want their children to take music lessons. Some children resist them by refusing to practice so that their parents give up. What we know about activation energy, however, advises parents to push their children hard enough or to give them skills that will enable them to engage in activities that produce flow.

Flow may sometimes occur only in certain settings or activities. It is instructive to look at places where flow does and does not occur. Science writer Winifred Gallagher reports the experience of a psychiatrist, who because he was familiar with Csikszentmihalyi's work, decided to study the time use of a hospitalized schizophrenic patient. An analysis of the woman's time use revealed that she had been happy in a state of flow only twice. During both these times, she had been caring for her nails. The psychiatrist recommended that the woman enroll in a class for manicurists. The woman did and loved the work. She was discharged from the hospital to work in the community as a manicurist. She remained in the community with weekly visits from a nurse. A manicure salon, an art studio, a tennis court, or a band camp – these are all places that may structure our lives in such a way to precipitate the experience of flow.[8]

Evolutionary Heritage and Biological Basis of Flow

Csikszentmihalyi argues that evolution has shaped humans to enjoy activities that are necessary for survival. Think about it; the species would not have endured if we did not experience pleasure from food and sex. Flow is pleasurable. Finding flow and maintaining it is self-rewarding for humans.[9] So, according to Csikszentmihalyi and his colleague Susan Jackson, evolutionary success depends on our ability to structure the environment in a way that produces flow:

"People are happy when they have a purpose and are actively involved in trying to reach a challenging goal . . . . It seems that evolution has provided us with a powerful survival mechanism: the feeling of joy we experience when we overcome a challenge."[10]

Humans derive pleasure in being absorbed in a goal-oriented activity, such as one that produces flow. The part of the brain involved in processing pleasure is the behavioral activation system (BAS). The BAS is buried in the cerebral cortex and is responsible for stimulating us to engage something in the environment that causes pleasure (or relief from pain). Dopamine is the chemical neurotransmitter in the brain that is released when the BAS is stimulated. Dopamine also is released in the brain when drugs are used (e.g., marijuana, cocaine, nicotine, alcohol). Scientists hypothesize that when a person cannot get dopamine-mediated pleasure through involvement in flow activities, then drugs can be an artificial substitute.[11] So, when a child participates in flow activities and experiences that she is competent, she will seek other opportunities to — quite literally — experience that same "rush." At the same time, chemically-induced pleasure cannot substitute for flow because it lacks a vital component: the person having achieved it through skill and effort.[12]

To summarize, flow activities cause youths to come alive in ways that rarely happen in other activities.[13] Youth naturally increase their involvement in flow activities that provide feelings of esteem and efficacy.[14] Psychologist Albert Bandura has developed the theory of self-efficacy, which is defined as an individual's belief that he can successfully accomplish a task that tests ability. Self-efficacy plays a central role in flow and the motivational process.[15] The next section deals with the concept of "initiative," which is a character trait with motivation at its core.

Initiative

As discussed in the last section, if a teenager experiences flow when involved in the area of a talent, he will enjoy it and want to continue improving. The development of talent becomes intrinsically rewarding. Quite simply, the flow experience is so pleasurable that the youth wants to repeat it.[16]

Unfortunately, many youths simply do not get on pathways that engage flow activities. Reed Larson summarizes the phenomenon:

> **"Many youth do their schoolwork, comply with their parents, hang out with their friends, and get through the day, but are not invested in paths into the future that excite them or feel like they originate from within. A central question of youth development is how to get adolescents' fires lit, how to have them develop the complex of dispositions and skills needed to take charge of their lives."[17]**

Larson has identified a single, core quality that appears to be critical for youths. It is the development of initiative. He defines it as "the ability to be motivated from within to direct attention and effort toward a challenging goal."[18] Larson says that initiative is a central requirement for other aspects of healthy development, such as creativity, leadership, and altruism. Larson's thinking on the subject of initiative is set forth in a seminal article published in the year 2000 in *American Psychologist*.[19] Elements of this article are summarized below.

Activities that develop initiative are often organized by adults. Extracurricular school activities and community youth activities are examples. Sometimes activities that develop initiative are activities that youths participate in on their own, such as hobbies, keeping a diary, building a music library from the Internet, or playing in a band. The key element is that the activities are voluntary (i.e., not required for school) and have structure, which Larson says involves participation in an activity involving constraints, rules, and goals. According to Larson, youths who participate in these kinds of activities often experience a shift in their way of thinking. They appear to develop skills for directing and implementing plans. They embrace an assertive mode of action. As a result, they feel able to affect the world.

Larson uses the example that during activities that involve the learning of initiative youths learn to think like chess players. They learn to see different options and judge the consequences of each. Larson says this develops the tools of initiative, including "tools for anticipating, planning, adapting to others, monitoring progress, and adjusting behavior over time to achieve a goal."[20] According to Larson, youths must focus their attention on a specific course of action without being put off by the first barrier they encounter. Hence, initiative involves sustained effort over time to achieve a goal.

Structured youth activities provide an ideal setting for the development of initiative. During these activities, youths experience inner motivation and attention that is not present in most of their daily activities in school and during unstructured leisure.

Practicing Adulthood

The structured youth activities discussed above create exemplary learning environments that keep youths involved. Such activities allow youths to *practice adulthood* in safe places, while pursuing meaningful experiences, and with role models and mentors in older peers and adults.

The late anthropologist Ruth Benedict noted that many societies provide a set of steps that educate youths in the responsibilities of adulthood. In American society, there is a larger difference in what is expected of children and what is expected of adults, especially regarding initiative. Children in American society are given few responsibilities, whereas adults are expected to be entirely independent. This is not the case in many societies. American adolescents have less responsibility and are given fewer opportunities to participate in meaningful activities, compared to teenagers in many societies. American adolescents experience less scaffolding to help develop initiative. They have few experiences of planning and implementing an endeavor. The result is that many young adults in America fail to accomplish the goals they set for themselves.[21]

Regarding flow, sometimes it doesn't occur because parents do not push their children to learn the skills that will enable them to fully commit to an activity. They don't make them practice the clarinet or stick with their yoga lessons. Parents don't always have to push, either, according to psychologist Dan Kindlon: "We teach our kids through example, whether it's practicing the guitar or honing our fly-fishing technique, that doing something well, and sticking to it, is important and will pay off in the long run."[22]

One of the ways that a child's belief that he will succeed can be weakened is when he can't handle frustration. A critical component of personal maturity is the ability to be unperturbed by roadblocks; to persist in the face of hardship. To help children achieve this quality, parents need to refrain from overindulging children. We must allow children to learn to wait their turn, delay gratification, and resist temptation. Only then will the neural changes in their brains take place that are needed to engage in healthy activities.

How do we teach children skills such as frustration tolerance and coping with stress? There is only one way: Children must experience frustration and stress. Of course, many parents try to help children avoid all pain, but experiencing failure and learning from it is a critical part of developing character. A little pain, then, is actually desirable; children grow from the experience.

At the same time, adults play an important role teaching youths about ways to handle obstacles and frustration. For example, we can specifically teach children how to take an adverse event and redefine it as a challenge – one that helps children learn a skill that will make it easier the next time adversity is confronted.[23]

Many people associate happiness with having free time to engage in whatever one wants. But this is not sufficient to activate flow. Sports psychologist Susan Jackson and Mihaly Csikszentmihalyi point out that a person must have something to do that will focus the mind:

"Most people believe that material comfort and relaxing leisure are what make life happy and enjoyable. Heaven on earth, they think, consists in having nothing to do and plenty of entertainment to amuse oneself with. But in the long term, this belief is mistaken. Contrary to popular opinion, the most enjoyable and satisfying moments, the ones that make life meaningful and happy, are usually those when we make something happen, when we achieve something difficult by the use of brains or muscle."[24]

In this chapter, we have discussed the concept of "flow" in the lives of children. Flow is a state of pleasure derived from achievement in an activity. We want to precipitate the experience of flow in children's activities, because flow activities cause youths to come alive in ways that rarely happen in other activities. It is flow activities, and the environments that contain them, that spur the development of skills needed for youths to take charge of their lives.

In the following chapters, we are going to analyze the major behavior settings and activities that affect children and teenagers. I have divided the contexts of childhood into 10 different settings. To a great extent, these categories are arbitrary; they overlap and intermingle. So as you read, you will need to keep in mind that the categories are fluid. For example, a chapter is devoted to the influence of the electronic environment, including television. Obviously, this environment overlaps with the home environment, which also gets its own chapter. As you will see, the categories pretty much correspond to the principal areas of a child's time use, identified in Csikszentmihalyi's studies. Parents, teachers, professional counselors, and others charged with organizing the contexts in which children and teenagers develop need to understand these environments to effectively meet the needs of youths:

- Home Setting
- Neighborhood Setting
- School, Co-Curricular, and Service-Learning Settings
- After-School Settings
- Electronic Setting
- Friends Setting

- Faith Setting
- Work Setting
- Recreational and Leisure Settings
- Sports Settings

Each of these behavior settings offers a maze of choices. Each chapter will help map out some of the key choices in the settings. Along with information about the setting to help guide parental decision-making, each chapter will provide a tool to help you incorporate the information into the lives of children: a five-question quiz. Complete the quiz before proceeding to the next chapter. In Chapter 16 you will collate all the scores from your quizzes to help you take a look at your child's lifestyle profile, with the goal of identifying some practical strategies to ensure that your child is on positive pathways. If you do not have children, complete the profile on a child you know well.

---

[1] Csikszentmihalyi, M. (1997). *Finding flow: The psychology of engagement with everyday life.* New York: Basic Books.

[2] Kindlon, D. (2001). *Too much of a good thing: Raising children of character in an indulgent age.* New York: Hyperion, p. 49.

[3] Csikszentmihalyi, M. (1999). If we are so rich, why aren't we happy? *American Psychologist, 54,* 821-827.

[4] Csikszentmihalyi, M. (1997). p. 67.

[5] Csikszentmihalyi does not explain why television shows up as producing flow. Technically, watching TV could not produce flow, though it can be a pleasurable experience. The fact that these are self-reported states may account for it.

[6] Csikszentmihalyi, M. (1997).

[7] *Ibid.* p. 32.

[8] Gallagher, W. (1994). *The power of place: How our surroundings shape our thoughts, emotions, and actions.* New York: Harperperennial Library.

[9] Csikszentmihalyi, M., & Csikszentmihalyi, I. (1990). Adventure and flow experience. In J. Miles & A. Priest (Eds.), *Adventure education* (149-155). State College, PA: Venture Publishing.

[10] Jackson, S., & Csikszentmihalyi, M. (2002). *Flow in sports: The key to optimal experiences and performances.* Champaign, IL: Human Kinetics. p. 35.

[11] Kindlon, D. (2001).

[12] Csikszentmihalyi, M. (1999).

[13] Larson, R. (2000). Toward a psychology of positive youth development. *American Psychologist, 55,* 170-183. p. 170.

[14] Shanahan, M., & Flaherty, B. (2001). Dynamic patterns of time use in adolescence. *Child Development, 72,* 385-401.

[15] Klint, K. (1990). New directions for inquiry into self-concept and adventure experiences. In J. Miles & S. Priest (Eds.), *Adventure education* (pp. 163-172). State College, PA: Venture Publishing.

[16] Csikszentmihalyi, M., Rathunde, K., & Whalen, S. (1993). *Talented teenagers: The roots of success and failure.* New York: Cambridge University Press.

[17] Larson, R. (2000). p. 170.

[18] *Ibid.* p. 170.

[19] *Ibid.*

[20] *Ibid.* p. 178.

[21] *Ibid.*

[22] Kindlon, D. (2001). p. 49.

[23] Csikszentmihalyi, M., & Larson, R. (1984). *Being adolescent: Conflict and growth in the teenage years.* New York: Basic Books.

[24] Jackson, S., & Csikszentmihalyi, M. (2002). p. 50.

CHAPTER 4

Home Setting

THERE WAS A TIME WHEN THE HOME ENVIRONMENT was the main context of a child's development. Further, the home typically has been the setting of focus when professionals write about child development. Researchers have emphasized communication and interaction between parents and children in the home. Without diminishing the importance of these human relationship factors, this chapter considers how the time-related rhythms of the home and the way families structure their time and activities affect child development. Typical activities in the home environment are outlined in the table on the next page. In this chapter, we will be concentrating on a subset of these activities.

The home setting is especially critical for elementary-age children, because they spend 35 percent of their waking hours with the family. This is an age period when children play, watch TV, and engage in other family-centered activities. As children grow older, they become less influenced by the family environment and more involved in "creating their own environment."[1] Adolescents have a widening set of social contexts and growing involvement with peers. Consequently, the amount of time spent with their parents declines significantly — teenagers spend only about 14 percent of their waking hours with family.[2] While the family continues to have influence, the influence changes as adolescents participate in many environments outside the home.

Typical Activities in the Home [3]

- Reading or writing for pleasure
- Thinking, relaxing, meditating, praying, etc.
- Listening to radio or music
- Watching TV
- Speaking on the telephone
- Drinking beverage
- Studying, doing homework
- Sleeping or resting
- Talking with a family member
- Eating a meal
- Entertaining or being with friends
- Caring for other family members
- Spending time with pets, e.g., feeding, grooming, playing with them
- General personal hygiene, e.g., showering, bathing, brushing teeth, using toilet
- Dressing, undressing, applying make-up
- Watering plants or gardening
- Doing laundry (ironing, folding clothes, washing, hanging out clothes)
- Tidying house, e.g., making bed, putting things away
- Cleaning house: dusting, polishing, vacuuming, taking out garbage
- Clearing, washing, or drying dishes
- Preparing food, cooking meals
- Playing a group game (cards, Monopoly, etc.)

As we will see in the upcoming chapters, society is imposing many time-use rhythms on our lives. It has significantly altered how families spend their time, and consequently, how families interact. Many changes have meant the loss of positive developmental opportunities. William Doherty offers a bit of an anecdote to this societal onslaught in his practical book entitled *The Intentional Family*.[4] In it he explores the home life-space of families and how families can make a concerted effort to reorder the organization of their time and maximize the health of the home environment. He shows how families can create time-use "rituals," that help keep family bonds strong, such as mealtime and other family-group activities. Doherty defines a ritual as a coordinated activity that the family does over and over again and that has emotional meaning to family members.[5] I will share some of his suggestions here, but I highly recommend that you consult his book.

Doherty notes that families are starved for time: "cars, television, busy work schedules, consumerism, and a host of other forces propel family members along fast-moving, diverging tracks."[6] He says that by ensuring that a few rituals are sustained in home life, families experience many benefits. Doherty lists the following ritual suggestions:

- Share family meals together.

- Have a regular chore responsibility for each child.

- Have a regular homework time for children.

- Have a bedtime routine for each child.

- Have a ritual for the time of re-entry to the family after being away for the day.

- Have rituals for monitoring children's whereabouts. (I've added this one to Doherty's original list.)

- Celebrate holidays, birthdays, Mother's Day, Father's Day, graduations, weddings, etc. with special rituals.

Let's take a look at opportunities for rituals in each of these categories:

Mealtime. The custom of families eating their meals at home together around a table and discussing the morning's news or the day's events and sharing ideas has been around for a long time. However, such family-focused mealtime has become the exception rather than the norm in America today. Most families rarely eat together anymore; instead, individuals grab their meals as they come and go. Many factors have conspired to create this situation. First, the family lunch disappeared when family members began eating at work or school. Then the family breakfast fell by the wayside when everyone began leaving the home in the morning on different schedules. Now, with the hectic lifestyles of single parents or two working parents, only a small number of families sit down to dinner together every night, and many of those who do are grouped around the television set. According to a study by the Kaiser Family Foundation, when families have dinner together, 60 percent usually have the television on.[7]

This haphazard meal situation is mostly a new American habit. In many countries, mealtime is a special gathering time for families. In places where the food budget can take up to 40 percent of a family's income, eating is not taken for granted. Evening mealtime becomes a time for relaxation and family conversation, a time to discuss how the day went for everyone.

I have a colleague who gives the evening meal highest priority in her family. The rule is that on school nights dinner is at 6:30 sharp. If one of the teenagers is late, the penalty is grounding (in her room) on the weekend, one hour for every minute after 6:30. She enforces the rule rigorously. You may find this harsh, but it simply indicates how important it is to her. You do not have to share this value so strongly. It is not necessary to have a sharing meal every night – even once a week is better than never. When you can arrange for your family to share a regular meal together, make sure it's TV-free and turn on the telephone answering machine. Make sure it's a pleasant time for everyone by avoiding stressful topics of conversation. Save disciplinary discussions or heated debates for other times.

The transition from work to home for adults, and from school to home for children, can be stressful. The pent-up tensions from the day can collide. During the 5–7 p.m. period, dinner must be prepared, homework begun, and everyone must decompress. A further complication is that sports practices or other activities sometimes intrude on this time period. One solution to arranging a relaxing family meal may be to schedule it for a later time, as they do in some European countries.[8]

Household chore time. It is important for children to participate in the upkeep of the family home by having regular chore responsibilities. The point is for children to have the experience of working together for the common good of the family. For example, in rural families in Kenya, children participate in the shared cultural understanding that household responsibilities contribute to the well-being of household members. This attitude has wider approval within the community.[9] Children take great pleasure in being told to do small duties and show great satisfaction in their accomplishment. The adults believe that without such training in responsibility and communal sharing, children do not grow into adults who have the respect of the community.

One American study revealed that boys from dual-earner families who are highly involved in household tasks see themselves as more competent and rate their relationships with their parents more positively than do their peers who perform fewer chores around the house.[10] While it is desirable for all school-age children to have assigned chores, the amount of time and responsibility should be reasonable. For example, in some households, older siblings are expected to care for younger ones. Parents must monitor such responsibility so it doesn't become excessive.

Homework time. Another home-centered activity with various behavioral implications is completing school homework. Not surprisingly, increased study time is associated with better academic performance. Parents should provide children with the proper environment, adequate time, and constant encouragement to do their homework. You can make homework activities more successful and enjoyable by creating rituals. Designating a specific time each day when homework studying is to begin is generally helpful. Some children benefit from a special, private, quiet space to complete homework assignments. If a motivator to complete homework is needed (and it often is!), you may need a rule that requires completing all homework before engaging in some other desirable activity, such as watching TV or talking on the phone.

According to Larson and Kleiber, a child's desire for companionship during homework time may reflect an increasing need for peer interaction in the upper grade levels. Parents of these young teenagers would do well to encourage group study with friends or collaboration with a classmate over the telephone. Larson and Kleiber also found that homework done with a parent or other family member present is associated with the highest attention levels and better performance.[11]

Bedtime. In some families, going to bed at night and awaking in the morning are random, chaotic events. Much research indicates that a more calming routine creates an environment of security, and the importance of a bedtime routine for children has become a mainstay of parenting advice. Typically, it involves a standard time when a bath is taken, followed by preparation for bed, perhaps a bedtime story for younger children, and a ritualistic conveying of "good nights." Such a ritual, appropriately adapted for all members of the family, can create a calm, nurturing atmosphere in the home. In some families, for example, a younger child starts to bed at 8 and, after hearing a bedtime story, is tucked away by 8:30. The hour of 8:30–9:30 is a time that a mother and teenage daughter can talk and perhaps review plans for the weekend or tackle a difficult homework problem. Then in the hour from 9:30–10:30, the parents have personal time to share their day while preparing for bed. A half-hour of reading together in bed is a nightly ritual cherished by many spouses.

Keeping a reasonable bedtime during the weekdays ensures that family members get enough rest and that children go to school refreshed and ready to learn. Unfortunately, research studies report that Americans generally get less sleep than they need. Children and teenagers need lots of sleep. Many teenagers get as little as six hours of sleep a night, although, as a group, they may need as much as nine and one-half hours to maintain optimum physical and emotional health. When conflicts and stress arise with children, a good thing to check first is whether they are getting enough sleep. Adequate sleep for all members of a household helps maintain good feelings overall.[12]

Time of re-entry to the family. William Doherty recommends that families create a ritual for the time of re-entry into the family after the long day. He offers the example of the re-connection that occurs each day between a dog and its owner. He refers to this as a re-bonding ritual. While it may only be brief, such a ritual can jump-start family members toward a positive evening.[13] In one family I know, when the mother returns home with the children after school, the re-bonding ritual involves sitting at the kitchen table to discuss the dinner menu. When the father returns home, he seeks out the children and gives a big cheek kiss to the daughter and heaves his son into the air in a re-bonding hug.

Monitoring children's whereabouts. Because parental supervision of children can be such an important issue, it is recommended that monitoring rituals be established early in a child's life. Monitoring children as they grow older and seek more autonomy will be easier if they are used to reporting their whereabouts to you. While technology has a down side, which we will explore in Chapter 8, in this case cell phones can be vital to monitoring teenagers' activities when you are not with them.

> American teenagers spend far more time without adult monitoring of their activities than teenagers of my generation. This change has been blamed, in part, for the significant increase in problem behaviors among adolescents.[14] Scott Henggeler and his associates at the Medical University of South Carolina have found that helping parents supervise their teenagers more closely is often an effective intervention when adolescents are having behavior problems.[15]

It is interesting to step outside of American society and look at the issue of parental supervision. In the East Asian countries of Japan and Korea, parents monitor the whereabouts of adolescents much more closely in comparison. Of course, in those countries, adolescents have less time to be out and about. School consumes many more hours in Japan and Korea, leaving much less unstructured time for teenagers. In addition to the fact that there is simply less "free time," parents in East Asia generally limit teenagers' activities outside the home, including staying out late in the evening.

Other societal factors affect this issue also. In many parts of the world, stores close much earlier than in the United States. There are fewer outside-the-family activities in the evening too, and fewer teenagers are employed. As I've already mentioned, in many countries, the evening meal occurs later in the evening than in the United States. This mealtime not only results in a shared family meal more often but also leaves little post-meal time for family members to leave the home. Sundays are often reserved for family activities. In America, Scout meetings, softball practice, and music lessons all compete for this same time.[16]

> Another issue to put into this equation is what social scientists call "risky time." This is time spent in settings that increase the likelihood of negative experiences, for example, when youths may be exposed to accidents, violence, or peer pressure concerning drug use, sex, and criminal activities. Research clearly indicates that as the amount of unmonitored time increases with adolescents, these risks grow accordingly. Time spent driving around *without* adults in the car may be especially risky. Studies have identified 3-6 p.m. on school days as the time of greatest risk for many teenagers. Parents must walk the tightrope of providing both adequate supervision and the independence necessary for teenagers. Finding this balance is critical.[17]

Celebrations. Many families have well-established rituals for holidays and special-person days, such as birthdays, Mother's Day, etc. I remember that a birthday ritual in my family involved a picnic dinner with friends at a riverside park, always followed by the trip home in which my father pretended to get lost. We screamed from the back of the car for my dad to turn here or there, and he always turned the wrong way as we rolled in hysterics in the back of the station wagon. Creating these kinds of celebration rituals does much to build lasting bonds in the family.

Importantly, celebration rituals can promote pride in one's ethnic and cultural heritage. The Hays family celebrates Kwanzaa each year. They decorate their home with Kwanzaa symbols and they place a *mkeka*, a straw mat, on the table. Corn (one ear for each child in the family) and other foods are placed on the *mkeka* to signify the earth's abundance. Candles are placed in a *kinara*, a wooden candle holder, with a black candle in the center as a reminder of the richness of African-American skin. A candle is lit for each day of Kwanzaa. Such rituals can help children and teenagers learn to embrace their own cultural and ethnic identity. It is the first step toward knowledge of and comfort with people of different cultural, racial, and ethnic backgrounds.[18]

Summing Up

Keeping some key family rituals in your home setting will create a nurturing sanctuary that can help counteract some of the negative influences that can creep into the other environments of childhood.

Action Steps:

- Limit the amount of time that the TV is on in the home.
- Have at least two slow-paced family meals together each week (and make sure the TV is off).
- Make bedtime a predictable, special time, especially for younger children.
- Give children a regular chore responsibility, starting at about age 6, increasing the complexity and time commitment as they grow older.
- Create a regular homework time and place.
- Celebrate family with special rituals: holidays, birthdays, annual vacation.

Before moving on to Chapter 5, complete the short quiz about your home environment on the next page.

QU IZ

Home Environment

_____ 1. Do you have at least two meals together as a family every week, with the TV turned off?

_____ 2. Do you have regular holiday and birthday celebration rituals in your household?

_____ 3. Do you have homework rules in your family, to ensure that homework is completed in an orderly fashion?

_____ 4. Does your child have a regular bedtime which is consistently followed?

_____ 5. Does your child have regular chores around the house?

Scoring: Give yourself 2 points for "yes," "often," or "usually" answers, 1 point for "sometimes" answers, and 0 points for "no" and "never" answers. Total your points for questions 1 through 5 and write the answer below.

Your total score = _____ (0 to 10 points)

[1] Scarr, S., & McCartney, K. (1983). How people make their own environments: A theory of genotype-environment effects. *Child Development, 54,* 424-435.

[2] Benson, P. (1997). *All kids are our kids.* San Francisco: Jossey-Bass.

[3] Smith, S. (1994). The psychological construction of home life. *Journal of Environmental Psychology, 14,* 125-136. p. 127.

[4] Doherty, W. (1997). *The intentional family: How to build family ties in our modern world.* Reading, MA: Addison-Wesley.

[5] Doherty, W., & Carlson, B. (2002). *Putting family first: Successful strategies for reclaiming family life in a hurry-up world.* New York: Henry Holt and Company. pp. 28-29.

[6] *Ibid.* p. 9.

[7] Roberts, D., Foehr, U., Rideout, V., & Brodie, M. (1999). *Kids & media @ the new millennium.* New York: Kaiser Family Foundation.

[8] Larson, R., & Richards, M. (1994). *Divergent realities: The emotional lives of mothers, fathers, and adolescents.* New York: Basic Books.

[9] Wenger cited in Belle, D. (1999). *After-school lives of children.* Mahwah, NJ: Lawrence Erlbaum Associates. p. 92.

[10] Belle, D. (1999). *After-school lives of children.* Mahwah, NJ: Lawrence Erlbaum Associates.

[11] Larson, R., & Kleiber, D. (1993). Daily experience of adolescents. In P. Tolan & B. Cohler (Eds.), *Handbook of clinical research and practice with adolescents* (pp. 125-145). New York: Wiley.

[12] Kindlon, D. (2001). *Too much of a good thing: Raising children of character in an indulgent age.* New York: Hyperion.

[13] Doherty, W. (1997).

[14] Felson cited in Larson, R. (1994). Youth organizations, hobbies, and sports as developmental contexts. In R. Silbereisen & E. Todt (Eds.), *Adolescence in context: The interplay of family, school, peers, and work in adjustment* (pp. 46- 65). New York: Springer-Verlag.

[15] Henggeler, S., Schoenwald, S., Borduin, C., Rowland, M., & Cunningham, P. (1998). *Multisystemic treatment of antisocial behavior in children and adolescents.* New York: Guilford Press.

[16] Crouter, A., & Larson, R. (Eds.). (Winter, 1998). Special issue: Temporal rhythms in adolescence: Clocks, calendars, and the coordination of

daily life. *New directions for child and adolescent development, 82.* San Francisco: Jossey-Bass.

[17] *Ibid.* p. 85.

[18] Lucero, M. (2000). *The spirit of culture: Applying cultural competency to strength-based youth development.* Denver, CO: Assets for Colorado Youth.

CHAPTER 5

Neighborhood Setting

THE CHILD'S FIRST TURF UPON VENTURING OUTSIDE the family home is the neighborhood. For young children, the neighborhood is more than a simple geographical setting; it is the child's social universe. Since young children are only minimally mobile, the things they do from day to day are, in part, shaped by the nature of the physical environment in which they live. Parks, schools, libraries, rivers and other "places" serve as resources that influence children's activity patterns in a number of ways. Further, the social environment of the neighborhood, from adult neighbors to the types of friends and peers available to children, has a powerful impact on children's time use.[1]

Neighborhoods vary in terms of the opportunities for peer-to-peer contact they provide to children. Some neighborhoods may have barriers, such as busy streets, which separate children from each other and from places to play. How variations in the quality of neighborhood environments impact children was studied by Elliott Medrich and his colleagues at the University of California.[2] These researchers identified a number of factors, such as terrain, distance from commercial areas, child population density, and safety, that affect the number and types of social experiences that occur among neighborhood children. Basing their findings on interviews with sixth-grade children, they reported that in neighborhoods in which houses are widely separated and sidewalks are scarce, children tended to have fewer friends and had to travel longer distances in order to make contact with peers. Also, in these types of neighborhoods, friendship patterns were generally more formal and rigid. (For example, play opportunities often had to be scheduled and transportation to meet a friend often had to be arranged.) In contrast, in neighborhoods with little distance and few barriers between houses, children generally reported a higher number of friends and more-informal and spontaneous play patterns.

Pedestrian safety is another neighborhood factor that can affect children's development of peer relationships. Children in neighborhoods with traffic safety hazards, such as major thoroughfares and unregulated traffic (i.e., few traffic lights and stop signs), reported much less autonomy in visiting playmates and gaining access to play areas. Such constraints not only limit the number of friends and amount of large-group play, but also may result in fewer friendships. Research shows that these children often compensate by playing more with siblings than do children in safer neighborhoods.[3]

Finally, the density of the childhood population in the neighborhood is also an important factor in determining the quantity and quality of peer relationships among children. Neighborhoods with large populations of children generally provide a child with a greater number of friends, more large-group play, and more spontaneity in play. In neighborhoods with low child populations, children usually report having fewer friends and more formal friendship patterns.[4]

To understand how to seek out neighborhood environments that provide healthy developmental opportunities for your children, first think back to your own childhood neighborhoods. What was good about the neighborhood that you grew up in? As I reflect on growing up in my own neighborhood, it is easy to understand what a profound effect this context has. I was an athletic child, and my neighborhood offered a wide variety of opportunities for football, basketball, baseball, and sledding in wintertime. A nearby wooded area was a virtual Sherwood Forest of adventure where we climbed, built forts, and held secret club meetings. Most of my friends lived in adjacent houses and our parents easily supervised the whole neighborhood. As I grew older, I ventured to nearby parks, rivers and commercial areas. I either walked or rode my bike to school each day from elementary school up through junior high school. Take a moment to reflect on your own experiences growing up in your neighborhood, and then try to identify the advantages and disadvantages for the children living in your current neighborhood.

Robin Moore, professor of Landscape and Architecture at North Carolina State University, has written a wonderful book about how children use their neighborhood environment for play and learning. *Childhood's Domain* looks at the world through children's eyes: how they perceive their neighborhood environment, how they navigate its territory, and how this physical environment contributes to their development. If you forget what it was like back then, I encourage you to consult Moore's text for an in-depth review of the geography of childhood.[5]

Restorative Environments and Natural Settings

A related line of research being explored is nature's impact on people's mental functioning, social relationships, and even physical well-being. Psychologists Rachel and Stephen Kaplan at the University of Michigan have been on the forefront of this research studying "restorative environments." They have found that particular environments can contribute to emotional well-being – relaxation, calmness and comfort – as well as positive mood – happiness, enjoyment, and even excitement.

The Kaplans asked people to list their favorite places for relaxing and "getting away from it all." The most common responses identify natural settings, which are named by 61 percent of participants.[6] Why are scenic outdoor environments so special and restorative? The Kaplans have found that restorative environments make fewer demands on attention and provide a chance to rebuild energy resources.[7] Related research shows that viewing natural scenery stimulates a part of the brain that has a calming effect on people under stress.[8] As a result, it has been theorized that such effects may have an evolutionary basis. It is called the *Biophilia Hypothesis* and proposes that natural selection may have favored those who can relax in a natural setting.

Playing in a wooded area stimulates children's inventiveness and encourages them to engage in more fantasy.[9] Researchers have found that children who live in more natural environments have a greater capacity for paying attention, and are better able to delay gratification and inhibit impulses.[10] For example, one study looked at nature's impact on children with Attention Deficit Hyperactivity Disorder (ADHD). It was found that children exhibited fewer ADHD-related symptoms after spending time in areas with grass and trees than when they spent time indoors or in areas outside without grass or trees.[11] Could it be that we can increase the attention of children with ADHD and minimize other behavior problems simply by having these children spend more time in natural settings? Is it possible that all children will have better attentional skills when we incorporate natural settings into where they live, learn, and play?

The suggestion that natural settings promote well being and even healing is not so surprising when you consider some of the reports coming from the field of medical research. For example, one researcher studied the effect that views from windows had on patients recovering from surgery. Patients whose hospital rooms overlooked trees recovered more easily than patients in rooms with views of brick walls. The patients with natural views were discharged sooner, had fewer complications, and required less pain medication compared to the other patients.[12]

For most of human history, people have spent most of their time outside, so you would expect that we are born to love the outdoors. Unfortunately, in today's society, fewer and fewer children grow up incorporating plants, animals, and natural places into their sense of neighborhood. In 1900, only 10 percent of the United States population lived in cities. In the year 2000, 38 percent of Americans lived in urbanized areas where there is little natural wildness.[13] Rachel and Stephen Kaplan use the term "nearby nature" to describe the vacant lots, creeks, and ditches that make up a city or suburban child's "wilderness."[14] Adults need to do everything in their power to give children strong, satisfying connections to nature.

As we have found, natural environments offer many positive developmental opportunities. There may be other benefits as well. For example, youths who spend more time in the woods have been found to be less prone to illness. It seems that their increased exposure to dirt and bacteria helps them develop resistance to allergies.[15]

Developing a connection with the outdoors is also a way to help youths engage in physical activity. Outdoor recreation is viewed by most Americans as the best way to be physically active. Charles Cook, a respected authority on outdoor activity and communing with nature, has noted that our lives have become so stressful and hectic and that we now spend most of our time in artificial space. He says that our innate need to connect with nature must be fulfilled in order to maintain harmony in life. His book, *Awakening to Nature*, contains hundreds of suggestions on how to reconnect with the natural world.[16] Sometimes, it can be as simple as a short hike in the woods – good for body, mind, and spirit. Mother, and Asheville, North Carolina resident Julie Corey, has captured in a brief vignette (on pages 54-55) the magic of a child's relationship with nature.

Summing Up

For young children especially, the neighborhood is their social universe. If you can choose your neighborhood, here are some good choices.

Action Steps:

- Select a neighborhood with shorter distances between houses and less automobile traffic. Such an atmosphere usually results in more friends and more spontaneous play for children (with the fringe benefit of less time spent with "canned entertainment" such as television).

- Select a neighborhood with close availability of libraries, community centers, parks, and child care – these places can enhance family life and activities.

- Select a neighborhood with "nearby nature" for access to unique play areas and connections to the restorative and imaginative quality of natural settings.

53

Simple Hikes Bring Mother and Son Closer

By Julie Corey

Green eyes twinkling, eyebrows furrowed in thought, Joey pondered my question. A seemingly tough decision for a 3 year old. What to do today? His contemplation was really for show, though. His answer is always the same. Playground, library, or the woods? Ummmm . . . let's go for a hike!

Planning a hike with a 3 year old may sound ambitious — little ones tire easily and seem to need such elaborate entertainment. But Joey will accept a simple walk in the woods as a hike. Exploring along the river's edge, skipping stones in the water, throwing a stick for the dog to fetch are all adventures. Walking to the base of a waterfall to marvel at the sight is packed with entertainment value.

Some days it actually is a hike — the days I can spare three hours to cover the span of two miles. My little guy just wants to take it all in. A cool-looking rock gets two full minutes of attention. And look, there's a perfect climbing tree. I wonder if I can walk along that fallen tree without losing my balance. Hey, look at this leaf. Finding just the right walking stick is a mission not to be taken lightly.

I witness my child discovering the wonderment of nature . . . We are potentially as removed from the basic elements of life as any living creature ever has been. There are so many distractions steering us from enjoying the simple, basic things in life. Cars,

TVs, computers, telephones, toys, homes with so many comforts it sometimes doesn't occur to us to venture out.

Joey enjoys all the amenities of his easy life; he loves the Rugrats and his Matchbox cars as much as the other boys in his preschool class. But he has discovered something really cool out there in the woods. It's really quiet. You never know what you're going to come across, but it's so fun finding out.

It's the simplicity of life playing out — holding Mom's hand, talking easily, and asking a million questions (What are trees made out of? Why do people have noses?) No radio, phone, or e-mail to distract Mom today.

Breathing in the clean air; feeling the warmth of the brilliant sun on your skin; looking up at the fluffy clouds filtered through the tall trees. Hearing the crunch of leaves under foot; hearing the river rush past; the cool crisp smell of autumn in the air. (I think that's why we have noses.) A squirrel drops an acorn on a rock and busily sets to work extracting his snack from the nut. My 3 year old's innocence soaks up these sights, and his senses are filled with the beauty of nature.

We've come so far as a civilized society. But as I walk through the woods with my son I understand what he and I are enjoying together today has been enjoyed by other mothers and sons for thousands of years before us. There's something very grounding in understanding that in some distant future when this world is a very different place, a mother and son will walk in the woods together enjoying these same benefits of nature. She'll see the wonderment in her son's eyes and be thankful for these simple joys, as I am.

QUIZ

Neighborhood Environment

Answer Each Question 2, 1 or 0

2 = Yes, Often, or Usually   1 = Sometimes   0 = No or Never

_____ 1. Does your child visit with grown-ups in the neighborhood?

_____ 2. Can your child walk to a nearby school or park to play or socialize?

_____ 3. Are there other children in the neighborhood whom your child plays or socializes with?

_____ 4. Is it easy to supervise your child in your neighborhood?

_____ 5. Are there natural places (woods, etc.) in your neighborhood where your child can play?

Scoring: Give yourself 2 points for "yes," "often," or "usually" answers, 1 point for "sometimes" answers, and 0 points for "no" and "never" answers. Total your points for questions 1 through 5 and write the answer below.

Your total score = _____ (0 to 10 points)

[1] Medrich, E., Roizen, J., Rubin, V., & Buckley, S. (1982). *The serious business of growing up: A study of children's lives outside school.* Berkeley, CA: University of California Press.

[2] *Ibid.*

[3] *Ibid.*

[4] Belle, D. (Ed.). (1989). *Children's social networks and social supports.* New York: Wiley.

[5] Moore, R. (1986). *Childhood's domain: Play and place in child development.* London: MIG Communications.

[6] Korpela, K., Hartig, T., Kaiser, F., & Fuhrer, U. (2001). Restorative experience and self-regulation in favorite places. *Environment & Behavior, 33,* 572-589.

[7] Kaplan, S. (1983). A model of person-environment compatibility. *Environment & Behavior, 15,* 311-332.

[8] Sundstrom, E., Paul, A., & Asmus, C. (1996). Environmental psychology, 1989-1994. *Annual Review of Psychology, 47,* 482-512.

[9] Gallagher, W. (1994). *The power of place: How our surroundings shape our thoughts, emotions, and actions.* New York: Harperperennial Library.

[10] *Ibid.*

[11] Clay, R. (April, 2001). Green is good for you. *Monitor on Psychology, 32* (4), 40-42.

[12] *Ibid.*

[13] Nabhan, G., & Trimble, S. (1994). *The geography of childhood: Why children need wild places.* Boston: Beacon Press.

[14] Kaplan, S. (1983).

[15] Braun-Fahrlander, C., Riedler, J., Herz, U., Eder, W., Waser, M., Grize, L., Maisch, S., Carr, D., Gerlach, F., Bufe, A., Lauener, R., Schierl, R., Renz, H., Norwak, D., & von Mutius, E. Environmental exposure to endotoxin and its relation to asthma in school-age children. *New England Journal of Medicine, 347,* 869-877.

[16] Cook, C. (2001). *Awakening to nature.* New York: Contemporary Books.

CHAPTER 6

School, Co-Curricular, and Service-Learning Settings

SCHOOL IS THE PRINCIPAL COMMUNITY INSTITUTION for children and teenagers from about age 5 through adolescence. A great deal more than just a place for learning to read and write and do math, school is a place where children and teenagers spend a large portion of their waking hours engaged in the social, emotional, and psychological challenges of preparing for adulthood. Time spent involved with school, including homework, accounts for about 25–35 percent of children and teenagers' waking hours (including weekend time).[1] A national longitudinal study, *Protecting Adolescents from Harm*,[2] identified a key factor in youths' school experience as "perceived school connectedness," – that is, whether or not the child feels engaged or alienated at school. A number of elements in the school environment affect this feeling of connectedness, including teacher-student relationships, the classroom instructional strategies used, student-peer group relationships, the home-school linkage, student-school match, and school size.[3] Each of these factors is discussed in this chapter.

Teacher-student relationships. Teachers who are interested in and show that they care about the students they teach play a big role in helping students feel connected. A teacher's message that "I care" may take the form of taking extra time to critique a paper and write constructive comments. For other students, a teacher's use of humor or constant patience or provision of after-school one-on-one assistance may get the message across. All students value specific, positive statements about their personal worth, so teachers who make it a point to provide positive reinforcement are helping to establish their students' feeling of connectedness. Quite simply, students want to feel connected personally to their teachers. Students like teachers who draw on personal experience and share their own ideas. Students become more involved in their learning when teachers teach in a way that communicates excitement and enthusiasm. Also, teachers who can show that they understand the stresses of students' lives connect better. It takes a special type of person, with concern for and dedication to youths, to be a good teacher, and students are adept at spotting "phonies."

Instructional methods. Proper concern and the best of intentions can only take you so far, however. If teachers are to connect, they must use effective instructional strategies that engage all learners. This requires first understanding and appreciating each child's unique characteristic learning style. Such approaches expand the view of intelligence to a wider range of skills and concepts than is generally acknowledged, as Harvard psychologist Howard Gardner has so aptly pointed out.[4] Gardner believes that we have traditionally focused too much attention on verbal and logical thinking, and neglected other equally legitimate ways of coming to know the world. His studies indicate that human beings possess a range of innate cognitive processing styles – different ways of meeting and making sense of one's environment. Gardner coined the term "multiple intelligences" to refer to these various learning preferences, such as spatial intelligence, musical intelligence, and bodily-kinesthetic intelligence.

Without negating each individual's unique style, we can certainly make some generalizations. Girls generally prefer to learn by watching or listening, whereas boys more often than not prefer to learn by doing, by engaging in some action-oriented task that they find captivating. Same-gender classes are sometimes more supportive for a particular boy or girl. Instructional methods that diminish competition, such as cooperative learning, may be the best approach for some students. The bottom line is that traditional instructional methods may be ineffectual with some students, so in order to connect with those students, less-conventional teaching methods must be used. Take, for example, the Outward Bound Program or other group-team activities that build on a boy's or girl's physicality.

Student-peer group relationships. Peer group membership exerts a powerful impact on a student's feeling of school connectedness. When you were in school, where were you located within the school's social structure? In some cases, students can move easily among diverse peer groups, whereas in other school situations students are typically confined to a narrow range of interactions. A student's intergroup relationships profoundly affect that student's interactions and performance in the classroom. Chapter 9 is devoted to the friendship environment, so here it is simply acknowledged that a child must have friends in school in order to feel connected to the school experience.

Home-school linkages. Evidence suggests that a teacher's ability to connect with students' families and life outside of school, goes a long way toward encouraging the students' willingness to work hard toward academic goals.[5] There is a strong relationship between parental school involvement and a child's school behaviors, including academic performance, attitudes, and motivation. This involvement may take many forms: helping with homework, calling the school with questions when there are problems, attending school meetings, and even volunteering at the school. Schools must make an explicit effort to involve parents, and each teacher must reach out to all students' lives beyond the classroom. When the home-school linkage is present, children feel more connected to their school experience.

Student-school match. For connectedness to occur, there must be a good fit between what makes each child thrive and what the school provides for the child. Pluralistic schools, that is, schools that offer diverse learning environments, provide an opportunity to meet the unique needs of every student. Offering diverse classroom settings creates more niches for more students. In such schools, a student is placed in a classroom only after her most appropriate learning environment is identified by gathering information from the student, teachers, and parents.

When I was a student teacher in the Ann Arbor (Michigan) Public Schools in the early 1970s, there were five different high schools. A few years earlier, when I had attended the same school system, there had been only one high school. In the intervening years, the school system had made a commitment to providing pluralistic schools. Instead of trying to "fit" all students into one high school, the district enabled students to attend the high school which best fit their learning style. Of course, there was still the traditional college preparatory high school. In addition, there was a "community" high school, which had only a small faculty augmented by volunteer instructors from the community. The informal classes were often conducted at a community site. There was also a so-called "free school," an experiment of that era, in which students individually designed their own learning curriculum with faculty mentors. Another option was a high school attended mostly by students who were failing in school because of poor academics or behavior. A charismatic and experienced inner city principal was hired to take charge of this school, which was often called "Boot-Camp High" but the students learned and succeeded because of an extraordinarily dedicated administration and faculty. Lastly, there was a high school that emphasized vocational training primarily for students who did not plan to attend college.

Of course, many parents address a child's needs for a particular school environment or instructional strategy by sending the child to a private school. For families who cannot afford private school, charter schools with various educational philosophies and strategies are available in some communities. In some locales, all-boy and all-girl schools have become a popular alternative, and have been shown to have certain benefits for many youths.[6] When alternative schools are not available or feasible, parents must work with school administrators and teachers to customize the best options for their child within the existing school setting.

When a child is in a bad fit for the school environment, it can lead to problem behaviors, and in some cases, misdiagnosis. Many mild to moderate cases of Attention Deficit Hyperactivity Disorder (ADHD) fall within the normal range of a boy's behav-

ior, easily corrected by a better fitted classroom environment and attentive adults who intervene with support and appropriate structures. In a classroom that keeps a child motivated and energized with a variety of learning activities, and with a teacher who is sensitive to a boy's unique learning style, ADHD often never manifests itself. Mismatches are rampant in our schools and the number of prescriptions for psycho-stimulant medications to slow children down and make them more attentive is increasing exponentially every few years.

School size. For decades now, school districts around the country have sought to consolidate small schools into larger schools. The belief is that heating and cooling larger schools is cheaper, and savings can be made in staffing, busing, and construction. Nonetheless, students who attend smaller schools tend to perform better on standardized tests. One reason may have been identified in a classic study by Roger Barker and Paul Gump; the study supports the role of small schools in promoting school connectedness.[7] In 1964, these University of Kansas psychologists studied how school size influences children's social relationships. They found that small schools offer better opportunities for students to participate directly in school activities, to develop leadership skills, and to experience a sense of belonging. Larger schools, on the other hand, were often "overmanned," a term invented by Barker and Gump. They were referring to the phenomenon that in large schools there are too many students compared to the number of "positions" available in the setting (the term "position" meaning student government representative, cheerleader, drama co-star, shot putter, etc.). In the small schools surveyed, positions were generally "undermanned," and therefore, more students participated in school activities, and in many cases, were actively recruited. Suppose, for example, that the school orchestra of your small school needs five percussionists to handle a musical arrangement in which five different percussion instruments are used simultaneously. You are a mediocre drummer, but because of the circumstances, you are needed – and you drum. In a large school, the same situation would not benefit a discouraged twelfth-chair drummer, who might decide to drop out of band. We'll revisit this issue in the next section as part of the next topic, co-curricular activities.

Co-Curricular Activities

Co-curricular activities are optional, structured activities that are physically or mentally challenging to the student, as opposed to unstructured activities in which the student is less active.[8] Historically, these activities have been referred to as "extracurricular" activities. The new term emphasizes that these types of activities complement the regular educational curriculum as opposed to standing apart from it. Co-curricular activities may be athletic in nature, including intramural, junior varsity and varsity teams of various sports, or they may be associated with other groups such as choirs or orchestras, theater groups, or debating teams.

Because participation in co-curricular activities is voluntary and because these activities occur outside the regular school hours, they can be considered recreational in nature. However, because they occur within the school setting, they offer unique opportunities apart from recreational activities that are not associated with school. (I am treating the co-curricular activities separately here, saving a discussion of recreational and leisure settings in general for Chapter 12.) As an example, school sports strengthen the bond to school personnel, increase social status in school, and usually provide entry into positive peer groups. As a result, participation in school athletics draws students into the social mainstream of the school, thereby enhancing school connectedness and putting youth on a healthier pathway in that setting.[9]

Educators almost universally agree that participation in co-curricular activities has a positive impact on students. It has been found that during their period of participation, students usually perform better in the classroom, spend more time completing homework, have better grades, and manage their time better. Further, educators cite that co-curricular activities help students develop important qualities such as commitment and determination, and such interpersonal skills as cooperation and personal sacrifice. Ronald Jeziorski has identified some of the benefits that can be gained through participation in co-curricular activities; they are summarized in the chart on the next page.

Co-curricular activities may have special importance for so-called "high-risk" youths. In one study, youths with multiple adjustment problems who became involved in a co-curricular activity were significantly less likely to drop out of school or engage in criminal activities. This benefit may depend on the extent to which the youths are involved in positive social relationships surrounding the activity.[10] Co-curricular activities can determine who a child spends a great deal of time with, and often result in friendships between youths who otherwise would never have developed formal relationships.

Common Benefits of Co-Curricular Activities [11]

- Participants learn to persevere and keep trying in difficult times.
- Participants learn to overcome defeat.
- Participants learn to strive for self-improvement yet sacrifice self-interests to "the good of the team" when necessary.
- Participants learn to cooperate with teammates, even when tensions develop.
- Participants carry the structure of the co-curricular activities into their core curriculum activities.
- Participants have a sense of purpose and of being a part of something bigger than themselves as members of a team.
- The discipline and work ethic exercised in co-curricular activities carry over into the classroom.
- The mentors of participants evoke positive behaviors that carry over to other settings.

In addition to their importance as settings for developing potentially positive peer social networks, co-curricular activities generally include ongoing relationships with adults. Participants often develop a relationship with the same coach or mentor for several years. Relationships with teachers, on the other hand, are typically interrupted each semester in middle school and high school. While some students do maintain ongoing relationships with particular teachers over time, the co-curricular setting offers a unique opportunity for continuity. Often the same mentor guides an activity as the team or group develops new goals and strives for higher achievement from year to year.[12]

Some communities may have barriers to participation in co-curricular activities. In these situations community leaders, school officials, and parents must work together to provide these enriching opportunities for youths. For example, in rural areas where youths must ride buses home immediately after school, schools must offer flexible bus schedules. In communities where there are few activities in general for youth, schools must be willing to sponsor activities and locate certain activities (e.g., Scout meetings) in the school setting. Schools need to get directly involved in each student's co-curricular life. Students should be introduced to the range of co-curricular activities, and teachers and school counselors must take the initiative in communicating to parents the importance of their child's participation. The school can make an explicit effort to monitor whether every child is involved in a co-curricular activity.

Small schools may have advantages when it comes to encouraging participation in co-curricular activities. Consider a co-curricular activity such as a school drama. Students at a small school have a much better chance of landing a role in the play, since there are fewer students to compete for the roles. In some cases, students must be outright recruited to fill all the roles. There are fewer opportunities per person in a large school.[13] One way large schools can overcome this disadvantage is to optimize participation in co-curricular activities by "double-casting." In the example above, the school could stage two plays if there is a sufficient number of participants for two casts.

"Double-casting" can be a good idea in school sports also. My own success in school athletics was due, in part, to the double-casting phenomenon. My junior high school made a point of having three football teams for 7th grade boys: light, middle and heavyweight teams. While the school's rationale was to prevent larger players from injuring smaller players, the result was that everyone who wanted to was able to participate without regard to ability. While I have never considered myself small in stature, I was assigned to the lightweight team – I missed qualifying for the middleweight team by a mere two pounds. It was a two-pound blessing. The fact that I was able to excel on the team, even though I had only moderate ability compared to my larger schoolmates, gave a huge boost to my self-confidence. My grades improved and it put me on a trajectory of athletic involvement for life. Co-curricular activity participation continued to have positive influences beyond my years of schooling. In my case, these activities resulted in friendships that endured over time, through the transition to adulthood.

Relationship Between School Success and Co-Curricular Activities

There is a close connection between in-school performance and out-of-school activities. Studies have found that, on average, students who participated in co-curricular activities had higher school satisfaction and higher academic self-concept, which in turn led to higher grade-point-averages, more time spent on homework, and taking of more advanced courses.[14] It also appears that participation in co-curricular activities contributes to a student's sense of school connectedness, described earlier. These activities may enhance a student's identification with school and its values, resulting in more academic success.[15]

Of course school-sponsored sports and clubs represent only a small fraction of the enriching co-curricular activities available to youths. Reginald Clark's research corroborates the finding that children who have a chance to participate in quality out-of-school activities generally do better in school than their peers who have no co-curricular experiences. Furthermore, Clark identifies a diverse array of worthwhile activities:

"I have discovered that we can more accurately predict a young-ster's success or failure in school by finding out whether or not he or she typically spends approximately 20 to 35 hours a week (of the 60 to 70 [nonschool] waking hours a week that are avail-able to a youngster) engaging in what I call constructive learning activity. In a given week, this would consist of four or five hours of discussion with knowledgeable adults or peers, four or five hours of leisure reading, one or two hours of writing of various types (whether writing grocery lists, writing in a diary, taking messages on the telephone, or writing letters), five or six hours of homework, several hours devoted to hobbies, two or three hours of chores, four or five hours of games . . . that require the player to read, spell, write, compute, solve problems, make decisions, and use other cogni-tive skills and talents transferable to school lessons. This constructive learning activity also includes exposure to cultural activities, theater, movies, and sports."[16]

Taken together, activities such as these represent a vast, informal system of education through which children learn a broad spectrum of skills, attitudes, and values that can support and enhance in-school learning.[17] Unfortunately, the youths who would receive the most benefit from these types of activities are usually the least likely to seek them out. Consequently, parents, teachers, and professional counselors must be proactive, creative, and persistent in steering these "at-risk" children and adolescents toward investing their out-of-school time in co-curricular activities.[18] Certainly not all co-curricular activities are alike in their influence. Computer club, cheerleading, soccer team, how are they different? In Chapter 12, which discusses recreational and leisure activities, we will see if there are any answers.

Service-Learning Activities and Community Service

In American society today, there are still a few youths growing up on farms and in other settings where they contribute to their family's well being by doing valued work. Having such an experience, however, is far from the normal youth experience it was a century ago. Typically, today's adolescents are not contributors to the family economy, and unfortunately, adolescents often do not have a meaningful role in the social framework of their communities. Some theorists feel that this lack of a broader purpose or meaning in their lives may contribute to a sense of alienation. Today's adolescent can also be characterized as exhibiting an increased self-absorption, including an over-emphasis on physical appearance and materialism.[19] The theorists suggest that giving youths ample opportunities to work with people – and for people – in the community by volunteering can help counteract some of this inordinate focus on the self. By giving of themselves in this manner, youths become partners with adults in contributing to the betterment of their communities. This experience enables youths to assume meaningful roles and feel needed.

What is the difference between service learning and community service? In *service learning*, students participate in organized activities that address real community needs. Examples of common service-learning projects include participating in a "river-keeper" program which protects water quality and "adopting" a local nursing home. These activities are closely coordinated between the school and the community. Further, the experience is integrated into the academic curriculum and there is typically structured time to process and discuss the service experience. By contrast, *community service* is a volunteering activity in the community without a formal attachment to the school curriculum.[20] Almost six out of 10 teenagers participate in some kind of community service.[21]

Although many high schools offer or require community service, too often they do not set the context or teach about the larger problems the students are trying to address. For example, schools may organize activities for students at a homeless shelter but fail to discuss the lack of affordable housing in the community. Students may volunteer to help feed the hungry without being asked to explore why some people can't afford to eat. The challenge is to create community service experiences that inspire youths to get involved in creating solutions to problems when they enter adulthood.[22]

Why do youths participate in community service? Thirty percent volunteer because they were asked to by a church acquaintance or friend, 24 percent because it makes them feel good, and 21 percent because "it makes a difference." Only 6 percent reported volunteering because their school requires it.[23] Some of the benefits of service learning and community service reported by teenagers are outlined below.

More and more schools across the country are linking academics to volunteer experiences in the community. While many such efforts by the schools have been small-scale add-ons to the curriculum, increasingly schools are realizing that service learning should be a fundamental component in education. Take these examples:

In Michigan, a first-grade teacher works with students to raise funds for a charitable group. The effort is directly linked to a social studies unit on community. In New Mexico, students regularly visit

Benefits of Service Learning Reported by Teenagers [24]

- I learned to respect others.
- I learned to be helpful and kind.
- I learned to get along with and relate to others.
- I learned about the satisfaction that comes from helping others.
- I learned to understand people who are different from us.
- I learned how to relate to younger people.
- I learned to be a better person.
- I learned to be more patient with others.
- I learned leadership skills.

the local Meals on Wheels Program. Students help deliver meals, share their school work and gifts with seniors. In Georgia, sixth-grade students research the history of African Americans, write plays about their ancestors, and help restore an abandoned African-American cemetery.

In North Carolina, 9th-, 10th- and 11th-grade students volunteer one Saturday a month during the school year to participate in a youth leadership program. The goal is to develop leadership skills, encourage innovative problem solving, and instill a lifelong ethic of service and community involvement. Discussion topics include diversity and race relations, local government, education, and economic development. At the end of their training, students are put on local boards, giving them an opportunity to use their newly developed skills and abilities.

Community organizations sponsor service-learning projects too. For example, Boy Scouts, Girl Scouts, and 4-H Clubs have their members participate in community service efforts. Parents also may independently involve their children in volunteering, such as a parent who works as a nurse and has her teenager manage the reading cart at the hospital on Saturday mornings once-a-month. Another example would be where a parent and teenager volunteer together to sort materials one Saturday afternoon a month at the local recycling center.

There is impressive research showing that adolescents who participate in voluntary community service have better long-term adjustment compared to youths who do not participate in such activities.[25] Further, when the community service ethic is instilled in youths, it leads to greater giving and volunteering in adulthood, across every age group and income level.[26] Author Barbara Lewis has created a useful directory of over 500 service project ideas, *The Kid's Guide to Service Projects*. Included are topics such as animals, crime, the environment, literacy, politics, and others. Projects range from simple things anyone can do to large-scale commitments that involve whole communities.[27] If you wish to explore ways to involve children in service-learning and community service projects, Lewis' guide is highly recommended. Youth Service America, which is an alliance of more than 300 organizations involved in community service for youths, is another excellent resource, including their Web site.[28] There are other excellent sites on the Internet, as well, to help you find the right volunteer situation for a child.[29]

Summing Up

An essential element for school success is for a child to feel connected to the school. Following are some ways that you can encourage your child's connectedness.

Action Steps:

- Do some research (perhaps talk to a school counselor) to identify the best teachers in your child's school and try to see that your child benefits from these teachers. Students are more connected to school when they have a caring teacher who teaches with enthusiasm and responds to their special needs.

- If your child has a unique learning style that is not being accommodated by her current school, look for other educational environments that promise to provide a better fit for your child – alternative schools, charter schools, or even special learning tracks within a school. An alternative is to steer your child toward classes and teachers that better fit the child's learning style.

- Get involved in your child's schooling. Involvement may take many forms: helping your child with homework, calling the school with questions when there are problems, attending school meetings, and even volunteering at the school. There is a strong relationship between parent involvement and a child's school behaviors, including academic performance, attitudes, and motivation.

- Encourage your child to be regularly involved in a co-curricular activity, such as a varsity or intramural sport, choir, orchestra, theater group, debating team, student government, student yearbook or newspaper, or various school clubs. Co-curricular activities include relationships with one or more adults. These adults often become mentors who have an ongoing presence in the child's life, so get to know the coaches and teachers who lead your child's co-curricular activities. Co-curricular activities also are the best way to engender strong peer relationships in school. Peer relations in school must be positive for a child to feel connected.

■ Help remove barriers to your child's participation in co-curricular activities: advocating for schools to offer flexible bus schedules or forming a carpool with other parents are two ways you can help.

■ Talk to the school about available service-learning activities. Community service and service-learning activities enable youths to assume meaningful roles and feel needed.

QUIZ

School Environment

Answer Each Question 2, 1 or 0

2 = Yes, Often, or Usually   1 = Sometimes   0 = No or Never

_____ 1. Is the current classroom or school a good fit for your child's learning style?

_____ 2. Does your child study even when there is no homework?

_____ 3. Has your child participated in the school band, chorus or a drama presentation?

_____ 4. Is your child involved in a volunteer activity in the community?

_____ 5. Has your child participated in one of these types of school activities: cheerleading, student government, debate team, school clubs (chess, foreign language, science, etc.), newspaper or yearbook?

Scoring: Give yourself 2 points for "yes," "often," or "usually" answers, 1 point for "sometimes" answers, and 0 points for "no" and "never" answers. Total your points for questions 1 through 5 and write the answer below.

Your total score = _____ (0 to 10 points)

[1] Larson, R. (2000). Toward a psychology of positive youth development. *American Psychologist, 55,* 170-183.

[2] Resnick, M., Bearman, P. & Blum, R. (1997). Protecting adolescents from harm: Findings from the national longitudinal study on adolescent health. *JAMA, 278,* 823-832.

[3] Phelan, P., Davidson, A., & Yu, H. (1997). *Adolescents' worlds: Negotiating family, peers, and school.* New York: Teachers College Press.

[4] Gardner, H. (2000). *Intelligence reframed: Multiple intelligences for the 21st century.* New York: Basic Books.

[5] Schorr, L. (1997). *Common purpose: Strengthening families and neighborhoods to rebuild America.* New York: Doubleday-Anchor Press.

[6] Gurian, M. (2002). *Boys and girls learn differently: A guide for teachers and parents.* New York: Jossey-Bass.

[7] Barker, R., & Gump, P. (1964). *Big schools, small schools: High school size and student behavior.* Palo Alto: Stanford University Press.

[8] Gilman, R. (2001). The relationship between life satisfaction, social intrest, and frequency of extracurricular activities among adolescent students. *Journal of Youth and Adolescence, 30,* 749-767. p. 752-753.

[9] Crosnoe, R. (2002). Academic and health-related trajectories in adolescence: The intersection of gender and athletics. *Journal of Health and Social Behavior, 43,* 317-335.

[10] Mahoney, J. (2000). School extracurricular activity participation as a moderator in the development of antisocial patterns. *Child Development, 71,* 502-516.

[11] Jeziorski, R. (1994). *The importance of school sports in American education and socialization.* Lanham, MD: University Press of America. p. 5-6.

[12] *Ibid.*

[13] Bechtel, R. (1996). *Environment & behavior: An introduction.* Thousand Oaks, CA: Sage.

[14] Gilman, R. (2001).

[15] Marsh cited in Gilman, R. (2001).

[16] Clark, R. (1988). *Critical factors in why disadvantaged students succeed or fail in school.* New York: Academy for Educational Development, p. 4-5.

[17] Erickson, J. (1988). *Directory of American youth organizations.* Minneapolis, MN: Free Spirit Publishing.

[18] Medrich, E., Roizen, J., Rubin, V., & Buckley, S. (1982). *The serious business of growing up: A study of children's lives outside school.* Berkeley, CA: University of California Press.

[19] *Ibid.*

[20] Perkins, D., & Miller, J. Why community services and service learning? Providing rationale and research. www.quest.edu/content/Resources/ServiceLearningArticles/slarticle2.htm. Accessed 4/8/02

[21] Benson, P., Galbraith, J., & Espeland, P. (1998). *What teens need to succeed.* Minneapolis: Free Spirit.

[22] National Public Radio. (January 7, 2003). Civic lessons beyond the class-room: Volunteering may not teach students about problems' roots. http://www.npr.org/display_pages/features/feature_905341.html. Accessed 1/7/03.

[23] 2002 survey of Americans aged 15-25, conducted by the Pew Charitable Trust.

[24] *Volunteering and giving among American teenagers 12 to 17 years of age* cited in Benson, P., Galbraith, J., & Espeland, P. (1998).

[25] Allen cited in Mahoney, J., & Stattin, H. (2000). Leisure activities and adolescent antisocial behavior: The role of structure and social context. *Journal of Adolescence, 23,* 113-127.

[26] Independent Sector. (2002). *Engaging youth in lifelong service: Findings and recommendations for encouraging a tradition of voluntary action amongst America's youth.* Washington, DC: Author.

[27] Lewis, B. (1995). *The kid's guide to service projects: Over 500 service ideas for young people who want to make a difference.* Minneapolis, MN: Free Spirit Publishing.

[28] www.ysa.org

[29] Stories about what other children have done can be found at www.idealist.org/kt/youthorgs.html. Project ideas for teenagers to help other people by volunteering can be found at www.bygpub.com/books/tg2rw/volunteer.html. Family projects are emphasized at www.pointsoflight.org/for_volunteer/family.cfm. Finally, Volunteer Match allows children to enter their city to find organizations that are recruiting children volunteers: www.volunteermatch.org.

CHAPTER 7

After-School Settings

THE 1950s AND 1960s WERE A UNIQUE WINDOW IN American history when one income could support a family and the divorce rate was nowhere near the level of today. Most households included two parents and most mothers did not work outside the home. Today, only about one-quarter of children live in two-parent homes with stay-at-home moms.[1] While this figure is up 13 percent in a little less than a decade, the fact remains that most children are not supervised by parents after school. This phenomenon creates a challenge for the risky time, from 3 to 6 p.m., after school and before many parents return home from work. Research has shown that this is the time when youths are most likely to get into trouble. Youths are twice as likely to abuse drugs or alcohol, to have sex, or to engage in criminal activities when unsupervised after school.[2]

It is not a simple matter to categorize children's after-school arrangements. Some children are supervised by adults and others are not. Some unsupervised children spend after-school hours alone; others are in the company of siblings or friends. The environments where children spend their after-school time are diverse too: homes, libraries, schools or community sites hosting formal after-school programs, parks, friends' homes. And the varied options increase with age. Some children have considerable freedom to move around in multiple settings; others are confined to a single setting – even a single room.

Of course, the setting affects the after-school activities children are involved in. Some settings are rich with engaging activities, while others have few things of interest to children. For children at home, care for siblings or household chores may fill much of their time. Others may be involved in sports, music, or other recreational activities in supervised programs. Finally, some children are physically active, whereas others spend most of their time inert, watching television.[3] Here are some typical examples:

Billy is in second grade. After school he walks only 50 yards from his classroom to the school multipurpose room where an after-school program is conducted until 6 p.m. He spends time completing his homework, playing outside in good weather, and watching videos. Billy has friends from the neighborhood who attend the same after-school program. He likes the teachers and he generally enjoys the program.

Amanda is in the fifth grade. Two days a week she walks home from school and watches TV or uses her computer until her mother gets home from work at 6 p.m. Amanda calls her mother as soon as she gets home. Two afternoons after school, Amanda plays at a neighbor's house where the mother is at home. One day a week, Amanda's mother comes home early to take her to music lessons.

Arturo is in the second grade. He rides the bus home after school. His mother is unemployed. Arturo spends most of his time watching television. The family lives in a housing project and his mother discourages outside play because of potential dangers in the neighborhood.

As you can see from these examples, children's after-school arrangements are highly variable. Sometimes children go to the same place each day after school; sometimes arrangements vary by the day of the week or by the time of year. For example, one study found that 41 percent of fourth graders experienced at least one major change in after-school arrangements by the fifth grade.[4]

While parents often have a number of options for structured after-school programs for children in grades K-5, after-school programs are frequently unavailable for middle-school-age children. These young teenagers need to be given more responsibility and are often capable of taking care of themselves, but it opens a window of vulnerability. As noted earlier, this is a risky time in which adolescents can become involved in activities that threaten their health, safety, and positive development. I've already mentioned activities like drug or alcohol abuse and sexual experimentation. Let me add to the list of concerns: visiting Web sites with inappropriate material or chat rooms occupied by sexual predators and watching television that is sexually provocative or playing violent videogames.

> **Youths who participate in structured after-school activities show better behavioral adjustment than youths in unstructured situations, such as hanging out with friends or engaging in poor-quality recreation. Structured activities must be led by competent adults and have skill-building goals; good examples are Scouts, music activities, and sports teams. Psychologists Joseph Mahoney and Hakan Stattin conclude that the best opportunities for youths involve "engrossing activities and positive peer involvement in the context of thoughtful, consistent, adult supervision."[5]**

In a study of after-school activities, Boston University psychologist Deborah Belle concluded that time spent in organized activities is related to children's development. Children who spend more time in unorganized activities generally have poorer grades, work habits, and emotional adjustment. Children who spent more time in organized activities, such as music and gymnastics lessons, generally had better grades, work habits, emotional adjustment, and peer relationships. Time spent on academic activities with assistance from adults was positively related to better grades and conduct in school. The relationship between time use and children's adjustment was true for the whole sample as well as within the types of after-school care studied. Therefore, it appears that the children's organized activities and peer interactions were key, regardless of the care situation, even though some settings provided more opportunities for particular activities. There was one exception: Time spent with peers after school increased antisocial behavior for children in self-care but resulted in less antisocial behavior for children who attended organized programs. Clearly, peer activities have different outcomes under supervised and non-supervised circumstances.[6]

In a similar study, University of Missouri psychologist Harris Cooper and colleagues looked at five after-school activities and their relationships to the academic achievement of students in grades 6–12. The after-school activities included time spent doing homework, watching television, participating in extracurricular activities and other structured after-school groups, and in employment. After statistically controlling for the level of adult supervision, the researchers found that after-school activities contributed to the prediction of achievement. Students who did more homework after school earned higher grades. High amounts of TV viewing and after-school employment were related to poor achievement. Participation in extracurricular activities predicted higher grades. The research team concluded that knowledge about how students spend their after-school hours can predict their school performance.[7]

Finally, it must be acknowledged that highly structured after-school programs, following a day of structured classroom experience, may intrude on a child's need for simple down time and more independent time that is not directly organized by adults.

The quality of after-school programs varies enormously. It is clear from the research that the involvement in structured after-school activities does not in itself account for the reduction in risky behaviors. That is, the mere consumption of time is not the critical factor. Mahoney and Stattin found that adolescents who participated in structured after-school activities exhibited depression less often than other adolescents. The key factor was that the teenagers perceived high support from the adult activity leader. This perception of support was particularly important for youths who had poor relations with their parents.[8] Educational researcher Kim Pierce and his colleagues also found relationships with adults to be critical. In a study of first graders in after-school programs they found that positive relationships between the staff and children resulted in greater social skills.[9]

The supportive people available to children during the after-school hours are quite variable, ranging from babysitters to teachers, coaches, neighbors, relatives, and other adults. For some children, these adults make up an accessible support network that provides emotional support, guidance, and companionship. Some children readily engage such networks, while others do not take advantage of them.

Some relationships with adult activity leaders evolve into enduring mentoring relationships. Mentoring entails a one-on-one relationship with an adult who provides nurturance, assistance in problem solving, inspiration, and reassurance of worth. Such relationships often involve skill-building and goal-setting opportunities as well.[10] One study found that a majority of adolescents identified a nonparental adult who plays an important role in their lives.[11] Mentors can positively influence adolescents' behavior, school attendance, and sense of competence in school. Another study found guidance and support from a nonparental adult can lead to improvements in the quality of the parent-child relationship. It is important that parents do not feel supplanted by the additional adult support. Finding nonparental adult guides to look up to is an important, necessary step in adolescence.[12]

> **Read any autobiography and chances are that the writer will recount the importance of a teacher, a neighbor, or some other adult who was there for the writer at just the right time when growing up. It's not just the activity — the sport, the school play, or volunteering at the local hospital — which grows the child, it is often the adult relationship that makes the difference: the mature feedback, the teaching of self-reflection, the offer of praise during each step of success.[13]**

As children grow older, they are more likely to be involved in self-care. There are 3.5 million children in America who regularly spend their after-school hours unsupervised by adults or older teenagers. This phenomenon of the "latchkey" child has been a popular subject for research over the past two decades. Some studies have found that self-care can lead to problematic behavior. Other studies have found no difference between the behavior pattern of supervised and unsupervised children. Most of the studies have emphasized that there is great variation among self-care arrangements, making broad conclusions difficult.[14]

As with everything that involves children assuming more responsibility as they grow older, there is no specific age when children are ready for unsupervised time after school. Generally, however, a guideline used by many parents today is that starting at age 9 children may spend brief periods of time alone at home, increasing in amount until middle school, typically, age 12, when a child may spend the after-school time alone. These guidelines are variable, however, and each child's strengths must be considered as well as environmental hazards and supports. Parental expectations, too, will vary from family to family.

The locations where children spend unsupervised time can be an important variable. For example, self-care in a suburban neighborhood with a nearby supportive neighbor is generally very different than self-care in an urban neighborhood where crime is prevalent. Further, self-care when parents monitor a child from a distance (for example, by cell phone) is quite different than self-care when a child is left simply to hang out without a support line. Developmental psychologist Gregory Pettit and colleagues specifically looked at whether parental monitoring and perceived neighborhood safety affected behavioral adjustment. Unsupervised peer contact frequently led to problem behavior. Peer contact in the presence of adult supervision, however, did not as often lead to problem behaviors. Further, they found that the combination of an unsafe neighborhood and low monitoring often leads to aggressive behavior. The researchers concluded that parents who monitor their children and live in relatively safe neighborhoods buffer their children against many risks associated with unsupervised peer contact.[15]

However, on the whole, a review of the available studies to date shows that the overall behavioral adjustment of latchkey children is very similar to children who return home after school to a parent.[16] The lesson remains that we must be aware of each child's needs after school and look to the sources of support we can draw upon. In some cases, watching television may help a child cope with boredom and loneliness. Or perhaps a pet could be an important source of support for some children. Having responsibilities, such as household chores and homework completion, also may provide supportive structures.

Finally, in some homes, and particularly for low-income families and single-parent households, children must take care of one or more siblings. The experience of caring for a younger sibling may have negative repercussions, such as lost opportunities to pursue co-curricular activities. However, the experience may also teach care-taking skills and enhance nurturance as a value and sensitivity to others' needs. Sibling care-taking has been found to deepen the affection of siblings for one another and enhance the importance of their relationship in the lives of the siblings.[17]

Summing Up

There are numerous options for children's after-school care and participation. No one approach is the best for all children; each child's circumstances should be looked at individually. However, the time from 3 to 6 p.m. is the risky time in which adolescents can become involved in activities that threaten their health and safety. Unsupervised time spent with peers after school is related to increased antisocial behavior.

Action Steps:

- Involve elementary-age children in a structured after-school program. A guiding principle is that youths who participate in structured after-school activities show better behavioral adjustment than youths who are in unstructured after-school situations. By involving children in a structured after-school program, you enable them to form meaningful and enduring relationships with adult activity leaders. Such adults often become important mentors to children.

- Make sure children who need it have a chance for some "down time" during after-school programs. Highly structured after-school programs following a day of structured classroom experience can be a bit too much for some children.

- If your teenager must be unsupervised after school, remain in touch, for example, by having cell phone contact.

■ Minimize "risky time" for adolescents. This is the time from 3–6 p.m. when teenagers are most likely to encounter negative experiences or influences, such as suffering accidents or being pressured by peers to engage in risky behavior (drug use, dangerous sexual practice, criminal activity). Know where teenagers are and what they are doing!

After-School Environment

Answer Each Question 2, 1 or 0

2 = Yes, Often, or Usually   1 = Sometimes   0 = No or Never

_____ 1. Do you have a good child care arrangement when your child needs supervision?

_____ 2. Is your child involved in productive after-school activities?

_____ 3. If your child is alone after school, do you always stay in touch via phone?

_____ 4. Is your child under adult supervision after school?

_____ 5. Does your child participate in a co-curricular activity after school?

Scoring: Give yourself 2 points for "yes," "often," or "usually" answers, 1 point for "sometimes" answers, and 0 points for "no" and "never" answers. Total your points for questions 1 through 5 and write the answer below.

Your total score = _____ (0 to 10 points)

[1] Armas, G. (2003, June 17). Nineties brought boom in children with stay-at-home moms. *Asheville Citizen-Times*. p. C6.

[2] Gurian cited in Pollack, W. (1998). *Real boys.* New York: Random House.

[3] Belle, D. (1999). *After-school lives of children.* Mahwah, NJ: Lawrence Erlbaum Associates.

[4] *Ibid.*

[5] Mahoney, J., & Stattin, H. (2002). Structured after-school activities as a moderator of depressed mood for adolescents with detached relations to their parents. *Journal of Community Psychology, 30,* 69-86.

[6] *Ibid.*

[7] Cooper, H., Valentine, J., Nye, B., & Lindsay, J. (1999). Relationships between five after-school activities and academic achievement. *Journal of Educational Psychology, 91,* 369-378.

[8] *Ibid.*

[9] Pierce, K., Hamm, J., & Vandell, D. (1999). Experiences in after-school programs and children's adjustment in first-grade classrooms. *Child Development, 70,* 756-767.

[10] Mahoney, J., & Stattin, H. (2002).

[11] Greenberger, E., Chen, C., & Beam, M. (1998). The role of "very important" nonparental adults in adolescent development. *Journal of Youth and Adolescence, 27,* 321-343.

[12] Rhodes, J., Grossman, J., & Resch, N. (2000). Agents of change: Pathways through which mentoring relationships influence adolescents' academic adjustment. *Child Development, 71,* 1662-1671.

[13] Bloom, M. (2001). The uses of theory in primary prevention practice: Evolving thoughts on sports and after-school activities as influences of social competency. In S. Danish & T. Gullotta (Eds.), *Developing competent youth and strong communities through after-school programming* (pp. 17-66). Washington, DC: CWLA Press.

[14] Belle, D. (1999).

[15] Pettit, G., Bates, J., Dodge, K., & Meece, D. (1999). The impact of after-school peer contact on early adolescent externalizing problems is moderated by parental monitoring, perceived neighborhood safety, and prior adjustment. *Child Development, 70,* 768-778.

[16] Shulman, S., Peri Braja, M. (1998). Latchkey children: Potential sources of support. *Journal of Community Psychology, 26,* 185-197.

[17] Belle, D. (1999).

CHAPTER 8

Electronic Setting

THIS CHAPTER ADDRESSES ONE OF THE SETTINGS that is not a physical environment. However, using the various forms of electronic media involves some distinctive characteristics, regardless of the actual setting. It is this fact, along with media's strong pull on the child and adolescent psyche, that qualifies the electronic setting as an environment of concern when addressing child development. How much time are youths spending with the media? I will try to answer that question, as well as their effects on children's lives, including the other activities that are being displaced.

American popular media culture exerts an enormous influence in our lives. Sociologist Todd Gitlin, in his book *Media Unlimited*, says "the obvious but hard-to-grasp truth is that living with the media is today one of the main things Americans and other human beings do . . . they are wraparound presences with which we live much of our lives . . . an accompaniment to life that has become a central experience of life."[1]

Although the predominant medium that children spend time with is still television, new technologies like instant messaging and the Internet are emerging to consume their time. Youths today spend more time in media "activities" than in any activity other than sleeping. Clearly, the media have become a new second family. This means that the range of influences on children's cognitive and social learning has broadened. We must assess these effects, which may be either educational and enhancing or inane, distracting, and actually harmful to children's development.[2]

In past decades, through the 1970s, the media environment that children grew up in was much safer. Today's media landscape surrounds children with sex, violence, and an incessant focus on commercial values, where everything is dedicated to the purpose of selling something.

The immensity of the experience of media includes, to name a few, television, radio and audio systems, gaming systems and computers. Youths can choose from hundreds of television channels, thousands of videogames, and millions of Web pages. They also carry portable versions of their favorite media to go wherever they go. Most youth report having media that they can control and use in private, typically in their bedrooms. The simultaneous use of two or three media is not unusual, for example, instant messaging while researching a term paper on the Internet and listening to pulsating rap music on the stereo. Today, one in three teenagers has a wireless phone. By 2006, three out of four will have one, according to the Yankee Group, a technology research and consulting firm.[3] Youths' environments have become a multiplex, an arcade of amusements.[4]

James Steyer has written one of the most incisive reviews of media in the lives of children. I recommend *The Other Parent* to all parents. He notes:

"It is tempting to believe that we can trust the media with our kids, that we don't need to pay close attention to what movies or TV shows our kids are watching, what computer games they're playing, where they're surfing on the Internet, or what lyrics are coming through their Walkman headphones. It's much easier to believe – as our parents could – that we can trust the media. After all, we're only adding more work and worry to our lives if we admit that we now need to be as wary of the media as we are of strangers accosting our children on the street. As a result, many parents are in a state of 'media denial,' while others feel overwhelmed and helpless. But the fact is, we need to take as much responsibility for our children's media consumption as we do for their performance in school and their physical well-being."[5] Steyer's statement is sobering – we must take responsibility for the influence of the ubiquitous electronic environment. There are dangers in failing to do so.

There is one more issue regarding children's exposure to any of the various forms of media – and this relates more to the general nature of electronic media than to the content of what is presented. Children should have the maximum opportunity for talking in their daily lives. The use of language is critical for brain development. Anything that limits a child's verbalizations, such as TV viewing, solitary computer use, and videogame playing may be detrimental. Take for example the concept of metacognition, which describes the process of self-evaluation. The process entails monitoring what we are doing, figuring out why a particular behavior was successful or not successful, and then developing options for behavior for similar situations in the future. To develop this skill, children need to interact with adults and older children who model how to reflect on their thinking, use down time to pause and think things through, and develop the language ability to "think aloud" about their behavior. It is important to create sufficient conversational spaces for children during time not dominated by computers and other media.

In the discussion that follows, I will review some of the major forms of electronic stimulation in the lives of children.

Television

TV viewing shapes and changes children's behavior and their social environment. The portrait of a typical American child in the television age involves these facts:

- TV viewing consumes 30 percent of pre-adolescents' free time on weekday evenings and close to 50 percent of their time on weekends.[6] This amount increases by 50 percent or more during summer months.[7]

- The average teen watches 22.5 hours of television a week, which is about four times the amount of time devoted to homework.

- By age 18, the average child will have watched 22,000 hours of television, which is double the amount of time the child will have spent in classroom instruction.[8]

Outlined below are five major potential health effects of TV watching:[9]

- Unhealthy eating behaviors may accompany television viewing (e.g., eating snacks and drinking sugary soft drinks). About 80 percent of adolescents say they eat while they watch television.

- Family lifestyle may be disrupted. Families may eat with the television on or change mealtimes because of programming. Television viewing may compete with the time for cooking the family meal, resulting in more ready-made or take-out meals. Sleeping habits may be affected, especially if a favorite show is on at a late hour.

- Watching television may displace other skill-building leisure time activities. Television viewing also is primarily a solitary activity and steals time from possible real-life interactions with others, which helps develop interpersonal skills.

- Television viewing makes people physically inactive and robs time that could be spent in more physical pursuits.

- The content of television may sometimes be detrimental to healthy child development. Four decades of research on this issue shows that there is room for concern about what children watch.

Most of the talk and research about TV's harmful effects on children has focused on this latter issue, that is, TV programming. In reality, the likelihood of harm from viewing age-inappropriate violence and sexual acts on television may be matched or surpassed by the harm that comes merely from the act of watching television. When children are watching TV, they are not doing other things that are an important part of growing up and learning how to be human:

participating in hobbies, talking to others, learning how to do something when bored, reading, doing homework, and helping around the house. A new term has emerged to describe households where the TV is constantly blaring, even when no one is watching: *total television homes*. TV is an effective babysitter – keeping children quiet and out of the way – but this comes at a high price. Too much of "childhood" is being missed.

Watching TV is a passive activity; it doesn't challenge the mind. Developmental psychologist David Elkind has explained very nicely how television shapes behavior. Elkind compares TV to a digital watch; you just look at it and there's the time. But radio and books are like regular watches; you must use your mind and interpret what you see. For instance, when the big hand is on the one and the little hand is on the three, that means it's five minutes past three o'clock. So TV entails relatively little challenge, low demand, and usually little educational benefit.[10]

For children who are learning to read, watching a lot of TV may take its toll on the development of literacy skills. When children are spending a lot of time watching TV, or playing videogames, reading time is being displaced. Also, TV viewing can become habit forming, because the visual media offer instant gratification. Children may develop the need for quick satisfaction and constant entertainment. It's much easier to become engaged in TV than to work at reading. Consequently, reading may become much more difficult.[11] The American Academy of Pediatrics warns that TV viewing can negatively affect early brain development, especially for children under 2, an age when learning to talk and play are critical. The Academy recommends that these very young children not watch TV.[12]

Psychologist David Walsh also notes that TV viewing may have an important effect on critical aspects of language development: having a conversation with yourself, or what is called private speech. Private speech engages our critical thinking, helps us consider alternatives and consequences, and helps us make reasonable decisions. We use private speech to control impulses, that is, to think before acting. Reading skills facilitate the development of private speech.[13]

In a fascinating study, University of Michigan doctoral student, Wu Ping, found that watching an excessive amount of TV increases people's desire for material possessions. He also found that excessive TV viewing reduces personal contentment by about 5 percent for every hour a day we watch television![14]

One possible solution to the TV problem is to get rid of your television set. (Some families choose to keep a television set just to watch an occasional video or DVD.) There are many anecdotal reports that lots of good things usually begin to happen in families that give up TV. Family psychologist John Rosemond has been a proponent of "televisionectomies" for a long time. He notes that there is usually a withdrawal period (from four to six weeks), after which children quickly develop a variety of healthy interests, including sports, reading, and hobbies. He also observes that it is not uncommon for children to become straight-A students and for children with ADHD to improve remarkably within a relatively short period of time. Here, Rosemond relates the experience of one family that took his advice and eliminated television from the household when their daughter was 2 years old:

> "She is a voracious reader, Mom reports, and her teachers rave about what a joy she is to have in class. She and Mom swap books and then talk about what they've read, but Mom is finding it increasingly difficult to keep pace with her daughter's reading speed and comprehension.

> "Has not watching television caused any social difficulties for this youngster? No. In her own words (as quoted by her mother), 'Other kids look at me like I am crazy when I tell them my parents don't allow TV, but I think I matured more quickly than my peers, and I have different values.'"[15]

Children do not always act in their own best interest, however. We adults have to set some guidelines. If you can't bring yourself to eliminate TV from your family's life, at least keep TV out of children's bedrooms. Don't use TV as a babysitter. And set some clear rules about when kids can watch – "no TV before homework is completed" is a common restriction that helps children recognize priorities.

The history of television teaches an important lesson. Television was heralded as a great, innovative teaching tool that would help produce a generation of smarter children. The result has been minimal at best. True, watching prosocial programs on educational television has been found to have a positive relationship with prosocial behaviors. And children who watch *Sesame Street* grow up to have better grades in high school.[16] So while some educational programming on television fulfills the early promise of television, most of television is, in the words of former Chairman of the U.S. Federal Communications Commission, Newton Minow, a "vast wasteland."

Computers

While computers have burst onto the scene with much of the same fanfare and promised benefits as television did, it remains to be seen what the effects of computers will be on youths. The likelihood is that the place computers are given in the family will be a critical variable in determining their potential effects.[17]

Why do parents buy home computers? Surveys suggest that parents buy home computers and Internet access, in part, to enhance educational opportunities for their children and to prepare them for the technological age. Parents may be deceived, however, in believing that just because using the computer looks technologically sophisticated children are learning important things. Computers share some of television's disadvantages. Certainly, with their mesmerizing special effects, computers may be even more addictive than TV. We've begun to hear some parents say that they wished they had never purchased a computer. Many parents say they are disappointed that their children often use the computer mostly to play games, surf the Internet, or download music or pictures of popular stars. Generally, parents consider this to be wasted time, comparable to time spent in front of the television.[18]

Parents prefer that their children use computers for educational purposes. But what about that? Computers can facilitate the learning process, but do they really make a difference? University of Michigan Professor James Kulik studied whether computer-aided instruction improved achievement scores in elementary and high schools. Interestingly, when computer-aided instruction was compared to traditional learning, using paper, pencil and printed material, the traditional way of learning was as effective or better.[19] Schools are spending millions of dollars on computers and yet they may be less effective than traditional activities such as hobbies, games, and reading, which improve academic skills.

To understand the full impact of computers on children, it is important to know how much time children spend on computers and what possible alternative activities are being displaced. Early research shows that moderate computer use does not negatively impact children's and teenagers' social skills and activities. However, the impact of excessive computer use is not well-documented yet. Certainly, long hours spent using the computer may displace other important activities, such as recreational and social activities. Children in general still spend more time watching television than using computers, although children who use computers, watch less television.[20]

With the presence of personal computers in many homes, more and more families are using the Internet both as a tool for communication and as a resource for information. The number of households that are "connected" has grown so rapidly that any cited data are sure to be obsolete before they are published. The explosion of the Internet is no doubt dramatically affecting the ecology of child development.

Teenagers, who are heavier users of the Internet compared to their parents, spend most of their online time messaging or e-mailing friends, doing homework, or surfing the Web. While data on the use of the Internet among children and adolescents is scarce, the HomeNet study provides some early insights.[21] Boys are heavier users of the Internet than girls, even though girls have the same access to computers. The study also found that high Internet use is related to weaker social relationships. For example, low Internet users generally have better relationships with their parents and friends compared to high Internet users. Although computer use is often a solitary activity, e-mail and the Internet may facilitate communication and help sustain social relationships.

At the same time, the Internet harbors the potential for the exploitation of youth, such as sexual solicitations, pornography, and online harassment. The Youth Internet Safety Survey looked at the characteristics of youths who have formed close relationships with people they met on the Internet. The sample, consisting of Internet users aged 10–17, revealed that 14 percent of youths had close online friendships, 2 percent reported online romances, and 14 percent reported close online relationships. The study found that a disproportionate number of adolescents with close online relationships reported high amounts of conflict with their parents, had low communication with parents, and engaged in more delinquent activities. One implication is that parents should ask their children about online relationships just as they would monitor other close friendships.[22]

According to another study, increased use of the Internet is associated with decreased family communication and a reduced social circle.[23] Further, youths who spend an excessive amount of time online experience increased loneliness and decreased social support. It is conceivable that high Internet use restricts the social activities and interactions that are critical to building social support. However, as already noted, moderate use could actually increase social resources. The particular influence will depend on whether the social uses of the Internet supplement or supplant other social contacts that youths engage in. Clearly, the Internet has the capacity either to support or to constrain developmental processes and outcomes, depending on the particular circumstances.

Parents often ask questions such as: How much online time is appropriate for my child? What is the best age to introduce the Internet to my child? Is filtering software enough to protect my child from objectionable material and cyber-pedophiles? How do I choose the best software to protect my child? The Center for Online and Internet Addiction offers a selection of publications to educate parents on the dynamics of online relationships and Internet behavior and to help families wisely integrate the Internet into the home.[24] Parental oversight of children's Internet use is critical. While most parents gave up monitoring children's TV watching long ago, the Internet should be treated with more concern. Parents can use filtering devices to protect children from potentially harmful content on the Internet. A problem with Internet filters and "safe-haven" sites is that parents with limited computer skills are uncomfortable using them. Studies indicate that the majority of parents do not use them.[25]

Electronic Games

Games played on the computer are similar to games played on other platforms (e.g., X-Box) or interactive games played on the Internet. The reference to videogames here includes all formats.

Most parents, feeling that the computer is more educational than TV, will typically buy their children any software they ask for – usually that means software for game playing. Video and computer games have become a mainstay in most American homes today. Just as television and movie content should be monitored, videogames should be scrutinized. Some are innocuous; some are educational; some have no place in the home. Boys may be particularly vulnerable, because they spend about triple the amount of time playing videogames compared to girls.[26] Many computer games are so psychologically compelling to children that they become addictive.

Boys also are usually the consumers of the most violent games. In his book *Dr. Dave's Cyberhood,* psychologist David Walsh points to a disturbing fact regarding violent videogames. He cites David Grossman, a retired military officer who spent his career studying how to enable soldiers to kill. It turns out that killing does not come naturally to soldiers; it has to be taught. Human beings have some psychological resistance to killing their own. Grossman is an expert in the psychological conditioning techniques used to eliminate that resistance. Chillingly, the techniques that are used by the Army to enable soldiers to kill are identical to those employed in violent electronic games. According to Grossman, "Children don't naturally kill; they learn from the violence in the home, and most pervasively from violence as entertainment in television, movies, and interactive video."[27]

Should parents be concerned about violent media content, including violent interactive videogames? Journalist Gerald Jones, an author of videogames and cartoon series, writes persuasively in *Killing Monsters*[28] that fantasy violence plays an essential role in children's development. Jones argues that many of the new videogames which hold such appeal to youths can help them develop coping skills they desperately need. He draws mostly from anecdotes to make his case, such as the timid adolescent girl whose participation in make-believe violence helped her to tap into her own bottled-up emotions and discover feelings of personal power. But scientific evidence may diminish Jones' reassurance that fantasy violence can help children develop in healthy ways. For example, psychologist L. Rowell Huesmann and his associates at the University of Michigan's Institute for Social Research, found that both boys and girls who watch a lot of violence on television have a heightened risk of aggressive adult behavior, including spouse abuse and criminal offenses, no matter how they act in childhood.[29] And Craig Anderson, professor and chair of the department of psychology at Iowa State University, says emphatically, "The evidence is now clear that playing violent videogames increases aggressive behavior and decreases prosocial behavior in children and young adults."[30]

Educational games appear to be more available for computers, versus free-standing gaming systems. For example, there are some popular culture and simulation games. Parents may assert more control over the use of computer software, since they are more apt to be using the computer themselves. It is intuitive that parents may encourage educational games as opposed to action/adventure software, especially in light of their stated perception that computers give children an educational advantage. But this is speculation; we do not have empirical evidence.[31]

To be fair, there are instances in which computer games can help children learn. For example, some computer games help children develop certain forms of visual-spatial reasoning. However, the overall effect of how this ability may relate to school learning is not clear. As with the other forms of media already discussed, the key is for parents to monitor children's use of electronic games, both the content of the games and the amount of time spent playing them.

Music

Music is part of the metabolism of most teenagers and pre-adolescents. Four out of five teenagers say that music is an important part of their lives.[32] As they grow older, children spend increasing amounts of time listening to music and can establish intense loyalties to certain kinds of music and singers. Teenagers listen to music or watch music videos an average of four to five hours a day.[33] Studies show that teenagers buy the majority of popular music recording.[34] In general, as teenagers get older, they spend less time watching television and more time listening to music, although these activities are combined in music videos. Researcher Reed Larson and his colleagues conjecture that the popularity of music with teenagers is the result of growing concerns about independence, romance, and sexuality, and precisely because it flies in the face of adult concerns. They say that music offers adolescents relief from the constant pressures they face at home and in school.[35]

Interestingly, research has shown that most teenagers can name a song that has influenced a value they hold. Many parents are concerned about the values that children are exposed to in the world of music. Music videos frequently have sexual themes. The dancing promoted in some videos has lead to provocative imitation among teenagers. Most parents find the lyrics of some hip-hop and rap songs to be disgusting. These concerns have been widely reported in the popular press. I only mention them here, with the caveat that they are unlikely to change.

Impact of the Digital Revolution on Children and Families

The Kaiser Family Foundation has conducted the first study to examine the full pattern of media use among a representative sample of American youth. The study gives us a picture of how new media are impacting the development of children. The study found that the average child consumes seven hours of media per day. Since youth sometimes use two or more media at once, they are actually exposed to over eight hours of media content per day.

The authors of the Kaiser Foundation study highlighted a couple of resounding themes. They noted that if it were not for a great increase in listening to music, teenagers' media use drops precipitously as adolescence takes hold. Teenagers watch far less television, play videogames less, and go to fewer movies. The authors believe that this occurs because of the demands placed on teenagers' time. Hence, they conclude that the best predictor of media use is available time, that is, time not filled by more structured and attractive activities.[36]

The other compelling point made by the authors of the study is this: "Prior to television, parents could exert at least some control over children's access to messages. The seven or eight years it took most children to learn to read provided time for parents to establish the 'cognitive templates' which their offspring used to interpret the meaning of print and audio symbols."[37] In Chapter 9, we will discuss how friends have become more influential in children's lives as adults' time in interaction with youth has diminished. Here, we see that parents' ability to influence their children has become a daily battle with the media also.

A new research center has been established to help understand the proliferation and effects of new media. The National Science Foundation-funded Children's Digital Media Center[38] is based at Georgetown University. The Center is looking at two major questions: How does the interactivity that is a hallmark of the new technologies affect children's ability to learn? And how do the new technologies help children create their identities? Sandra Calvert, co-founder of the Children's Digital Media Center, is studying how online interactions allow adolescents to experiment with their identities. Teenagers create personae that role play and interact with others on Multi-User Domains (MUDs). They are able to express facets of themselves that they are uncomfortable with in a safe place. Calvert is looking at whether MUDs can enhance or undermine identity formation in adolescence. Another project is studying how "chat room" interaction relates to children's real-world social lives.[39]

So what are the implications of this dazzling array of digital media? The electronic environment is perhaps as pervasive and influential as any environment that children inhabit. The present generation of youth have come to expect this constant stimulation. We cannot generalize with an admonition that these media constitute a negative influence on children. These media are neither entirely good nor entirely bad. What becomes important is that we recognize their power. Our children's lives are enveloped by these media. Earlier in the book, I alluded to the diet of children. We would not let children subsist on a Twinkies-chips-and-candy diet. The same analogy applies here. Balance in the media diets of our children is the watchword.

> Is electronic stimulation replacing physical activity and interpersonal experience? Teachers often remark that today's children are overstressed and overanxious, in part due to a general lack of physical exercise. Physical activity — preferably outdoors — is vital for good health, including sleep patterns, dissipation of energy, stress reduction and socialization. During spontaneous play, important learning and problem-solving occurs that is important for psychological development.

Many teachers complain that students find everything boring. They feel like the students expect to be entertained. Children often require so much stimulation that they use multiple media simultaneously ("multi-tasking"). Take for example the child huddled in front of the television set watching the Cartoon Network while simultaneously playing with his Game Boy. Watching television, focusing on fast-paced, visually distracting images may actually change children's minds. It may make the sustained attention that is required for reading, listening, and problem solving, for example, less appealing, and in the worst cases, impossible.

Educational psychologist Jean Healy has succinctly described the neural basis for this concern: "Human brains arrive in the world with excess potential to make connections (synapses) between different types of neurons. As a youngster carries out certain types of activities, those connections are strengthened, whereas habits that don't get much stimulation or practice may lack a strong neural base. Repetition of an experience tends to 'set' connections – to make that particular form of learning more automatic. Many children with school problems lack strong automatic connections for particular academic skills, such as reading or math computation, or for learning habits such as attention, strategic problem solving, or self-control." Healy offers the guideline that preschoolers' media use should total no more than one hour a day and no more than two hours for elementary-age children.[40]

What can you do for your children? You can begin by keeping a media diary. Record how much time each day they spend watching TV, using the computer, listening to music, talking on the telephone, etc. The American Academy of Pediatrics now recommends that physicians routinely take a media history when evaluating their patients. This entails asking parents about the amount of and type of computer, television, and video use.

It would be ridiculous to reject all modern technology – there are many benefits to be gained. I find e-mail to be an invaluable tool for staying in touch with friends around the country. And listening to the radio provides many relaxing and informative hours for me. But, for many children and adolescents, electronic technology has become the dominant pursuit during their time spent outside of school. Taming the media flood and giving it a moderate place in the lives of family members can free up important time for alternative activities that are more meaningful.

> **When you read this book, even newer technologies may have emerged and may well even pervade our lives in as revolutionary way as the Internet has. But the guidance will be the same. While media must be given a reasonable place in the lives of children, we cannot let media consume the "precious space of childhood."[41]**

Summing Up

Research has clearly demonstrated that media play a significant role in the socialization of youth, and they can and do influence children's attitudes and behaviors across a wide range of areas. Youths today spend more time participating in media-related activities than in any activity other than sleeping. Our culture conditions children to develop the need for constant entertainment. Giving electronic and digital media a moderate place in the life of families can free up important time for more meaningful activities.

Action Steps:

- Set some clear rules about when children can watch television, such as no TV before homework is completed.

- Set limits for the maximum time allowed with media, especially on school nights. The American Academy of Pediatrics recommends no TV for children younger than two and a maximum of two hours a day of "screen time" (TV, computer, videogames) for older children.

- Keep TVs and computers, if possible, out of children's bedrooms.

- During "National TV-Turnoff Week" (the last week in April) turn off your TV for a week. You do not need to become an anti-TV zealot, banning TV forever from your children.

- Watch movies and TV shows with your child and have discussions about what you watch.

- Monitor your child's viewing – make sure the material is age appropriate.

- Regulate computer and electronic game use. Computers may be even more addictive than TV. Long hours in front of the computer may displace other important activities such as recreational and social activities. Learn how to monitor your child's Internet and instant messaging habits.

- Each day make sure your child is given the maximum opportunity to talk. The use of language is critical for healthy brain development. Anything that limits a child's verbalizations, such as solitary computer use, may be detrimental.

Electronic Environment

Answer Each Question 2, 1 or 0

2 = Yes, Often, or Usually   1 = Sometimes   0 = No or Never

_____ 1. For entertainment, does your child usually do something other than watch TV?

_____ 2. Does your child watch less than two hours of TV per day?

_____ 3. Does your child spend less than one hour per day on the telephone?

_____ 4. Does your child spend less than one hour per day playing videogames?

_____ 5. Does your child spend less than one hour per day online?

Scoring: Give yourself 2 points for "yes," "often," or "usually" answers, 1 point for "sometimes" answers, and 0 points for "no" and "never" answers. Total your points for questions 1 through 5 and write the answer below.

Your total score = _____ (0 to 10 points)

[1] Gitlin, T. (2001). *Media unlimited: How the torrent of images and sounds overwhelms our lives.* New York: Henry Holt and Company. p 5, 10, 17.

[2] Stokols, D. (1999). Human development in the age of the Internet: Conceptual and methodological horizons. In S. Friedman & T. Wachs (Eds.), *Measuring environment across the life span* (pp. 327-356). Washington, D.C.: American Psychological Association.

[3] www.yankeegroup.com; accessed 8-5-02

[4] Roberts, D., Foehr, U., Rideout, V., & Brodie, M. (1999). *Kids & media @ the new millennium.* New York: Kaiser Family Foundation.

[5] Steyer, J. (2002). *The other parent: The inside story of the media's effect on our children.* New York: Atria Books. p. 21.

[6] Larson, R., & Richards, M. (1989). Introduction: The changing life space of early adolescence. *Journal of Youth and Adolescence, 18,* 501-509.

[7] Larson, R., Kubey, R., & Colletti, J. (1989). Changing channels: Early adolescent media choices and shifting investments in family and friends. *Journal of Youth and Adolescence, 18,* 583-599.

[8] Gurian, M. (1999). *A fine young man.* New York: Tarcher.

[9] Van den Bulck, J. (2000). Is television bad for your health? Behavior and body image of the adolescent "couch potato." *Journal of Youth and Adolescence, 29,* 273-288. p. 273-274.

[10] Elkind, D. (2001). *The hurried child: Growing up too fast too soon.* New York: Perseus Books.

[11] Walsh, D. (2001). *Dr. Dave's cyberhood: Making media choices that create a healthy electronic environment for your kids.* New York: Simon & Schuster.

[12] American Academy of Pediatrics, Committee on Communications. (1995). Children, adolescents, and television. *Pediatrics, 96,* 786-787.

[13] Walsh, D. (2001).

[14] Wu, P. (1998). Goal structures of materialists vs. non-materialists: The effects of TV exposure on materialism and the relationship between materialism and happiness. Ph.D. Dissertation, University of Michigan, Ann Arbor, Michigan.

[15] Rosemond, J. (2002, January 26). Dare to unhook your children from the 'plug-in-drug.' *Asheville-Citizen-Times,* p. E-1.

[16] Jordan, A., Schmitt, K., & Woodard, E. (2002). Developmental implications of commercial broadcasters' educational offerings. In S. Calvert, A. Jordan & R. Cocking.

(Eds.), *Children in the digital age: Influences of electronic media on development* (pp. 145-164). Westport, CN: Praeger.

[17] Walsh, D. (2001).

[18] Subrahmanyam, K., Greenfield, P., Kraut, R., & Gross, E. (2001). The impact of computer use on children's and adolescents' development. *Applied Developmental Psychology, 22,* 7-30.

[19] Walsh, D. (2001).

[20] Subrahmanyam, K., Greenfield, P., Kraut, R., & Gross, E. (2001).

[21] *Ibid.*

[22] Wolak, J., Mitchell, K., & Finkelhor, D. (2003). Escaping or connecting? Characteristics of youth who form close online relationships. *Journal of Adolescence., 26,* 105-119.

[23] Sanders, C., Field, T., Diego, M., & Kaplan, M. (2000). The relationship of Internet use to depression and social isolation among adolescents. *Adolescence, 35,* 237-242.

[24] www.netaddiction.com.

[25] Jordan, A. (2002). A family systems approach to examining the role of the Internet in the home. In S. Calvert, A. Jordan & R. Cocking. (Eds.), *Children in the digital age: Influences of electronic media on development* (pp. 231-247). Westport, CN: Praeger.

[26] Wright, J., Huston, A., Vandewater, E., Bickham, D., Scantlin, R., Kotler, J., Caplovitz, A., Lee, J., Hofferth, S., & Finkelstein, J. (2001). American children's use of electronic media in 1997: A national survey. *Applied Developmental Psychology, 22,* 31-47.

[27] Cited in Walsh, D. (2001). p. 187.

[28] Jones, G. (2002). *Killing monsters: Why children need fantasy, super heroes, and make-believe violence.* New York: Basic Books.

[29] Huesmann, L., Moise-Titus, J., Podolski, C., & Eron, L. (2003). Longitudinal relations between children's exposure to TV violence and their aggressive and violent behavior in young adulthood: 1977 – 1992. *Developmental Psychology, 39,* 201-221.

[30] Anderson, C. (2002). Violent video games and aggressive thoughts, feelings, and behaviors. In S. Calvert, A. Jordan & R. Cocking. (Eds.), *Children in the digital age: Influences of electronic media on development* (pp. 101-119). Westport, CN: Praeger. p. 115.

[31] Roberts, D., Foehr, U., Rideout, V., & Brodie, M. (1999).

[32] Leming, J. (1987). Rock music and the socialization of moral values in early adolescence. *Youth and Society, 18,* 363-383.

[33] Walsh, D. (2001).

[34] Arnett, J., Larson, R., & Offer, D. (1995). Beyond effects: Adolescents as active media users. *Journal of Youth and Adolescence, 24,* 511-518.

[35] Larson, R., Kubey, R., & Colletti, J. (1989). Changing channels: Early adolescent media choices and shifting investments in family and friends. *Journal of Youth and Adolescence, 18,* 583-599.

[36] Roberts, D., Foehr, U., Rideout, V., & Brodie, M. (1999). p. 78.

[37] *Ibid.* p. 3.

[38] Children's Digital Media Center: http://kidtv.georgetown.edu/cdmc

[39] Calvert, S. (2002). Identity construction on the Internet. In S. Calvert, S. Cocking & A. Jordan (Eds.), *Children in the digital age: Influences of electronic media on development* (pp. 57-70). Westport, CT: Greenwood Publishing Group.

[40] Healy, J. (1998). *Failure to connect: How computers affect our children's minds – and what we can do about it.* New York: Simon & Schuster. p. 133.

[41] Walsh, D. (2001). Chapter 9.

Friends Setting

O F THE TEN DIFFERENT BEHAVIOR SETTINGS EXAM-
ined in this book, friendships and electronic settings are not
physical environments. All the others, such as home, school, and recreation are actual places. Friendships, of course, occur across all settings,
and friends can bring a behavior-altering factor into any environment. It
is for this reason that I elevate peer relations to its own behavior setting.

The peer environment is nested within a larger set of social contexts, which shape the influence of friends. The structure of each of
these environments influences the types of peer relationships formed,
the types of activities engaged in, and the depth of interaction that
develops among peers. Some environments may provide many opportunities to interact with numerous other children; other environments
may provide few or none at all. The structure of an environment may
encourage or even mandate peer interactions, or it may prohibit or
constrain them. Finally, an environment may provide a consistent set
of peers who become known over a period of time (for example, a co-
curricular activity), or it may present a constantly changing group of
peers (for example, a YMCA after-school program).[1]

Social relationships are the very center of life. Having friends who
care about us and who we care about is an essential part of human
existence. Friendships play a strong role in supporting our sense of
self-worth, in learning about life, and in growing in social competence. Friendship is a relationship between two people offering more

support to each other than mere acquaintances would. University of Nebraska Professor Beth Doll has identified six elements of friendship: a) affection and caring responsibility, b) shared interests and activities, c) commitment, d) loyalty, e) self-disclosure, and f) sharing of power in the relationship.[2]

> Friendships are a principal arena for the development of personal competencies throughout life. During the preschool years, friendships consist mostly of shared play activities. Between ages 9 and 11, peer interactions take on some of the characteristics of true friendship, such as reciprocity, affection, and empathy. More mature forms of friendship develop during middle adolescence. The transition to opposite-gender relationships begins during this developmental period, as strong same-gender relationships then transition to intimate relationships during late adolescence.[3]

A few years ago, Judith Rich Harris generated considerable controversy about peer relationships when she published *The Nurture Assumption: Why Children Turn Out the Way They Do; Parents Matter Less Than You Think and Peers Matter More.* Though not trained as a scientist, Harris was a writer of college-level textbooks about child development. It impressed her that many of the accepted truths about child development, and in particular the critical influence of parents, had scant empirical evidence behind them. While the popular media widely reported that Harris' book claimed that parents mattered little and that peers were the dominant influence in children's lives, this was an over-simplification. Nevertheless, Harris did argue that the universe that children share with their peers determines the kind of people they will be in adulthood.[4]

> After reviewing the empirical evidence, Harris concluded that all the things that parents do have not been shown to have substantial effects. She says that what children experience outside the home, in the company of their peers, is what matters most. Put another way — parents don't socialize children — children socialize children. She says that we cling to the "nurture

assumption," which is our unquestioned belief that, except for their genes, what makes children turn out the way they do is the way their parents bring them up.[5] Harris does recognize that parents have considerable power to influence their child's friendships, but she says that control diminishes as children move into adolescence.

Peer Groups

When teenagers are asked about when they have the most fun, many say it's when they are with a group of friends, furthest away from adult supervision. Mihaly Csikszentmihalyi and Reed Larson report that teenagers describe these experiences in terms of being rowdy, loud, crazy, and wild. Why is such "let it loose" behavior so important to the time with friends? The researchers conclude: "It appears to be a situation in which you are free to say anything, to do everything – friends will support your words and actions, they will come back with something even more crazy and bizarre, something that builds on the inverted reality you are creating."[6]

As children grow, they move from primarily a parent (adult)-focused orientation to more of a peer-focused orientation. Teenagers begin to separate into reputation-based clusters composed of youths with similar traits. Peer groups, or "crowds," typically have labels like jocks, druggies, Goths, brains, nerds, etc. As teenagers choose particular dress, grooming, and weekend activities, they place themselves within peer niches that can restrict the kinds of friendships they will have. Theories in the field of sociology maintain that joining a group leads to a process in which the adolescent takes on the groups' norms and develops an identity associated with the membership in the group. These groups are often quite fluid and close friendships, also, can change relatively frequently. For example, one study found that among seventh graders, only 12 percent of peer groups were intact after one year; a similar level of high turnover was found among individual friends.[7]

Adolescents who have close friendships and are generally accepted by their peers are typically more socially skilled and academically successful and exhibit higher self-esteem than their agemates who

are loners. For the most part, adolescents who lack supportive friendships or who are rejected by many of their peers show poorer psychological, social, and academic adjustment.[8]

Evidence suggests that the mere quantity of friends can be a factor in healthy behavioral adjustment. Children with a larger number of same-age peers in their networks tended to receive higher academic and behavior ratings from their teachers throughout the school year.[9] However, there are exceptions, and a few high-quality relationships may provide sufficient support to some children. At the same time, a child with a large network of mostly superficial friendships can have less support.[10]

Although it has been widely accepted that the quantity and quality of peer friendships is a strong predictor of future behavioral health, studies do *not* necessarily support this conclusion. For example, sociologist Peggy Giordano and her colleagues reported that adolescents with strong friendships do not necessarily exhibit higher self-esteem, better relations with parents, higher marital satisfaction, less psychological distress, less involvement in criminal activity, or less violence against one's spouse.[11] So what is the implication of this finding? Friendships are important but it is not essential for children and adolescents to have strong peer networks. Having some good friends throughout childhood is sufficient.

Children and teenagers are always trying to fit into their peer group. Fitting in and being a part of the collective is their driving motivation. Making friends from other ethnic and cultural groups and affirming one's own culture in the process can be an important step to the formation of self-identity, because cultural and ethnic identity is central to self-identity. For example, research indicates that personal competence can be built by involvement in interracial friendships.[12] Adults can serve as role models for discussing ethnicity and culture, and can assist youths in embracing friends who are culturally and ethnically different from them.

Mihaly Csikszentmihalyi's study of talented teenagers has highlighted some interesting issues about the conflict between investing time exclusively in friends of the opposite sex and investing time in more diverse pursuits. He notes that the preoccupation of some teenagers with their burgeoning sexuality is not necessarily natural; we all have seen teenagers whose time and energy appears to be wrapped up in artificially fueled sexual concerns. Csikszentmihalyi makes the point:

> "Teenagers can easily be swept away by the biological needs stirred up at puberty, especially when these are heightened by a constant barrage of commercially motivated exploitations of sexuality. They can lose perspective on the importance of sex in the context of a whole life. Talented adolescents, perhaps because they know they have more to lose or because they are better prepared by their families, do not let this happen."[13]

Peer relations may have special meaning for vulnerable youths; close friends may be a factor in children's behavioral adjustment. In fact, psychologists Shari Wasserstein and Annette La Greca at the University of Miami found that children from high-conflict marriages who had high levels of peer support showed fewer signs of behavioral problems. So, for youths who live in families with marital strife, building friendship support may be important.[14]

Children who are socially rejected by their peers tend to show more inappropriate behaviors. More than half of children with ADHD are subjected to social rejection. In working with such children, it is important to enhance their peer social status. Efforts to help these children should not be limited to the teaching of social skills but should include promoting friendships in their everyday environments.[15]

Is Peer Influence Predominantly Negative?

Parents are often quick to blame friends for leading their child toward deviant or illicit behavior. The reality may be that their adolescent had already been using drugs (or whatever the behavior might be) for some time, and merely became friendly with a group of peers who also used them. This is referred to as the "birds of a feather flock together" theory, for which there is some evidence. Quite simply, friends are chosen who have similar attitudes and behaviors, rather than friends changing teenagers to particular behaviors through example.[16] One researcher determined that increases in friends' similarity (in regard to behavior) during the year was due about as much to friendship selection as to friends' influence.[17]

One study found that most teenagers are not pressured by their friends to drink alcohol, smoke, use drugs or have sex, or participate in delinquent activities. The study found that peer pressure is more likely to support a teenager doing well.[18] Another study found that adolescents are susceptible to negative peer influences only when they are caring for themselves and have little parental supervision. For children whose parents practice an "authoritative" style (characterized by a high degree of structure and warmth in their parenting), negative peer influences were minimized.[19]

So, while the presumption that many teenagers are being led astray by their peers doesn't hold up to the scientific evidence, we can't conclude that peer pressure is never negative. As noted, parenting style may be a factor, as well as parental supervision. Parents sometimes say "I don't know who my child's friends are." During adolescence, parents fill the role of monitor of teenagers' friends. Monitoring is a composite measure of how well the parents keep track of their children's whereabouts, their friends, and the types of activities they engage in. A number of studies of parental monitoring indicate that parents of delinquent children do less monitoring and supervising of their children's activities, especially with regard to the children's use of evening time, than parents of non-delinquent children. Parents of delinquent sons tend to perceive themselves as being less in control of their son's choice of friends.[20]

Reflecting on my own peers in childhood, the friends "setting" exerted a strong influence. Until middle school, the neighborhood comprised my universe of social relations. The surrounding homes were full of children, many my own age, and we were always dreaming up some interesting activity. Several were classmates at school, and we played together as well as worked together on homework. My friends were from stable homes that instilled in them good values, and we had common interests, especially sports. During middle school, playing sports at school became our dominant activity, with personal and team development the focus of our world.

Peer friendships are in large measure determined by the places where children spend their time. Friendships depend on opportunity and are difficult to develop without a supportive environment. There are several steps parents and teachers can take to ensure that children establish strong friendships. First, assess how environments impact a child's peer relationships. Next, encourage the child to spend time in environments where other children have common interests.[21] For example, if your 8 year old enjoys riding his dirt bike, look for settings where children share that interest. You may notice that elementary-age children often ride their dirt bikes to the local skateboard park. You might accompany your child to the park to see if that environment promotes interactions that lead to friendships. While parents cannot pick children's friends, they can pick environments where children will select good friends.[22]

Structured activities such as hobbies and sports are some of the most development-enhancing ways for children to spend their time.[23] The complexity and content of these activities correlate with children's psychological growth. The kinds of activities children participate in offer different opportunities for the development of social relationships – friendships – and it is often these relationships, rather than the activities themselves, that explain the links between children's use of free time and their behavioral adjustment. Children's social contexts and the nature of children's free-time activities are interrelated. Some activities are solitary (e.g., reading); some involve nonparental adult supervision (e.g., sports); some activities are done in the presence of parents (e.g., family television viewing); and finally, some activities are done with peers, unsupervised by adults (e.g., hanging out). Susan McHale and her colleagues at Pennsylvania State University found that free time spent with parents and nonparental adults was related to positive behavioral adjustment. Time spent in unsupervised peer settings usually signaled behavioral adjustment problems.[24] So, the social context of everyday activities appears to be the key variable.

Time Without Friends

The majority (about 73 percent) of adolescents' time is spent in environments which are shared with friends and adults. What is striking about this statistic is that 27 percent of the time teenagers are alone. In the early 1980s, Mihaly Csikszentmihalyi and Reed Larson studied teenagers' time use.[25] For one week, 75 teenagers carried an electronic pager and pad of self-report forms. At a random time, once every two hours, the pager was activated. Participants were instructed to complete a self-report form each time the pager was activated. The form asked about a number of issues, including where the teenager was, who he was with, and what he was doing, as well as his mood when he was paged.

The researchers found that over one-quarter of these teenagers' lives was spent in solitary activities. Time alone was further broken down into these three categories. First, maintenance activities made up 42 percent of time alone. These activities consisted of eating, personal care, resting, transportation, chores, and errands. Next came leisure activities which consumed 36 percent of time alone. Leisure activities consisted of sports and games, watching TV, listening to music, arts and hobbies, reading, and thinking. Finally, "productive" activities made up 22 percent of time alone, consisting mostly of studying. Although the results of this study are somewhat dated, nonetheless Csikszentmihalyi and Larson have identified an essential aspect of growing up, solitude, whether it is at home, at schools or in other environments.[26]

> Time spent alone is a developmental necessity for youths. People need to be alone to develop their individuality; however, most teenagers dread to be cut off from interaction with others. When they are alone, adolescents spend more time thinking about themselves, and research shows that when people think about themselves, their moods are usually negative and they ruminate about the downside of life. When teenagers interact with someone else, their attention is structured by external demand, and therefore, they are not so preoccupied by negative thoughts.[27]

You'll recall from Csikszentmihalyi's study of talented youth, discussed in Chapter 2, that talented youth are involved in more solitary activities. The motivation to develop talent-related skills may require that teenagers be alone. According to Csikszentmihalyi and Larson, the capacity to use solitude is the capacity to structure one's own attention, to set one's own goals, and to provide oneself with meaningful feedback. This describes the concept of metacognition, the process of self-evaluation discussed in the last chapter. The process includes monitoring what we are doing, figuring out why our behavior was successful or not successful, and then developing successful strategies for similar situations in the future. To develop metacognition, children need to have down time to pause and think things through. It is important for parents to encourage spaces of solitude in children's lives, even if youths find solitary time to be less fulfilling.

Finally, in terms of sheer amount of time, friends are the greatest presence in teenagers' lives; they consistently report that the best part of their lives is the time spent with friends. It is noteworthy, however, that American adolescents spend more time with peers than teens in any other contemporary society. For example, teenagers in Russia and Japan spend only two to three hours per week with friends. In the United States, teenagers spend approximately 20 hours per week with friends.[28] Historically, adolescents in most societies have learned skills in preparation for adulthood by spending a considerable amount of time with adults – observing, imitating, and interacting with them.[29] A critical environmental variable in adolescence is who teenagers spend time with, for it is those people who socialize them, through the support and feedback they provide.

Summing Up

What children experience outside the home, in the company of their peers, has a profound effect on their development. Assessing how the environment impacts a child's peer relationships is an important step to improving the lives of children. Friendships are in large measure determined by where children spend their time, so the neighborhood you live in and the activity settings where your child lives are especially important.

Action Steps:

- Encourage school friendships by helping with transportation. Adolescents place a premium on friendships with school friends that extend to nonschool settings.

- Steer children toward activity settings where wholesome children can befriend your child. Peer pressure is more likely to support a teenager doing well.

- Keep track of your children's whereabouts, their friends, and the types of activities they engage in. This is critical for helping your children to find supportive activity settings and to avoid non-supportive ones.

- Insist on – and support – your child spending time in productive pursuits. During the teenage years, a conflict may arise between investing time in friends of the opposite-gender and investing time in more-productive pursuits. This is natural, but don't let it get out of hand.

QUIZ

Friends Environment

_____ 1. Do you know all of your child's friends?

_____ 2. Does your child have friends at school?

_____ 3. Does your child make an effort to make new friends?

_____ 4. Do your child's friends stay out of trouble?

_____ 5. Does your child have at least one very close friend he or she sees regularly?

Scoring: Give yourself 2 points for "yes," "often," or "usually" answers, 1 point for "sometimes" answers, and 0 points for "no" and "never" answers. Total your points for questions 1 through 5 and write the answer below.

Your total score = _____ (0 to 10 points)

[1] Searcy, S., & Meadows, N. (1994). The impact of social structures on friendship development for children with behavior disorders. *Education and Treatment of Children, 17,* 255-266.

[2] Doll, B. (1996). Children without friends: Implications for practice and policy. *School Psychology Review, 25,* 165-183.

[3] *Ibid.*

[4] Harris, J. (1998). *The nurture assumption: Why children turn out the way they do; Parents matter less than you think and peers matter more.* New York: Free Press.

[5] *Ibid.*

[6] Csikszentmihalyi, M., & Larson, R. (1984). *Being adolescent: Conflict and growth in the teenage years.* New York: Basic Books. p. 168.

[7] Meyer, L., Park, H., Grenot-Scheyer, M., Schwartz, I., & Harry, B.(1998). *Making friends: The influence of culture and development.* Baltimore: Paul H. Brookes.

[8] Berndt, T., & Savin-Williams, E. (1993). Peer relations and friendships. In P. Tolan & B. Cohler (Eds.), *Handbook of clinical research and practice with adolescents* (pp. 203-219). New York: Wiley.

[9] Salzinger, S., Antrobus, J., & Hammer, M. (1988). *Social networks of children, adolescents, and college students.* Hillsdale, NJ: Erlbaum.

[10] Frey, C., & Rothlisberger, C. (1996). Social support in healthy adolescents. *Journal of Youth and Adolescence, 25,* 17-33.

[11] Giordano, P., Cernkovich, S., Groat, H., Pugh, M., & Swinford, S. (1998). The quality of adolescent friendships: Long-term effects? *Journal of Health and Social Behavior, 39,* 55-71.

[12] DuBois, D., & Hirsch, B. (1990). School and neighborhood friendship patterns in Blacks and Whites in early adolescence. *Child Development, 61,* 524-536.

[13] Csikszentmihalyi, M., Rathunde, K., & Whalen, S. (1993). *Talented teenagers: The roots of success and failure.* New York: Cambridge University Press. p. 246-247.

[14] Wasserstein, S., & LaGreca, A. (1996). Can peer support buffer against behavioral consequences of parental discord. *Journal of Clinical Child Psychology, 25,* 177-182.

[15] Cited in Anhalt, K., McNeil, C., & Bahl, A. (1998). The ADHD classroom kit: A whole-classroom approach for managing disruptive behavior. *Psychology in the Schools, 35,* 67-79.

[16] Benda, B., DiBlasio, F. & Kashner, T. (1994). Adolescent sexual behavior: A path analysis. *Journal of Social Service Research, 19,* 49-69.

[17] Cited in Berndt, T., & Savin-Williams, E. (1993). Peer relations and friendships. In P. Yolan & B. Cohler (Eds.), *Handbook of clinical research and practice with adolescents* (pp. 203-219). New York: Wiley.

[18] Cited in Benson, P., Galbraith, J., & Espeland, P. (1998). *What teens need to succeed*. Minneapolis: Free Spirit Publishing.

[19] Belle, D. (1999). *After-school lives of children*. Mahwah, NJ: Lawrence Erlbaum Associates.

[20] Medrich, E., Roizen, J., Rubin, V., & Buckley, S. (1982). *The serious business of growing up: A study of children's lives outside school*. Berkeley, CA: University of California Press.

[21] Searcy, S., & Meadows, N. (1994).

[22] McIntosh, H. (1996, June). Adolescent friends not always a bad influence. *Monitor on Psychology, 27*, 16.

[23] McHale, S., Crouter, A., & Tucker, C. (2001). Free-time activities in middle childhood: Links with adjustment in early adolescence. *Child Development, 72*, 1764-1778.

[24] *Ibid.*

[25] Csikszentmihalyi, M., & Larson, R. (1984).

[26] *Ibid.*

[27] Csikszentmihalyi, M. (1997). *Finding flow: The psychology of engagement with everyday life*. New York: Basic Books.

[28] Csikszentmihalyi, M., & Larson, R. (1984).

[29] *Ibid.*

CHAPTER 10

Faith Setting

R ELIGION IS A POTENT FORCE IN THE LIVES OF MANY
families. About 94 percent of Americans believe in a God. There
are 350,000 religious congregations in the United States and on a typical
weekend, 41 percent of all families with children attend religious services.
More people have confidence in organized religion than in any other
social institution in America. Religion provides a set of rituals, traditions,
and beliefs that help members define personal identity pathways in life.[1]

In our current context, as an environment that affects child development, what can be said about religion – what about the faith lives
of youths? How many go to Sunday School? How many youths are
involved in the social ministries of their church? Do they spend time
praying? What are their relationships with adults in the church? In
this chapter, we will try to answer some of these questions.

A word of explanation: In this chapter, I will use the term "church,"
as a generic reference to religious institutions, with the understanding
that the discussion encompasses all religions.

**Adolescence emerges as an important time of development where-
in religion can emerge, with parental support, as a significant
influence. According to a Gallup Youth Survey, most American teenagers believe in a God and their religious beliefs are important
to them. Slightly more than half of American teenagers attended
religious services on the weekend.[2] About half of high school**

students participate in religious youth groups.[3] **Nearly two-thirds of youth say they pray daily or weekly.**[4]

Research indicates that belief in religion and participation in religious activities tend to divert youths away from high-risk behaviors.[5] In a study of problem behaviors in youths over time, adolescent religiosity was found to provide a personal control against problem behaviors. Church attendance and the expression of positive religious attitudes and beliefs among high school students were related to a lower incidence of deviant behavior and to less problem behavior in general. Findings from the study include:[6]

- *Reduced Suicide:* Teenagers who are involved in religious institutions are less likely to think about committing suicide.

- *Less Depression:* Teenagers who are involved in religious institutions and feel they experience a high level of support for their spirituality report less depression overall, and when they do experience depression it is usually in the normal range, compared to significant depression which requires mental health counseling or medication.

- *Less Casual Sex:* Teenagers who are involved in religious institutions are less likely to engage in casual sex and more likely to wait longer before they become sexually active.

- *More Resilient to Trauma:* Traumatized teenagers (for example, teenagers who have been abused) involved in religious institutions feel more social support, are more likely to experience lower distress, and recover faster than other teenagers.

- *Less Substance Abuse:* Teenagers who are involved in religious institutions and beliefs are less likely to use drugs and alcohol.[7]

Another study, conducted by sociologists Christian Smith and Robert Faris, found that religious involvement is associated with safer, healthier, more-constructive lifestyles. The chart on Lifestyle Advantages (page 123) summarizes the effects that they found in their study of religious involvement on 12th graders. Smith and Faris defined religious

Lifestyle Advantages of Religious High School Seniors [8]

- **Substance Abuse.** Students are less likely to smoke cigarettes and to start smoking at an early age. Students are less likely to drink alcohol and more likely to postpone their first experience getting drunk. When students do drink, they are less likely to drink to the point of drunkenness. Students also go to bars less often. Students are less likely to have tried any kind of drug, including hard drugs. Students also are more likely to postpone first use of marijuana and often never try it.

- **Safety and Danger.** Students receive fewer traffic tickets and are more likely to wear seat belts. They are also less likely to enjoy danger or take risks.

- **Crime and Violence.** Students are involved in fewer violent incidents, such as hitting teachers and getting into fights. Students also are less likely to commit a variety of crimes, including shoplifting or other theft, vandalism, trespassing, arson, and armed robbery. Students are generally less likely to get into trouble with the police.

- **School Problems.** Students tend to be better-behaved at school. They are less likely to be sent to detention, to skip school, or to be suspended or expelled.

- **Constructive Activities and Supervision.** Students are more likely to volunteer in their community and to participate in student government. They also play sports and exercise more. They are less likely to argue with their parents, who tend to be stricter than other parents.

involvement as regular service attendance, self-reported importance of faith, and many years spent participating in religious youth groups. The effects were present despite differences across race, age, sex, rural versus urban residence, religion, educational level attained by the parent(s), number of siblings, whether or not the mother worked, or presence of a father or male guardian in the home.

It is important to note that while religiously active teenagers are significantly less likely to engage in risky behaviors, from 20–40 percent of these teenagers are involved in risky behavior involving alcohol or drugs. For example, about 39 percent of religiously active high school seniors have used illegal drugs, including alcohol, in the past year. (Of course, a significantly higher percentage of non-religiously active students have done the same in the past year.) Clearly, active religious involvement does mitigate negative outcomes, but it does not eliminate them entirely.[9]

In addition to the reduction in risky behavior that generally accompanies involvement in religious activities, the evidence also suggests that frequent church attendance and perceptions of religion as meaningful are associated with psychological well-being.[10] Religious activities can take many different forms; for example, attendance at religious services, prayer, ritualistic events such as funerals and weddings, various activity groups, and support from the clergy or other church members.[11] Of course, not all religious groups and congregations will offer the same degree of support – and some affiliations, such as with cults, can be potentially destructive. Nevertheless, adolescent involvement with religious activities can create strong, positive supports. Youth groups, choirs, and various small group activities serve young church members. Often, there is a bonus effect: not only do the activities help the child who participates, but also, his family benefits by being accepted into a larger social system. In addition to providing positive self-image and status, this acceptance frequently brings with it nurturance, affection, and altruistic outlets.[12]

The faith environment may well have as pervasive an impact on the lives of some children as any environment. On the other hand, some youths have virtually no involvement in faith insti-

tutions. According to sociologists Mark Regnerus, Christian Smith and Melissa Fritsch, "Religion can be an irrelevant setting for youth. But it can constitute much, much more than that. It can vary in the lives of teenagers from a compulsory hour-per-week period of intense boredom to the setting that sprouts an entire network of friends to an all-encompassing lifeworld of belief, behaviors, and ritual practices."[13]

Many youth are involved in the activities of faith institutions that mimic those of other youth development organizations. Social, recreational, and service-learning activities predominate. They have pizza socials, movie nights, basketball games, and dances. They celebrate members' birthdays, take trips to amusement parks, bowling alleys, movies, etc. They volunteer at nursing homes and work at church fairs doing face paintings and arts and crafts. They volunteer at the community soup kitchens. They have speakers from various organizations come talk about their work. They hold car washes to raise funds for their program. In the paragraphs below, I have compiled the faith institution activities of several youths. These examples are taken from Christian denominations, but equivalent activities can be found in all religions.

Terrell participates in the church's Pilgrim Fellowship. Senior High Pilgrim Fellowship meets for fellowship activities, discussion, worship, and fun. The group is involved in occasional service projects, such as serving at soup kitchens and working at Habitat for Humanity projects. Each summer, the group attends the National Association of Pilgrim Fellowship meeting. Other summer activities that help fill the school void include various retreats and a week-long service project.

Nina loves music and participates in Starfire, a group of high-schoolers who gather weekly for rehearsal and who sing in worship every Sunday. They also go to retreats, have special outings, go on tours, and have good times together sharing music and fellowship. Music is an important and integral part of their life at church, and their youth choir is a fun and rewarding way of being involved in the life of the church. Nina is also an acolyte. Acolytes assist ministers by lighting the candles for the worship service, helping collect the Sunday offering, and helping with baptisms.

Kim belongs to Youth Crossroads at her church. The Youth Crossroads group is involved in many different types of activities – camping trips, lock-ins, trips to the beach, bowling, miniature golf, goofy game nights, and fellowships with other churches. They are also heavily involved in mission projects, such as ministering to the homeless, participating in the children's ministry, helping the elderly with house and yard work, and visiting nursing homes. Throughout the year, they have weekly youth meetings and retreats to focus on the spiritual lives of the members and they do week-long mission trips in the summer. The goal of the Youth Crossroads group is to be a partner as youths journey through their adolescent years by creating a place where youths feel comfortable being themselves, as free as possible from peer pressure or the need to meet others' expectations.

Finally, Candice participates in Journey to Adulthood at her church. This youth ministry is aimed at helping youths grow into responsible adults. Following sixth-grade confirmation, youths enter into Journey to Adulthood, with activities taking place during the Sunday morning education period and Sunday evenings after the 5 p.m. services. Journey to Adulthood provides a liturgical context for getting along in the world today, while celebrating each person's individuality and creative potential. Journey to Adulthood develops within youths the skills needed for participation in the church and in greater society.

There are three phases in Journey to Adulthood, each lasting two years. The first phase helps young people to move into their own lives. It creates a safe environment for younger teenagers to explore new thoughts and ideas. The second phase is the core of the program. There are six basic skills taught to prepare youths for adulthood: active listening, negotiation, assertion, research/information management, partnership, and leadership. In the third phase of the program, called Young Adults in Church, participants are encouraged to take on adult responsibilities in the church and community.

Despite the relative scarcity of scholarly writing on the subject, it is clear that religious institutions provide a major context

for the development of today's youth. As you can see from the examples above, some religious organizations strive very explicitly, through an "embedded curriculum," to engage youths in activities that teach the kinds of knowledge and skills that will help them succeed in school and life. In addition to the programs themselves, these types of activities frequently alter the scheduling of family life and dictate parental involvement and support, affecting everything from mealtimes to carpooling to voluntary group involvement. Although for some youths faith experiences may indeed be extremely positive and psychologically enhancing, for others they may be less so. The circumstances that determine these outcomes remain to be studied.

To help fill the gap in knowledge about the faith lives of youths, the National Study of Youth and Religion is being conducted at the University of North Carolina.[14] Some recent findings from the project include:

- There is a positive correlation between religious commitment and civic volunteerism in high school seniors.

- There is a positive correlation between religion (based on any amount of religious service attendance) and self-esteem among high school seniors.

- Youths who attend religious services at least occasionally and who consider themselves at least somewhat religious are more active in sports and exercise among high school seniors.

- Youths from religiously active families – at any level of religious involvement – are significantly more likely than their non-religious peers to have a positive relationship with their fathers, saying that they enjoy spending time with their fathers, that their fathers are helpful with things that are important to them, and that they admire their fathers.

Clearly, the few studies that have focused on these issues show links between adolescents' religiosity and prosocial behavioral adjustment. The many documented benefits include lower rates of delinquent activity, substance use, and sexual activity; more attachment to school; better grades; greater occupational achievement; more concern for others, and higher scores on tests of self-esteem and moral development.[15] How do religious variables lead to these indicators of prosocial development among adolescents? One answer is that religious involvement and commitment add some very important, positive elements to family relationships. Take the example of educational progress. Religious service attendance has an even greater impact on youth from high-risk neighborhoods. It may be that religious organizations provide functional communities amid dysfunction.[16]

Christian Smith, Director of the National Study of Youth and Religion at the University of North Carolina, has identified nine distinct factors that exert influence on religious youth. The nine factors are outlined in the table on pages 130–131. Professor Smith says that there are two opposing theories about the effects of religion. One theory claims that what appears to be religious phenomena at work is really due to other influences unrelated to religion. That is, these influences happen to be found in religious contexts but are not distinctly religious phenomena. For example, supportive social networks just happen to be found in religious groups, but the influence is not unique to religious settings; it just happens to be located there.

The second theory claims that there is something uniquely religious in religion that exerts influence. For example, a particular moral tradition (e.g., resting on the Sabbath) may produce a unique influence on youth not by a generic process but only because of the religious context.[17] More research is needed before either theory can be validated; however, Smith subscribes to the latter theory for the time being. Sociologists Darwin Thomas and Craig Carver offer this example of religion's unique influence:

"We assume that, as the individual becomes integrated into the religious social sphere and accepts the set of values surrounding those social relationships, he or she becomes more sensitive to interpersonal expectations from significant others, finds it easier to develop goals, and more readily identifies personal abilities needed to achieve those goals. We see such interpersonal skills as being transferable to an educational setting, which assists the religious person in becoming a better student."[18]

Christian Smith points out that the nine influences of religion do not operate independently, rather they work in combination. Further, he notes that some religious organizations provide many high quality experiences, while others may offer only a few, and some may be neutral or even detrimental. He suggests that religion's potential for antisocial effects deserve investigation, including the influences of abusive leaders, adult hypocrisies, and dysfunctional organization.

Again, it should be emphasized that religion is not the only place where these kinds of social influence exist. While acknowledging that similar experiences are available in voluntary associations and other community programs, Smith says "Religious organizations are uniquely pervasive organizations in American society that do strongly encourage youth participation. And religious organizations can provide cultural moral orders characterized by impressive scope, depth, and authority, often matching if not surpassing other kinds of American voluntary associations or purchasable services."[19]

How do the benefits of religious activities compare with the benefits of Little League or Girl Scouts? Does the spiritual aspect of faith activities make them different from other activities outside of the faith context in regard to supporting healthy youth development? Further data from the National Study of Youth and Religion may help answer these types of questions. In the meantime, we can say that although they are not necessarily unique in their socialization impact, youth faith experiences assume disproportionate significance in the psychological and social development of some children today. So far, the evidence is compelling that regular religious service attendance, high personal importance of religion, and time spent participating in religious youth groups are strongly associated with safer, healthier, and more constructive lifestyles for teenagers.

Finally, religion's influence on healthy lifestyle behaviors was studied in a large national sample of adolescents, which found that more-religious youth routinely eat better, exercise more often, get more sleep, and more consistently use seat belts than less religious or non-religious youths.[20] University of Texas sociologist Robert Hummer and his colleagues found that the magnitude of the influence of religion is huge. Although his data specifically looked at adults, we

Religious Effects on Youths [21]

Religious Effects	Explanation
Moral directives	As youths make the decisions that shape their lives, religion can provide them with the norms and standards to guide their choices. Example: treating one's body as the Temple of the Holy Spirit
Spiritual experiences	Religion provides a setting for personal spiritual experiences, and thereby, reinforces the moral orders that shape youths' lives. Example: an answer to a prayer
Role models	Religion supplies adult and peer role models who lead exemplary lives as shaped by the religious moral order. These role models provide an incentive for youths to live within the moral order. Example: a teenager prizes his relationship with a devout youth leader in the church
Community and leadership skills	Religion provides many opportunities to learn the skills of community life and leadership. Religious youth are exposed to useful skills like group decision making, public speaking, and resolving disagreements. Example: a teenager who serves as a youth delegate on a church committee
Coping skills	Religion promotes beliefs and practices that help congregants to cope with stressful situations and deal with life's problems. Example: a teenager who uses confession to gain forgiveness for an indiscretion

Religious Effects	Explanation
Cultural capital	Religion provides youth with increased opportunities for cultural experiences which lead to unique learnings. The youth who has been exposed to this distinct knowledge may have an advantage and will converse more easily in broad social contacts. Example: a teenager who because of his religious education is exposed to world civilizations
Social capital	Religion is one of the few social institutions that is not age-stratified. Religion affords age-variable and cross-generational ties which link youth to wider resources. Example: a teenager who attends a fellowship gathering meets an adult who links him to an after-school job fixing computers
Network closure	Congregations have relational networks of people who encourage positive life practices among youth. These resources outside the family may reinforce parental influences and oversight. Example: a choir director reinforces a parent's expectation about the importance of a teenager devoting more time to nightly homework
Extra-community skills	Religion provides youth with connection experiences beyond their immediate community. These experiences can increase knowledge, encourage maturity, and expand a youth's aspirations. Example: a teenager who participates in a denominational trip to the Holy Land

might assume the same is true of youths. Hummer found that going to weekly religious services provides a positive effect on lifespan that is comparable in size to the negative effect of smoking a pack of cigarettes a day: approximately seven years![22]

Summing Up

In seeking healthy developmental activities and supportive environments for children, parents would do well to consider the potential benefits offered by religious organizations. The faith environment may well have as powerful an impact on the lives of some children as any environment.

Action Steps:

- Encourage religious activities such as attendance at religious services and involvement in church youth groups. Research indicates that belief in religion and participation in religious activities tend to divert youths away from high-risk behaviors, toward more participation in sports and exercise, and toward more positive relationships with their parents.

- Choose a faith setting where your family feels comfortable and get involved in its activities. Faith experiences can assume considerable significance in the psychological and social development of children.

- Do some research before you choose a faith setting. Not all denominations and churches offer the same degree of support, and some affiliations can be potentially destructive. If a church that you have chosen proves to be unsupportive, find another one.

Faith Environment

Answer Each Question 2, 1 or 0

2 = Yes, Often, or Usually   1 = Sometimes   0 = No or Never

_____ 1. Does your child regularly attend services at a faith institution?

_____ 2. Does your child participate in a faith institution's youth group?

_____ 3. Do you hold family discussions concerning religious or moral issues?

_____ 4. Does your child participate in part of a faith institution's program (e.g., choir, altar boy, etc.)?

_____ 5. Does your child participate in an organized faith institution activity, such as a summer camp, etc?

Scoring: Give yourself 2 points for "yes," "often," or "usually" answers, 1 point for "sometimes" answers, and 0 points for "no" and "never" answers. Total your points for questions 1 through 5 and write the answer below.

Your total score = _____ (0 to 10 points)

[1] Pargament, K., & Maton, K. (2000). Religion in American life: A community psychology perspective. In J. Rappaport & E. Seidman (Eds.), *Handbook of community psychology* (pp. 495-522). New York: Kluwer Academic/Plenum Publishers.

[2] Gallup, G. (2000, July 1). Poll finds that religious beliefs continue to be important to American teenagers. *Asheville Citizen-Times*, p. B-2.

[3] Smith, C., Denton, M., Faris, R., & Regnerus, M. (2002). Mapping American adolescent religious participation. *Journal for the Scientific Study of Religion, 41*, 597-612.

[4] Smith, C., Faris, R., Denton, M., & Regnerus, M. (2003). Mapping American adolescent subjective religiosity and attitudes of alienation toward religion: A research report. *Sociology of Religion, 64*, 111-133.

[5] Carnegie Council on Adolescent Development. (1992). *A matter of time: Risk and opportunity in the nonschool hours.* New York: Carnegie Corporation.

[6] Jessor & Jessor cited in Wright, L., Frost, C., & Wisecarver, S. (1993). Church attendance, meaningfulness of religion, and depressive symptomatology among adolescents. *Journal of Youth and Adolescence, 22*, 559-568.

[7] Garbarino, J. (1999). *Lost boys: Why our sons turn violent and how we can save them.* New York: Free Press. p. 156-157.

[8] Smith, C., & Faris, R. (2002). Religion and American adolescent delinquency, risk behaviors and constructive social activities. Chapel Hill, NC: *National Study of Youth and Religion*, Department of Sociology, University of North Carolina.

[9] Smith, C. (2002). Significant numbers of religiously active teenagers are involved in serious risk behaviors involving alcohol and drugs. Chapel Hill, NC: *National Study of Youth and Religion*, Department of Sociology, University of North Carolina.

[10] Wright, L., Frost, C., & Wisecarver, S. (1993). Church attendance, meaningfulness of religion, and depressive symptomatology among adolescents. *Journal of Youth and Adolescence, 22*, 559-568.

[11] Pargament, K., & Maton, K. (Eds.). (1991). Religion and prevention in mental health: Conceptual and empirical foundations. [Special Issue] *Prevention in Human Services, 9* (2).

[12] Maguire, L. (1991). *Social support systems in practice: A generalist approach.* Silver Springs, MD: NASW Press.

[13] Regnerus, M., Smith, C., & Fritsch, M. (2003). Religion in the lives of American adolescents: A review of the literature. Chapel Hill, NC: *National Study of Youth and Religion.* p. 46-47.

[14] www.youthandreligion.org

[15] Gunnoe, M., Hetherington, E., & Reiss, D. (1999). Parental religiosity, parenting style, and adolescent social responsibility. *Journal of Early Adolescence, 19,* 199-225.

[16] Regnerus, M., Smith, C., & Fritsch, M. (2003).

[17] Smith, C. (2002). Theorizing religious effects among American adolescents. *Journal for the Scientific Study of Religion, 42,* 17-30.

[18] Thomas, D., & Carver, C. (1990). Religion and adolescent social competence. In T. Gullotta, G. Adams, & R. Montemayor (Eds.), *Social competence in adolescence* (pp. 195-219). Newbury Park, CA: Sage. p. 201.

[19] *Ibid.* p. 27.

[20] Wallace, J., & Forman, T. (1998). Religion's role in promoting health and reducing risk among American youth. *Health Education and Behavior, 25,* 721-741.

[21] Smith, C. (2002).

[22] Hummer, R., Rogers, R., Nam, C., & Ellison, C. (1999). Religious involvement and U.S. adult mortality. *Demography, 36,* 273-285.

CHAPTER 11

Work Setting

WHEN I CAME OF AGE IN THE 1960s, FEW TEENAGERS worked at paying jobs outside the home. Today, work has become a common part of adolescents' lives. Therefore, the workplace has emerged as an important context for adolescents' development. Although most regular jobs practically require that the individual has a driver's license and access to a vehicle, many teenagers also work during their early adolescent years (13–15 years of age). Work arrangements vary from those that are occasional or seasonal, such as grass mowing and leaf raking, to those that last all year. A recent study[1] found that:

- Minority youths tend to work less than do majority teenagers.

- Youths from economically disadvantaged families tend to start work earlier than do their counterparts from less economically disadvantaged families.

- In the early teenage years more boys than girls work, but by the senior year of high school, rates of work between the genders are comparable.

- Except for African-American boys, youths who started work by 13 or 14 years-of-age tend to be those who were well-engaged in school but not at-the-top achievers.

According to the Department of Labor, 2.9 million teenagers ages 15 to 17 worked during the 2000 school year. The number jumped to

4 million during the summer months. Teenagers typically work for the minimum wage, according to the Department of Labor data, and work for an average of 18.2 hours each week.[2]

The proportion of adolescents who work in the United States is higher than in most other developed countries. About 80 percent of American youths are employed sometime during their high school years.[3] In the U.S., there is no formal system to help adolescents make the transition from student to adult employment. In many European countries, on the other hand, high school students enter apprenticeships that are closely linked to their curriculum and that lead to adult employment. For example, the student apprenticeships in Germany involve a formal contract which outlines the learning opportunities as well as the knowledge and skills the apprentice is expected to master. In the United States, jobs for teens are not usually linked to the school curriculum and are not seen as career stepping-stones.[4] Some schools do have work-study programs, but they are not nearly as comprehensive as apprenticeships.

There is a common belief that working students usually hold jobs at fast-food outlets, spend their earnings on clothes or cars, and do poorly in school. While these generalizations are often true, they are not always supported by the research.[5] Let's take a closer look at each of these popular beliefs.

Who Works and Where?

Gordon Ruscoe, Jack Morgan and Cynthia Peebles at the University of Louisville School of Education studied 1,800 Kentucky high school students. They found that from an early age, most children work at home. By 13 years-of-age, they regularly perform an average of about four household chores. By the time they are of middle school age, the majority of children are involved in some paid work outside the home. Among youths from working-class families, 20 percent of boys and 11 percent of girls 12 years-of-age had a regular paid job that they performed at least once a week outside the home. Most jobs held by young adolescents are informal employment with relatives, friends, and neighbors – jobs such as babysitting, lawn mowing, etc. Sixty-nine percent of students began working during the summer at 13 years-of-age.[6] So, even before high school, many youths have begun the school-to-work transition.

In a classic study of the adolescent work experience in the 1980s, Ellen Greenberger and Laurence Steinberg reported that few adolescents worked in good jobs,[7] but more recent studies have found that even youths in service industry jobs do work that is a step above menial labor. For example, teenagers often help with carpentry, roofing, or plumbing, or work in nursing homes, greenhouses, or kindergartens. While these types of jobs are considered unskilled work, they can be challenging for young adolescents. By late adolescence, teenagers often progress to more formal employment in restaurants, grocery stores, and other retail outlets.[8]

Why Do Teenagers Work?

Teenagers work for a variety of reasons. The most common reason is to have spending money so they can participate in the American consumer society. More than half of teenagers interviewed report that they do not receive allowances, which would seem to support the need to "earn some spending money." According to Teen Research Unlimited, a marketing-research firm that specializes exclusively in teenagers, 32 million American teenage consumers spent $170 billion in 2002 on things like clothes, make-up, and cell phones – about $101 a week on personal expenses.[9]

How do working students spend their money? Again, in the Kentucky study, about one-third said they spend it on car-related expenses (repairs, insurance, gas) and only 15 percent mentioned clothes. However, one-third said that they saved their money, typically for college, and this is a common work motive for many teenagers. Teenagers who were employed in service/retail positions said that they liked the opportunity to work with people. Others said they liked their work because they enjoyed being outside and getting exercise. Some teenagers felt that their job provided important experience along with being a challenge. Helping others was another attraction for many employed teenagers. Finally, teenagers said they like jobs that offer flexible schedules so as not to interfere with their school and homework.[10]

School Performance and Work

Many researchers have claimed that working can have a negative effect on students' school performance. However, there is competing evidence that indicates working while in school can contribute to students' development. Work may be seen as "practical experience" or learning from the "real world," and, as such, is consistent with historical efforts to have "work-study" programs as part of the high school experience.[11] Parents often praise work for promoting responsibility, time-management skills, a positive work ethic, "people skills," and independence. Even the least-inspiring jobs require teenagers to mobilize effort, apply themselves to a task, and show some self-discipline.[12] While such benefits are irrefutable, the question remains: can the requirements of holding down a part-time job exert a negative effect on school performance?

Gordon Ruscoe and his colleagues found that students who worked had an average grade point average (GPA) of 3.02 (on a 4-point scale) compared to a GPA of 2.98, on average, for those who did not work.[13] This finding does not necessarily refute the common belief that students suffer academically as a consequence of working. However, researchers have identified a 20-hour work week as the point when work generally becomes detrimental. That is, when working does have a negative impact on students, especially on their school performance, this seems to occur when students work 20 or more hours in a week. So, whether or not a student works is not as critical as how many hours are worked.[14]

Studies also link these longer work hours with higher rates of drug use (i.e., smoking, alcohol, and illicit drugs).[15] Why might excessive work hours for teenagers be associated with negative outcomes like drug use? One reason may be that working long hours can lead to an increase in informal, unstructured, unsupervised activities such as hanging out with friends, cruising, and dating. Studies show that as unstructured social activities increase, substance abuse tends to increase.[16] One reason unstructured social activities may tend to increase along with increased work hours may simply be the nature of the part-time work scheduling. Jobs often require shift work, which can involve weekly schedule changes. This fluctuating work schedule makes it difficult for teenagers to commit to activities that follow a regular schedule, such as co-curricular sports. Unstructured activities have the advantage of being time-flexible, so they are much easier to fit around the adolescent's work schedule.

Another important question regarding the finding that long working hours can increase substance abuse and other problem behaviors is how the quality of the work experiences affects these outcomes. For example, there is some evidence that substance abuse is linked to work stress. Another study found that when adolescents were challenged at work and used skills, substance abuse decreased.[17]

The relationship between adolescent work and diminished school performance may have another explanation. If students who work excessive hours do less well in school, is it a result of work causing lower school achievement or could lower achievement lead to a student's decision to work? This chicken-or-the-egg argument has been studied by Laurence Steinberg, Suzanne Fegley and Stanford Dornbusch, who followed students over a number of years. Their data show that the negative factors that are associated with working usually precede working, rather than result from it.[18] Simply put, students who are not satisfied with school look for other ego-boosting opportunities, and employment offers an alternative way to establish some status.[19] These studies do not prove that students who already have problems select work as a result of those problems. Researchers must randomly assign teenagers to a workplace in order to make a causal connection, however, this link – called *selection effects* – remains possible.

It would be unfair and inaccurate to characterize employers of teenagers as slave drivers who sacrifice their young employees' educational well-being for money. Many employers are quite attuned to the challenges that working students confront and do show concern and support for their student employees' success in school.[20] Many teenagers who work in fast-food restaurants have even reported that their bosses are concerned about them. Clearly, many employers are serving as employee coaches, and perhaps because the teenage labor pool is shrinking, are going out of their way to be helpful and to demonstrate flexibility in scheduling.[21]

Other Effects of Working

Teenagers who put in long work hours may be displacing time that they would otherwise spend on important developmental activities, including health-related behaviors, schoolwork, co-curricular activities, and hobbies. This is called the "time trade-off" viewpoint, meaning that time spent in one activity (in this case, work), leaves less time for more developmentally helpful activities. The eventual result could be more negative outcomes for the youth, such as drug use, poor nutrition, lack of commitment to schoolwork, depression, or a poor relationship with parents.

The teenage years are a critical time to develop health habits, and teenagers who work longer hours spend less time on health maintenance activities.[22] Physical health habits include ensuring proper nutrition (e.g., eating breakfast), getting sufficient sleep, and exercising daily. Mental health activities include having down time and opportunities for solitude, as a way to nourish one's emotional energy. Interestingly, while teenagers who work longer hours spend less time on health behaviors, they continue to spend more time in unstructured social activities, as noted above.

Regarding stress at work, University of Minnesota sociologist Jeyland Mortimer studied 750 teenagers over a decade to see how jobs during high school affected their adaptation to work later. She found that those who had to cope with work stress as teenagers coped better with job stress in their early 20s compared to teenagers who did not work or who had stress-free work. According to Mortimer, this advantage disappears by age 27.[23]

Finally, today's teenagers often make a considerable amount of money. What is the effect of having such "premature affluence" during this developmental stage? One concern is that teenagers may develop lifestyles and standards based on what they want versus what they need.[24]

So, what have we learned about employment during the teenage years? How the adolescent experiences work is dependent on how the employment is related to commitments in other contexts, such as school, family, recreation, and others. More recent research does not support some of the popular impressions of the adolescent work experience. Work, clearly, is not a developmental wasteland for adolescents. The majority of working students who do not work excessive hours do not suffer in school, and some youths are employed in more challenging jobs in a wide variety of settings, not just fast-food restaurants. Working students do not spend their money only on cars and clothes — they spend their money in diverse ways. When students are not over-worked, they incur benefits from employment, including becoming personally, interpersonally, and socially more mature.[25] The work context establishes an important pathway through which adult maturity is pursued and dictates to a great extent many of the competencies teenagers will develop.

The question is no longer whether adolescents should be employed; most will be. The question then is how much time they devote to work and what kind of work. What constitutes a good work experience remains the pivotal question for researchers. For example: To what extent does work enable adolescents to apply what they learn in school or present them with other learning opportunities? What is the quality of teenagers' relationships with their supervisors and other adults in the workplace? What is the degree of stress of different adolescent work experiences?[26]

One day as I was perusing a book in a mall bookstore, a young teenage girl excitedly ran up to her father, embracing him while she exclaimed that she had just been given her first job at one of the mall stores. The father reciprocated her excitement. It was obviously a big step for both of them, but youth employment includes both advantages and disadvantages. Parents should carefully consider the consequences at this critical time of an adolescent's development.

Summing Up

Employment during the teenage years has become a norm in American society. By their senior year, 80 percent of adolescents will be employed part-time. Working less than 20 hours per week while in school may contribute to students' academic development. Jobs often help adolescents become personally, interpersonally, and socially more mature.

Action Steps:

- Insist that some of your teenager's earnings be saved.

- Monitor your child's work time. Working over 20 hours per week can be detrimental, probably because long work hours can lead to an increase in unstructured time.

- Do not allow work to displace time for important developmental activities, such as schoolwork, co-curricular activities, and hobbies.

- Do not allow long work hours to diminish time spent on important health maintenance activities (nutrition, sleep, exercise, stress-reducing down time).

- Visit your child's work setting to know first-hand its attributes and get to know your child's supervisor. Work-related adults can be influential mentors for a child. Many employers are quite attuned to the challenges that working students confront and do show concern and support for their youthful employees' success in school.

Work Environment

(To Be Completed for Teenagers Only)

Answer Each Question 2, 1 or 0

2 = Yes, Often, or Usually   1 = Sometimes   0 = No or Never

_____ 1. Does (or did) your child do informal jobs (babysitting, yard work, shoveling snow) during his or her early adolescent years?

_____ 2. Is your child's school work always a priority over paid work?

_____ 3. Does your child work in a good environment where he or she is exposed to good peers and adults?

_____ 4. Does your child spend some of the money earned at work on something other than nonessential material things?

_____ 5. Does your teenager work 20 hours or fewer per week?

Scoring: Give yourself 2 points for "yes," "often," or "usually" answers, 1 point for "sometimes" answers, and 0 points for "no" and "never" answers. Total your points for questions 1 through 5 and write the answer below.

Your total score = _____ (0 to 10 points)

[1] Entwisle, D., Alexander. K., Olson, L., & Ross, K. (1999). Paid work in early adolescence: Developmental and ethnic patterns. *Journal of Early Adolescence, 19,* 363-388.

[2] Wirth, J. (2003, June 15). Teens earn, but parents still pay. *Asheville Citizen-Times,* p. D6.

[3] Institute of Medicine. (1998). *Protecting youth at work: Health, safety, and development of working children and adolescents in the United States.* Washington, DC: National Academy Press.

[4] *Ibid.*

[5] Ruscoe, G., Morgan, J., & Peebles, C. (1996). Students who work. *Adolescence, 31,* 625-632.

[6] *Ibid.*

[7] Greenberger, E., & Steinberg, L. (1986). *When teenagers work: The psychological and social costs of adolescent employment.* New York: Basic Books.

[8] Ruscoe, G., Morgan, J., & Peebles, C. (1996).

[9] www.teenresearch.com

[10] Ruscoe, G., Morgan, J., & Peebles, C. (1996).

[11] *Ibid.*

[12] Institute of Medicine. (1998).

[13] Ruscoe, G., Morgan, J., & Peebles, C. (1996).

[14] *Ibid.*

[15] Safron, D., Schulenberg, J., & Bachman, J. (2001). Part-time work and hurried adolescence: The links among work intensity, social activities, health behaviors, and substance use. *Journal of Health and Social Behavior, 42,* 425-449.

[16] *Ibid.*

[17] Institute of Medicine. (1998).

[18] Steinberg, L., Fegley, S., & Dornbusch, S. (1993). Negative impact of part-time work on adolescent adjustment: Evidence from a longitudinal study. *Developmental Psychology, 29,* 171-180.

[19] Silbereisen, R., & Todt, E. (Eds.). (1994). *Adolescence in context: The interplay of family, school, peers, and work in adjustment.* New York: Springer-Verlag.

[20] Ruscoe, G., Morgan, J., & Peebles, C. (1996).

[21] *Ibid.*

[22] Safron, D., Schulenberg, J., & Bachman, J. (2001).

[23] Elias, M. (2002, August 27). Teens take lesson from job stress study: Work builds coping skills for later. *USA Today*, p. 7-D.

[24] *Ibid.*

[25] Ruscoe, G., Morgan, J., & Peebles, C. (1996).

[26] Institute of Medicine. (1998).

CHAPTER 12

Recreational and Leisure Settings

EXCEPT FOR SCHOOLWORK, THE MAJORITY OF CHIL-dren's time is spent in recreational and leisure activities, about 40–50 percent of waking hours during the school year (including weekends) and even more during the summer.[1] A large block of this time is spent using electronic media or participating in co-curricular and sports activities, both of which are the subjects of separate chapters in this book. The focus in this chapter is on broader generic issues about recreational pursuits and leisure activities in the community.

Contemporary American culture may make children more dependent on recreational activities. The sheer amount of time spent in recreational activities is one reason they have grown in importance as behavior settings for youths. Also, with the absence of formal apprenticeship structures during adolescence and the scarcity of career-oriented job opportunities for youths, recreational activities may help facilitate the transition to adulthood, that is, from full-time education to employment. Recreation provides an arena for role experimentation in confronting challenges.[2]

Researchers Leslie Raymore and her colleagues report that youths identify recreational pursuits as the most enjoyable activities in their lives.[3]   Recreational activities provide an opportunity for youths to explore beyond some of the day-to-day restrictions of family life and school settings. As already noted, youths experience "flow" more often during recreational activities than during anything else they do. Participation in nonschool activities, such as a boys or girls club, or a hobby club, can increase the status of the child within school or increase the child's social involvement with school peers.[4]

Australian researchers Anne Passmore and Davina French have proposed three categories of recreational and leisure activities. *Achievement leisure* involves activities that are demanding, including competitive activities, and that provide a sense of personal challenge. *Social leisure* entails being with other people, especially peers. *Time-out leisure* is a way to relax and pass time. It is usually undemanding. Achievement leisure usually has measurable or observable developmental benefits, whereas time-out leisure typically does not. However, time-out leisure used wisely and productively may be developmentally essential, such as time spent alone thinking and sorting through one's thoughts. In fact, this need may too often go unmet in today's hectic, entertainment-focused, stay-"busy"-at-all-costs society. So it could be argued that there are two types of time-out leisure: vapid media-oriented activities, and more meaningful, productive, and necessary "reflective" activities, such as thinking, reading, going for walks, etc. Passmore and French's three types of leisure and recreation are summarized in the table on the following page.

In the study by Passmore and French, 45 percent of teenagers listed a sport as their primary achievement activity, whereas about 15 percent reported artistic activities (playing a musical instrument, dancing, painting) as their primary achievement activity. The most common social leisure activities were talking, visiting, going out, talking on the phone, and eating with friends. The most common time-out leisure activity was entertainment (listening to music or watching television), which was selected by 34 percent of teenagers, followed by 26 percent who reported reflective activities such as lying in bed thinking or reading.[5]

Adolescence is a critical time for the formation of patterns of leisure behavior, as this is typically when children begin

Types of Leisure and Recreation [6]

Type	Examples
Achievement	Sports, playing a musical instrument, dance, hobby, creative arts
Social	Being with other people, especially friends
Time-Out	Listening to music, watching TV, surfing the Net, lying in bed thinking

making leisure decisions themselves. Some leisure may become core activities that remain with the individual throughout life.[7] Most importantly, these activities are regular and predictable sources of pleasure and enjoyment in adolescents' daily lives. Participating in sports, socializing with friends, or becoming involved in a club introduces youths to settings and experiences that can be high points in their lives. These experiences are often what teenagers look forward to, what gets them out of bed in the morning, and what sustains them through times when school stress or family tensions fill their lives.[8]

Recreation and leisure activities can range from those having no structure to complex activities with a great deal of structure. For example, school- and community-sponsored athletics, music organizations, and church groups are highly structured. These activities usually operate on a formal schedule, require sustained attention, and give the participating youths feedback about their performance. Less-structured activities are often relatively spontaneous and generally do not involve formal rules, adult supervision, or skill development. Watching TV and hanging out with friends are examples.[9]

There are an immense number of leisure and recreational pursuits that are available to youths: Junior Achievement, Boy and Girl Scouts, YMCA/YWCA, Campfire Girls and Boys, 4-H. There are over 17,000 private non-profit organizations, parks and recreation programs, school-based after-school programs, sporting organizations, museums, libraries, and other independent youth organizations in the United States providing youth recreation programs.[10] There are also numerous less-official groups and annual activities. A proper accounting of them would require a volume the size of this book, but they include Dungeons and Dragon clubs, summer camps, hometown festivals and fairs, video arcades, and teenage night clubs. Here are a few examples of some established programs:

Odyssey of the Mind teaches youths creative thinking skills through problem-solving activities. Each year teams are given a problem to solve, and they then display their solution in regional, state and national competitions. There is an adult coach for each seven-member team. The challenges given to the teams run the gamut, from staging a drama performance to solving mechanical problems.

New Scenes is a filmmaking interest group for high school students. Participants produce videotaped movies to share with their peers. The diverse topics include adolescent pregnancy and the importance of voting. Students research the topic, write the script, and then videotape the movie. Local college students help edit the movies, which are screened in school libraries.

Adolescent Creative Theater (ACT) is an improvisational workshop for students in middle school. These groups meet weekly to conduct various exercises in improvisational theater. The emphasis is on learning extemporaneous speaking. ACT groups typically perform twice-annually for parents.

Promoting Social Competency Through Recreation

It has been widely claimed that positive recreational and leisure activities contribute to the healthy development of youths. Some examples: Studies suggest that participation in arts, hobbies, and youth organizations reduces the risk of delinquency.[11] Participation in structured activities correlates with less antisocial behavior.[12] (One theory is that structured activities impose organization on a youth's recreational pursuits that makes parental monitoring easier.[13]) Teenage boys who are active in "socially valued" recreational activities are less likely to become involved in risky behaviors like drinking and using drugs.[14] It must be stressed that antisocial behavior has not been linked to a lack of participation in community activities, but rather to participation in the wrong types of activities. Therefore, the issue is not whether or not a youth is engaged in activities, but rather what activities the youth is engaged in, and with whom. When it comes to the risk for antisocial behavior, it may be preferable for a youth to be uninvolved than to participate in unstructured activities, particularly if it involves deviant peers.[15]

Pick up any newspaper and it is not uncommon to find a story about a group of at-risk youths whose lives have changed for the better because of involvement in a positive activity. Take for example the story of a chess master who adopts a junior high school class. The kids, all from the inner city, become preoccupied with chess, too engrossed in their activity to be enticed by the street life. They win the national junior high championship. The kids talk about how they apply strategic chess thinking to the rest of their lives. Reed Larson hypothesizes that recreation is a "context in which there is often a higher density of growth experiences."[16]

It is noteworthy that studies have consistently found that a child's increasing age is related to increased problem behavior (for example, poorer school grades, decreased enjoyment of and effort in school, and increased alcohol use). Participation in certain recreational activities is related to decreased risks and problem behaviors associated with increasing age level. However, it is not fully understood what specific elements in recreational programs make them successful.[17]

One theory is that these kinds of activities provide a special environment which facilitates *agentic* behavior, that is, behavior in which an individual makes things happen by one's actions. Further, the activities redirect the natural motivations of teenagers into behaviors that are more adult-like. Larson puts it this way:

> "This combination — intrinsic motivation with challenge and deep attention — has led us to think of these activities as 'transitional,' on the theory that they provide a developmental bridge between the positive motivational states experienced in childhood free play and the structure and challenge of adult obligatory activities."[18]

Reverend Howard Hanger, an Asheville, North Carolina, minister, provides a personal account of his daughters' experiences with recreational activities, in *Life Gets Dark; Leave Delight On* (pages 158–159).

Scouting

Girl Scouts and Boy Scouts are classic examples of recreational programs that build character. Scouting fulfills a number of needs of growing boys, according to Michael Gurian.[19] I am sure these characteristic needs apply to girls as well:

- *Goal-Setting.* The system of merit badges teaches youths how to set goals and work step-by-step to attain them.

- *Healthy Hierarchy.* Scout troops provide youths with an emotionally healthy hierarchical system in which their position is clear.

- *Mentoring.* Youths desire adults to emulate. Scouting provides both healthy adult and peer mentoring.

- *Experience of Nature.* Youths need to bond with nature. Scouting takes them into the natural environment for camping and other activities.

- *Spiritual Development.* Youths need a spiritual language with which to understand moral concepts. Scout leaders teach a spiritual language.

- **Character Development.** The importance of character has lost emphasis in today's society, but Scouting sends a resounding message that character counts.

- **Discipline.** Scouting provides a structure of discipline; this helps youths construct their own form of self-discipline.

Today, Scouting competes with activities that didn't exist several decades ago: soccer, computers, the Internet. Scout troops are not alone in this struggle to win teenagers' allegiance and time. Boys and Girls Clubs, Little League, and 4-H Clubs find themselves competing for youth participants. Programs today must be exciting. "In this day and age, there is a challenge to holding any child's attention," says Rene Fairrer, Associate Director of Communications for Boy Scouts of America.[20] The Boy Scouts recently developed a high-energy adventure program, Venturing, to keep older youths involved. The Boy Scouts are not without controversy. Their stance on homosexuality has been under fire. (See below.)

Boy Scouts'
Stance on Homosexuality

The Boy Scouts began in the United States in the early 1890s and has become known for its emphasis on character development and values-based leadership training. Today, Boy Scouts is more popular than ever. In the 1990s, the Boy Scouts dismissed a scout leader for his public statement of homosexuality. The case went all the way to the U.S. Supreme Court, which upheld the Boy Scouts' right to such action. Because it is a private organization, the Boys Scouts may discriminate against another person because of his or her sexual orientation. Some readers will agree with this policy; others may not. In the latter case, parents will have to weigh the extraordinary opportunities provided by this premier youth development organization with a moral stance that they find objectionable.

Adolescent Pursuits

Adolescence is a time when teenagers become more independent from parents and navigate their life space more freely. They spend more unsupervised time with friends and explore new environments. Socializing is the most frequent free-time activity of high school students, accounting for 16 percent of their waking hours.[21] It includes a wide variety of behaviors, from rowdy parties to intimate conversations with friends. For older teenagers, Friday and Saturday nights are prime time for congregating to socialize. It includes hanging out at shopping malls, video arcades, skating rinks, and multiplex cinemas, as well as driving around, partying, and dating.

But without a doubt the most cherished privilege of independence granted to adolescents is the license to drive.[22] Teenage drivers and their riders engage in such activities as cruising the streets, and they find places along the "strip" where they can meet to talk and gawk. Cars not only provide mobility but also confer social status and make socializing easier. Riding around in a car for fun is a popular amusement for teenagers. Driving fast is common; adolescents often experience a high level of excitement as they "drag Main."

Alcohol and drugs are part of weekend activity for many teenagers; about half of all 16 and 17 year olds report drinking at least monthly. Most alcohol use occurs in groups of seven or more, typically at a friend's house or at a public location after dark. The more unsupervised time that teenagers spend with peers on weekend evenings, the more likely they are to use alcohol. "Partying" typically leads to higher rates of substance use. Once again, unstructured time is associated with higher substance use and delinquent activity. Friday and Saturday nights are the peak times for such high-risk behaviors.[23]

Another activity with a high degree of enjoyment for adolescents is being with a romantic partner. Over half of 9th to 12th graders spend time with a person of the other gender on a weekend night. One of the great challenges that adolescents face is the development of appropriate romantic friendships. Teenagers will often change their preferred recreational and leisure settings in order to increase the likelihood of making the right kind of interpersonal contacts. So, instead of spending time in contexts where there is close supervision, such as the parental home, teenagers naturally gravitate to community environments known to provide the right kind of encounters.

Arts-Based Youth Groups

There is a great need for additional research to broaden our understanding of what types of recreational activities are most likely to benefit particular children. Shirley Brice Heath at Stanford University, in collaboration with Milbrey McLaughlin, has done breakthrough research on the merits of adolescent participation in drama, dance, music, and the visual and media arts in community-based (that is, nonschool) organizations. Her research placed anthropologists in selected communities to look at arts-based groups and their effect on the development of adolescents. Heath's data reveal ways that the youths use language as they plan, practice, and perform their arts. In studying these groups over a decade, Heath found that the environments of arts groups were different from groups that were involved in community service or sports, particularly in the language used by adult leaders and the youths.[24]

Heath compared adolescents who participated in arts organizations with students in a national database. One hundred teenagers completed a selection of questions used in a longitudinal national survey of secondary school students sponsored by the United States Department of Education. Comparisons between students in the arts organizations were made with students in the national sample in order to answer these questions: how do they compare in areas of academic performance, leisure-time use, and their appraisal of their ability as planners, problem solvers, and community participants? What happens in arts activities that develops adolescents' sense of identity as creative, expressive, and independent? Just what is the essential process of learning within the arts?

Community organizations provide youths with substantial learning and practice opportunities with adult professionals and older youths, who serve as teachers and models. It appears that youths in arts-based organizations gain special practice in thinking and talking as adults. Heath's research team did frequency counts of the teenagers'

Life Gets Dark; Leave Delight On

By Howard Hanger

My oldest daughter, Windsor, is a ballerina. Tutu's, tights and toe-shoes...the whole hooha. She has studied dance for several years now. She loves it.

My youngest daughter, Kelsey, is a soccer player. She tried track, but likes the team thing better. She's played indoor and outdoor soccer with several different leagues. She's into it big time.

Windsor had her Spring recital last week. She was elegance incarnate. Grace made visible. Through tear-filled daddy eyes, she was a supple willow in the wind. A wispy mist spiraling in a morning breeze. A frisky candle flame on the stage/altar, calling my heathen heart to praise.

Kelsey has a game every Saturday. She's fast, long-legged, lithe and limber. Gazelle-like, she jets down the field, feet barely skimming the grass. Never quite earthbound, never quite sky-borne, she turns on a dime into a ball scramble, feet flying with surgical precision and speed that an Irish step dancer would offer a pint for.

Neither of my daughters does dance or soccer because she thinks she should. Neither of them does it because she thinks it will make her a better person. They don't do it because it will make them lots of money — or get them into college — or help them find a boyfriend. They don't do it to lose weight or tone their bodies or to look good in a bathing suit. They don't even do it because it's the "cool thing" and "all the kids are doing it."

My daughters play soccer and dance ballet for one reason and one reason alone: It brings them great delight — pure and simple. They enjoy what they do. They relish it. They take great pleasure in it.

Is it easy? No. Both soccer and dance require regular, consistent practices and rehearsals. Both demand discipline, regularity, and unending repetition. They work hard at it. Sweat, strain, and exhaustion are a constant part of the picture. Again and again, when I pick them up from rehearsal or practice, they'll be sweaty and beet-faced, hair matted or frazzled, face drained. They say, "My coach (or teacher) killed us today. They worked us sooo hard!"

"Ooooh!" I sometimes say, with tongue deeply embedded in cheek, "that sounds tough. Maybe you should quit and find something easier."

"Get serious, Dad," they retort. "I love it."

What a way to live! What a way to spend your days . . . whatever time you've been given in this crazy, wonderful and sorrow-filled life: To delight in what you do. To simply enjoy the doing of it. When you find such a magical enterprise, it hardly matters how much effort, training, and exertion are required.

Life is hard. Of course it is. Life is full of pain and struggle and heartache and broken dreams. I'm not trying to do a Pollyanna to get you believing that it's possible to live without stepping in excrement every now and then. But children know something that adults seem to have forgotten: that life offers delight. Over and over in countless ways, life offers delight. "And if you're wise," teach the children, "you'll jump into delight — whatever is your delight — headfirst."

Maybe that's why Jesus said that unless you become like a child, you ain't got a snowball-in-heck chance of even seeing the kingdom of heaven. If you're alive, you're going to struggle and sweat. Since we all have to go through that anyway, doesn't it make sense to go through it for something worthwhile? Something that serves up a big platter of delight to your heart and soul?

How do you live the perfect life? I'm not sure. But my kids have taught me this: Life gets pretty hard sometimes, so always leave delight on.

verbal interactions to identify their use of certain types of language. As the time of a production or performance neared, over 80 percent of the talk involved proposed explanations to situations. Seventy-six percent of their talk during practices involved "pointing out" terms with technical specialized vocabulary. The young artists also had extensive opportunities to use language that involved critical judgment and reasoning, such as identifying problems, devising solutions, and identifying steps. This meant that the students got considerable practice explaining their ideas, arguing for a particular solution, and defending their point of view.

By contrast, students who were not involved in organized arts-based activities or extracurricular activities at school, engaged in only 15–20 minutes weekly of sustained conversations with adults that included planning. These youths had little or no practice in talking through future plans, developing ideas for implementation, or evaluating next steps from a current situation. Heath concluded that the intensity of practice for key types of language uses is rarely available in other settings. Adolescents have few opportunities to work in a "planful" way to implement a project with an adult guide. Heath notes:

> **"Young people across all socioeconomic classes have almost no time with adults to hear and use forms of language critical for academic performance and personal maturation. Making decisions, thinking ahead, and building strategies make up most of what adults have to do in their everyday lives. But facility in these skills does not come easily. Most certainly, the linguistic competence necessary to talk oneself through tough situations cannot develop without hearing such language modeled."**[25]

Heath also found that when students worked in arts activities at least three hours-a-day, three days-a-week, for one full year, they demonstrated improved academics and ability to plan for the future for themselves. Further, she found that during their free time, adolescents who were involved in arts found ways to use time for specific learning goals. Compared to peers in the national sample, these "arts" students:

- Attended music, art and dance classes nearly three times as frequently.

- Participated in youth groups nearly four times more frequently.

- Read for pleasure nearly twice as often.

- Performed community service more than four times as often.[26]

To summarize, Heath found that key areas of learning in the arts groups to be the development of adult-like language, planful behavior, and collaborative attitudes and interactions. According to Heath, the ability to collaborate, be persistent, show discipline, be expressive, and work with peers who hold different viewpoints, all transfer well to the arena of adult work, and in particular, the business world. These skills are readily learned by adolescents who participate in arts-based activities. As we will see, similar skills can be learned in the most common of all youth recreational and leisure activities: sports. The next chapter takes up the role of sports in children's lives.

Summing Up

With the absence of formal apprenticeship structures during adolescence, recreational and leisure activities can provide experiences that help adolescents transition to adulthood, that is, from full-time education to employment. Some benefits of these types of activities can be fairly subtle – parents must be perceptive.

Action Steps:

- Involve your child in a youth organization which provides substantial learning and practice opportunities with adults and older youths who serve as teachers and models.

- Specifically, you might want to involve your child in an arts activity. Studies show that youths who participate in arts-based organizations have opportunities to practice thinking and talking as adults. When students worked in arts activities at least three hours-a-day, three days-a-week, for one full year, they demonstrated improved academics and the ability to plan for the future for themselves. Also, during free time, adolescents who are involved in arts tend to find ways to use time for specific learning goals.

- Limit the time that teenagers spend in unstructured activities with peers on weekend evenings. Unstructured time is associated with higher substance abuse.

- Provide safe, supervised opportunities for teenagers to have the excitement and emotional climax of weekend evenings. For teenagers, there must be a balance between adult supervision and independence.

QUIZ

Recreational and Leisure Environment

_____ 1. Does your child take part in a supervised recreational activity?

_____ 2. Does your child take lessons in support of some hobby or interest?

_____ 3. Do you participate in a recreational activity together as a family?

_____ 4. Does your child use leisure time to improve himself or herself?

_____ 5. Does your child rarely spend time just hanging out with friends, with nothing special to do?

Scoring: Give yourself 2 points for "yes," "often," or "usually" answers, 1 point for "sometimes" answers, and 0 points for "no" and "never" answers. Total your points for questions 1 through 5 and write the answer below.

Your total score = _____ (0 to 10 points)

[1] Larson, R. (2000). Toward a psychology of positive youth development. *American Psychologist, 55,* 170-183.

[2] Silbereisen, R., & Todt, E. (Eds.). (1994). *Adolescence in context: The interplay of family, school, peers, and work in adjustment.* New York: Springer-Verlag.

[3] Raymore, L., Barber, B., Eccles, J., & Godbey, G. (1999). Leisure behavior pattern stability during the transition from adolescence to young adulthood. *Journal of Youth and Adolescence, 28,* 79-103.

[4] Gilman, R. (2001). The relationship between life satisfaction, social interest, and frequency of extracurricular activities among adolescent students. *Journal of Youth and Adolescence, 30,* 749-767.

[5] *Ibid.*

[6] Passmore, A., & French, D. (2001). Development and administration of a measure to assess adolescents' participation in leisure activities. *Adolescence, 36,* 67-74.

[7] Raymore, L., Barber, B., Eccles, J., & Godbey, G. (1999).

[8] Larson, R. (2000).

[9] Mahoney, J., & Stattin, H. (2000). Leisure activities and adolescent antisocial behavior: The role of structure and social context. *Journal of Adolescence, 23,* 113-127.

[10] Carnegie Council on Adolescent Development. (1992). *A matter of time: Risk and opportunity in the nonschool hours.* New York: Carnegie Corporation.

[11] Larson, R. (2000).

[12] Mahoney, J., & Stattin, H. (2000).

[13] *Ibid.*

[14] Raymore, L., Barber, B., Eccles, J., & Godbey, G. (1999).

[15] Mahoney, J., & Stattin, H. (2000).

[16] Larson, R. (2000). p. 178.

[17] Butcher-Anderson, D., Newsome, W., & Ferrari, T. (2003). Participation in boys and girls clubs and relationships to youth outcomes. *Journal of Community Psychology, 31,* 39-55.

[18] *Ibid.*

[19] Gurian, M. (1999). *A fine young man.* New York: Putnam.

[20] Clark, P. (1999, December 6). Boy scouts get adventurous to keep teenagers' interest. *Asheville Citizen-Times,* p. B-1.

[21] Csikszentmihalyi, M., & Larson, R. (1984). *Being adolescent.* New York: Basic Books.

[22] Hartos, J., Eitel, P., Haynie, D., & Simmons-Morton, B. (2000). Can I take the car? Relations among parenting practices and adolescent problem-driving practices. *Journal of Adolescent Research, 15,* 352-367.

[23] Crouter, A., & Larson, R. (Eds.). (1998). Temporal rhythms in adolescence: Clocks, calendars, and the coordination of daily life. *New directions for child and adolescent development,* No. 82. San Francisco: Jossey-Bass.

[24] Heath, S. (2000). Making learning work. *About Afterschool Matters, 1,* 33-45.

[25] Heath, S. (undated). Imaginative actuality: Learning in the arts during nonschool hours. In E. Fiske (Ed.), *Champions of change: The impact of arts on learning* (pp. 30-34). New York: The Arts Education Partnership, The President's Committee on Arts and the Humanities. p. 26.

[26] Heath, S. (1998). Living the arts through language & learning: A report on community-based youth organizations. *Americans for the Arts Monographs, 2* (7). p. 8.

CHAPTER 13

Sports Settings

A GROUP OF GIRLS IN SOUTHERN CALIFORNIA LEARNS to square their shoulders to the volleyball net. A group of boys plays touch football at a middle school in rural Kansas. A Mississippi teenager practices free throws at home with his little brother. A Michigan high school student swims laps to the encouraging voice of her coach. A group of girls in Texas chatters before cheerleading practice. A baseball team in Missouri chants as they do calisthenics.

Millions of youths in the United States are engaged in sports as part of school or after-school activities. For many youths, sports are a significant part of their lives. According to a Gallup Youth Survey, half of American teenagers have played on a sports team recently, divided about equally between school teams and community athletic teams. Most youths say they see sports as a way to be part of a group and make friends.[1]

In this chapter, we will look at a number of aspects of sports in childhood and adolescence. We begin with the effects of sports involvement and the experience of team participation. I'll also discuss the grooming of young athletes and early specialization in a single sport. They have become controversial topics with the recent dominance of athletes like Tiger Woods. Then we'll look at the role of adults in youth sports – both parents and coaches. Because girls' sports involvement has exploded in the past three decades, we'll examine the implications.

The role of sports in the lives of children with behavioral challenges is another special topic we'll explore. Finally, we'll revisit the concept of flow and the special role that sports may play in it.

Effects of Sports

Adolescence is a time when youths are especially vulnerable to at-risk behaviors. These behaviors are sometimes misguided attempts of teenagers to assert control over their lives. Parent/authors Jean Zimmerman and Gil Reavill have this to say: "What does it take for a girl to feel confident, secure, and in control of her world? Children learn to feel good about themselves through accomplishment. The crucial element in self-worth is not consistent success, but the experience of progressing, of becoming better, of succeeding where you've failed before. . . . Athletes are constantly encouraged to achieve, to overcome obstacles, to practice to the point of proficiency. They may learn about sacrifice, commitment to the greater good, responsibility to others."[2]

Psychologist Maureen Weiss and her colleagues at the University of Oregon have demonstrated in numerous studies that sports have tremendous potential to increase children's self-esteem and motivation.[3] Educational psychologist Ronald Jeziorski's work has shown that youths who participate in sports generally get better grades and tend to be better adjusted in and out of school.[4] Further, sports psychologist Tara Scanlan at UCLA says that learning achieved in sports settings can teach children important life skills.[5]

Most of us can point to sports participation as an opportunity to learn about winning and losing, competition, and fairness. Perhaps an even greater benefit to be gained from participating in sports is the opportunity to learn lessons that shape character. I believe we can all agree on the value of developing perseverance, fortitude, dedication, commitment, and responsibility. Sports psychologist Caroline Silby notes that two of the most critical skills in life, taking risks and putting forth effort, can be developed through sports participation.[6]

Sports serve as an important anchor in many youths' lives, helping them cope with the normal challenges of growing up – the demands of school, the struggle for acceptance by a peer group, changing physical appearance, and bubbling emotions. Fourteen-year-old Mandy has an explosive temper. She often swears and has a tendency to mouth off if upset. However, her soccer coach and referees will not tolerate such behavior. In order to remain on the team, she has learned to control herself. The skill has carried over to her friendships. When she gets mad, she doesn't explode as much as she used to.

> **Sports involvement can make a tremendous demand on teen-agers' time. Varsity-level athletic training consumes about 20 hours-per-week on average. However, this time demand usually helps clarify academic priorities rather than detracting from them. Since athletes have a limited amount of time for studying, they must learn to manage their time more efficiently.[7]**

Sports may help teenagers get through some of the normal distractions of adolescence. For example, athletes may change their focus from the normal adolescent preoccupations with music, cars, spending money, and opposite-gender relationships. Olympic swimmer Summer Sanders says, "I never worried about my appearance; I never dieted; I never obsessed about what I ate or what I weighed; I never fussed over makeup or fashion, because these were all nonissues in my world."[8] Being on a team requires commitment to the sport and to teammates. If a girl, for example, is feeling good about herself because of her accomplishments on the field, she may be less inclined to pursue sexual relationships. Studies show that adolescent athletes tend to delay having sex.[9]

Team Participation

When basketball superstar Magic Johnson retired from sports, he said that more than anything else he missed being part of the team, the group of friends who strived together to get better, and who cared for each other as brothers do. He missed the daily camaraderie, the bonding experience. As I reflect on my own experience in sports, though I was not a superstar by a long shot, this also was the most important aspect of sports involvement for me – being a part of a team and forming strong relationships with my peers. There was a strong sense of belonging and mutual caring. Being part of a team meant that I was part of something important, something special. We got to do things that others didn't get to do. It brought both security and empowerment. It is noteworthy that sports often satisfy the needs of youths in a fashion similar to gangs. Teenagers who join gangs are typically looking for excitement, status, protection, and a sense of belonging. One might consider sports to be a positive gang, replacing the negative culture of gang involvement.[10]

> The athletic team experience provides a common mission for youth participants. The goal is always individual and team improvement. There is mutual sharing of celebrations as well as the experience of hard times together. There is an added sense of meaning to all participants. Even for players who don't make the varsity or the traveling team, or who are only allowed to practice, there is a mutual respect because each participant passes the test by hanging in when challenged and persisting through adversity. Also, in team sports, youths can feel a sense of accomplishment by making even small contributions to the team's success.

Sports Specialization and Grooming Young Athletes

By age 3, Tiger Woods was playing nine holes of golf. Chris Evert took up tennis at age 5. With the considerable media coverage (and the considerable financial rewards that can follow) given to elite athletes these days, there appears to be an increasing pressure on children to specialize in a sport at an early age. Is this good for a child? Is there any worthwhile payoff?

The book *Little Girls in Pretty Boxes* describes the struggle of young female gymnasts groomed for the Olympics. Years later, many of these girls are beset with eating disorders and burnout.[11] Decades ago, Eastern Bloc countries steered their athletes toward specialization at a young age. They achieved quick results and created child prodigies, but the youths did not improve as they matured. They lacked the solid, carefully developed foundation necessary for reaching new heights. Today, even countries such as Cuba have replaced specialization with a balanced approach to youth sports.[12]

According to the American Academy of Pediatrics, research does not support the presumed advantage of early sports specialization. Youths who participate in a variety of sports and who specialize only after reaching puberty (if at all) are generally more consistent performers, have fewer injuries, are less prone to delayed menstruation and eating disorders, and struggle with less emotional stress.[13] The implication, thus, is that children should be encouraged to participate in a variety of different sports activities and to develop a wide range of skills.

Age 15 appears to be the coming-of-age year for many athletes. At about this time, youths can assume responsibility for their athletic future. It is also a time in their adolescence when they make the transition from child to adult. I recall that at about age 15, I began to specialize in one sport, and at the same time rejected many of the trappings of *just* being a teenager. I distinctly remember wanting to be an adult from that point on. Sports, which presented many responsibilities of an adult nature, enabled me to enter a pseudo-adult world. According to psychologists Reed Larson and Douglas Kleiber, "the application of effort and concentration and the demand for persistence to improve skills give [sports] a worklike character that is comparable to other demanding situations that an adolescent faces increasingly in the transition to adult life."[14]

A recent phenomenon tied closely to the issue of specialization is individualized instruction for athletes. Once limited to individual sports such as tennis this has become popular in team sports, too, particularly for basketball, baseball, football, and soccer. Parents often pay free-lance coaches thousands of dollars to work intensively with their children, with the hope of gaining college athletic scholarships and stardom. Some of these private coaches appear to have considerable success in molding star athletes. Nevertheless, it is still too soon to judge whether or not successes are the exception and the majority of hopefuls experience failure and negative experiences.

Parental Involvement in Youth Sport Participation

There is nothing wrong with parents coaching their own children if it is done thoughtfully and carefully. Tens of thousands of mothers and fathers coach in America's youth sports leagues. In team sports, parent coaches must be sure to treat their child(ren) equally with teammates. In individual sports, parent coaches must guard against the possible distortion of the parent-child relationship. Problems quickly arise, however, when parents become obsessed with grooming their children for a professional career.

Some parents start coaching for practical reasons, saying that coaches are not available or are too expensive. Many sports psychologists oppose parental coaching, claiming that non-family coaches are better able to induce the best performance from a child athlete. The key issue for all involved adults is to ensure that youth sports are oriented toward the children's enjoyment, not toward the interests of parents and coaches. A point of compromise is for parents of talented child athletes to hand over coaching duties to someone else as the child matures, generally around 12 or 13 years of age.

What do parents want their children to get out of playing sports? Responses vary but the development of athletic skills is usually not a priority. Personal growth is typically the primary reason as evidenced by these statements: "I wish my daughter wouldn't give up so easily; I want her to be able to stick with an activity." "I wish my daughter wouldn't be so shy, that she would be more assertive." "My son drives me crazy with the way he wastes time; I wish he would learn to get on a schedule."[15]

With so many potential benefits to be gained through sports participation, it is disturbing that about 80 percent of youths who begin organized sports drop out between the ages of 12 and 17.[16] The number one reason teenagers give for dropping out of sports is the lack of enjoyment.[17] Olympic swimmer Summer Sanders says, "Anything that takes work down the road has got to be fun right from the start. It must involve friends, or the opportunity to make new ones. And there must be some reward for effort, some sense of progress, so that it's never pointless to try harder. Personal satisfaction, however small, should always be within reach."[18]

Parents are in a unique position to ensure that children remain active in sports and to ensure that sports participation teaches positive life skills. When a child faces stress resulting from sport participation and competition, parents must be supportive and help to mediate the stress. Parental pressure, which is defined as behavior perceived by a child as creating expectations that are unattainable, can be detrimental.[19] However, encouraging a young athlete toward excellence and success can be positively motivating. There is a fine distinction between being supportive and challenging for personal growth and stressful pushing for some other perceived payoff. Parents must be careful not to cross the line.

Another way a parent can make a difference is by helping a child get a healthy perspective on what is typically called "failure." Summer Sanders makes the point: "A child who tries something that's beyond her capabilities doesn't need a parent stepping in to redefine 'appropriate' goals – that only underscores her sense of failure. Instead, the parent should help her child see that not meeting a goal isn't any reflection on her self-worth. Failure is not something to be ashamed of; it means you tried something a little beyond your reach. It means you've just learned a little bit more to help you get a little closer to realizing that goal the next go-around. If a parent can help a child see that failure carries no penalty, then it shouldn't matter what goals the child sets for herself. Her best might not be good enough to win at first, but that doesn't mean it's failure."[20]

It is difficult to make generalizations about the appropriate level of parental involvement in children's sports activities. At one end of the continuum may be someone like Summer Sander's mother, who attended most of her practices and competitions, often traveling long distances. At the other end of the continuum might be my own parents. I recall my father attending only one of my competitions in high school and my mother attending one of my wrestling matches, but primarily because she wanted to express concern to the coach about how rundown I was from trying to lose weight. My parents filled the traditional roles of "taxi driver," chief nutritionist, and main fan, but sports were my love and they pursued their own interest in golf. There is no right way. Parent and child personalities differ and sports vary in their demand on family life.

Parents must be careful as fans, however. While pushy Little League fathers have been around for a long time, a new level of parental rage seems to have developed over the past decade. Some parents have become so invested in their children's sports that it erupts into violence at sporting events. The National Association of Sports Officials says there are at least two or three reports of violent parents at youth sports events each week![21] Harvard Psychiatrist William Pollack believes that the phenomenon may be due, in part, to some parents trying to live vicariously through their children.[22] Social critics have cited instances of parental rage in condemning all youth sports; therefore, I am going to address such criticisms and potential solutions in the next chapter, which addresses how to make sports a positive experience.

When you play catch with your child, take him to the park to play on the monkey bars, or sign her up for gymnastics class or a soccer league, you are providing opportunities for your child to develop a lifetime relationship with sports and physical activity.[23] Parents who encourage their children to participate in sports early in life can pave the way for lifelong benefits. Former college gymnastics champion Susan Wilson offers this perspective: "Hopefully she'll stay active in recreational activity because at the most basic level it enhances her in some way. Every time she does something physical, she'll realize something about herself. No matter what direction you'd like to see her grow – having fun, staying healthy, representing her high school team, keeping her weight under control, staying away from drugs and early sex – the bonanza of benefits she'll gain by playing sports will serve her throughout her entire life."[24]

Parents are not the only adults who need to show through actions and words that it's great to be involved in sports; relatives, neighbors, and other caregivers all need to communicate this important message to today's youth. Stanford University psychologist Albert Bandura has shown in his research that learning through example is the most effective form of learning. Simply put, people learn best by imitating the behavior of someone who effectively performs a task. Positive adult role models readily participating in sport activities are a vital link

in healthy youth development and the acquisition of physically and socially healthy habits.[25]

Coaches

The vital life skills that can be learned in sport activities must transfer from the activity to other areas of life such as in the school and home, and eventually to the workplace. The coaching process is an important aspect of making the lessons learned in sports transferable to other life settings. Gymnastics coach Susan Wilson uses goal setting as a way for girls to learn to discipline themselves. She talks about making sports lessons manageable – something the child can grasp: "When I am coaching girls, I frequently ask them, "What goal are we working toward? . . . I'll bet I say the word 'goal' fifty times during a practice. . . . I mostly work with short-term goals, because setting long-term ones is often unrealistic for early elementary school children. Make goals small and attainable."[26]

Wilson also notes that coaches can help children make the connection between reaching goals and taking risks by first starting with little goals with little risk. She says that it's important for coaches to teach the difference between goal-oriented and tension-relieving decisions: "A tension-relieving decision provides only immediate relief from a problem without considering the long-range implications. A goal-oriented decision is one that calls for planning and a step-by-step approach."[27]

Teacher Stacey Bess, in her poignant book about a school for homeless children in Seattle, describes how she engineered the involvement of one of her students in a summer basketball program. In the vignette outlined below, she encounters the coach after the boy, Alex, has had a rough day:

"Alex has gotten a little too rough, his coach said. I explained Alex's territory problem . . . . Then Alex's coach said with great compassion, 'He's definitely different . . . . What can I do?'

"He really hasn't been talked to enough, I offered. 'Just yelled at. If you get down at his level and explain things, he's a good listener.' The coach nodded with new understanding and returned to the court. I looked over later to see him on one knee beside Alex, talking to him, listening, nodding his head. I could see Alex warming up to him . . . . That night Alex told me he thought his coach was one of the coolest people he's ever met."[28]

The story goes on to recount how participating in that summer basketball program taught Alex a lot about life: what some rules were for and how they can work for you; that if you work hard, you get rewarded; that honesty can bring greater rewards than deceit. According to Bess, Alex learned mostly "that there were people in this world who love kids, no matter how they look and where they live – even if they sometimes break the rules."[29]

Adults must encourage youths to transfer the lessons they have learned to all areas of their lives.[30] Adults are an important element in the equation, often making the difference between a good and a bad experience. In teaching youths how to play games, it is the adults' responsibility to create life-enriching lessons.

Girls in Sports

On a recent Saturday morning at a local college celebrating National Girls and Women in Sports Day, Amy, a straight-A student in middle school, said "I love playing soccer, but some girls don't think it's fun; they think it takes too much work." Dawna, also a middle-school student, added "And they don't want to get all sweaty. You have to be pretty self-disciplined."

Beginning early in life, gender role stereotyping and socialization result in significant differences between boys and girls. In the first grade, girls feel less competent in sports than do boys, despite comparable skills. They are less involved in sports too and view sports as less important than boys do. However, playing catch with a parent can be a fundamental part of a girl's childhood, just as it can be for boys.

A number of years ago, the Nike sporting goods company ran a newspaper ad with the image of a young girl emblazoned across a full page. The caption read:

"If you let me play . . . I will like myself more; I will have more self-confidence; I will suffer less depression; I will be 60 percent less likely to get breast cancer; I will be more likely to leave a man who beats me; I will be less likely to get pregnant before I want to; I will learn what it means to be strong . . . if you let me play sports."

The ad was more than self-promotion. Girls who play sports tend to experience a number of benefits:[31]

- High school girl athletes earn higher grades and have better standardized test scores than non-athlete girls.

- Girl athletes are less likely than non-athlete girls to drop out of high school and are more likely to go to college.

- Teenage girl athletes have lower rates of pregnancy than their peers who don't participate in sports.

- Female athletes are more likely than non-athlete females to abstain from sex, and if they do have sex, are more likely to use contraceptives.

- Female athletes have one of the lowest rates of smoking among high school students.

- Female athletes have a significantly lower suicide rate than the teenage population as a whole.

- Sports participation can enhance the mental health of adolescent females, including improving self-esteem, increasing self-confidence, increasing positive feelings about body image, and providing experiences of competency and success.

With so many potential benefits to be gained, the statistics related to girls' involvement in sports are sobering:[32]

- Only a third of high school freshman girls play sports. By their senior year, the number drops to 17 percent.

- Sports participation declines steadily between ages 10 and 17 for girls.

- If a girl does not participate in sports by age 10, there is only a 10 percent chance that she will participate when she is 25.

- 62 percent of girls ages 6 and 7 play organized sports. At age 16 the number is 30 percent. In college the number drops to 18 percent.

According to the President's Council on Physical Fitness and Sports, the benefits of athletics to girls is so great and the protection against at-risk behaviors so pronounced, that any barrier which prevents young girls from participating in sports may well be a barrier to their lifelong health.[33] For many girls, involvement in sports is not only beneficial, but a lifesaving experience.

Although girls still lag behind boys in sports participation, the situation has improved over the past few decades. In 1972 when Title IX[34] was passed by Congress, one in 27 girls (4 percent) played high school sports. Now one in three high school freshman girls (33 percent) plays sports. Likewise, the number of female college students who participate in sports has increased dramatically, as has athletic scholarship money.[35]

Because girls' physical activity levels decrease markedly at about puberty, the Children's Nutrition Research Center in Houston makes these recommendations:[36]

- Take middle-school age girls to girls' high school sports events to expose them to role models.

- Downplay weight and body shape changes while reinforcing a positive self-image.

- Support involvement in sports and other physical activity, but don't force it.

- Be a good role model. Go swimming with girls. Go for nightly walks. Rake leaves together. Learn how to rollerblade together.

Children with Behavioral Challenges

A common characteristic among youths who are referred for behavioral problems at school is their lack of success in sports.[37] A study by University of North Carolina developmental psychologists Robert and

Beverly Cairns, found that the development of an admired skill seems to be important in adolescence. Sports success seems to be the easiest way for boys to earn this admiration, but involvement in other activities, such as the performing arts, provided successful avenues to acceptance in the school as well. When students excelled in these activities, they were more likely to be integrated into a positive social network.[38]

There are usually marked adaptive differences between well-coordinated students and poorly coordinated students. Poorly coordinated students perceive themselves as having less social support from their peers, teachers, and parents than well-coordinated students. Also, this group tends to have lower perceptions of close friendship than physically skilled classmates.[39]

If exhibiting socially valued skills reduces inappropriate behavior, it's logical that improving the sports performance of unpopular boys could result in increased peer acceptance and self-confidence. Psychologists Kevin Armstrong and Ronald Drabman found this to be true; they have developed tutoring sessions which focus on physical skill acquisition for unpopular boys. The sessions use skill-building drills which are arranged in order of difficulty, using small steps, to help boys master more complex sports skills.[40]

Children with Attention Deficit Hyperactivity Disorder (ADHD) sometimes do better when they are enrolled in organized sports activities that are supervised and highly structured. These children don't do well in sports that require a lot of standing around. Parents and coaches should take note of this and make decisions accordingly. In baseball, a child with ADHD will likely do better in the infield, where the action is, compared to standing around in the outfield. With well-informed adult support, team sports can provide the ADHD child with an opportunity to complete tasks as part of a group effort, as well as develop positive peer relationships. Sports also may help children with ADHD learn to control their impulses and thoughts and adhere to rules. While sports activities do not replace other treatment methods for ADHD, they can be an important part of the overall management of the disorder.[41]

Martial arts may be particularly useful in helping aggressive adolescents to learn self-control. Such programs use the philosophy of the gentle warrior, as instructors stress nonviolence. Learning-disabled youths who participate in martial arts sometimes show significant improvement in their ability to focus and perform academically.[42]

Planned adventure experiences, which are used not only with at-risk youths but with all groups of youths have been shown to boost emotional development. The original Outward Bound program was developed in 1941 in England by Kurt Hahn. He designed the program to help British merchant sailors during World War II develop the endurance and conviction needed to survive the stresses of war. The name comes from a nautical term, "outward bound," which refers to when a ship leaves the safety of the harbor for the unknown challenges of the open sea. Hahn wanted to have an outdoor adventure which creates a controlled environment to test a person's limits, allowing people to discover that they can go beyond the limits imposed on themselves.[43] Karen, a high school junior who has participated in the program says, "Whenever I'm in a hard situation, I think about that Outward Bound day and think I can do it. Outward Bound opened my eyes to a new outlook on life. It made me open to make decisions for myself."

Educational researcher John Hattie and his colleagues completed an analysis of Outward Bound and similar adventure programs.[44] They found that the programs have shown similar results, including increased self-confidence, fewer relapses into delinquent behavior, and increased motivation. The most fascinating finding was that the effects increased over time, rather than diminished, which is more typical of one-shot programs. Reed Larson conjectures that the "participants may have acquired some new quality, such as initiative, that is generative of additional post-program positive growth."[45]

Flow in Sports

Sports may present a unique opportunity for flow to occur. You will recall that youths feel much happier when they are participating in sports than when watching TV or engaging in other passive leisure activities. Youths often do not have meaningful opportunities for action; sports activities provide concrete experiences of overcoming challenges. Sports psychologist Susan Jackson and Mihaly

Csikszentmihalyi have written an entire book devoted to flow in sport.[46] Here are a few highlights:

To experience flow, one must know what one is trying to achieve. Sports provide structures that define each sport activity. Sports are so enjoyable because they provide clear goals and rules, enabling us to become completely involved in the activity.

Often in sports, we experience the realization of flow after the playing is over. It is the reflection on what you have accomplished, including the hard work to get there, which triggers flow. Jackson and Csikszentmihalyi say that being able to get flow from sports, whether you are an elite athlete or a weekend warrior, is a special opportunity to experience the satisfaction of excellence that everyone seeks.

Finally, I'd like to conclude this chapter with a quote from one of my favorite authors. I think acclaimed novelist Pat Conroy may have summed up best the lessons learned from sports, in this passage from his book, *My Losing Season*:

> **"The lessons I learned from playing basketball . . . have proven priceless to me as both a writer and a man. I have a sense of fair play and sportsmanship. My work ethic is credible and you can count on me in the clutch. When given an assignment, I carry it out to completion, my five senses lit up in concentration. I believe with all my heart that athletics is one of the finest preparations for most of the intricacies and darknesses a human life can throw at you."[47]**

Summing Up

Participation in sports presents opportunities to learn lessons that shape character traits, such as perseverance, fortitude, dedication, a strong work ethic, commitment, and responsibility.

Action Steps:

- Encourage your child to try different sports until he or she finds a favorite. Youths will naturally tend to stick with sports that mesh more with their natural abilities.

- Provide plenty of support and encouragement for young athletes. Positive parental support is directly associated with the child's greater enjoyment.

- If possible, encourage youths to get engaged in sports before adolescence; it may help teenagers avoid some of the normal distractions of adolescence. Sometimes "normal" adolescence leads to preoccupations with music, cars, spending money, and opposite-gender relationships.

- Encourage other kinds of activities, if your child is not athletic. When students succeed in an activity, they are more likely to be integrated into a positive social network. The development of an admired skill seems to be important in adolescence. Sports are one way to gain this status, but involvement in other activities, such as the performing arts, also provides successful avenues to acceptance in school.

Sports are the last of the environments we'll focus on as comprising children's life space. Because sports have generated so much controversy concerning their potential negative effects on youth, I have devoted Chapter 14 to those controversies, with some thoughts about how to ensure that sports are a positive activity.

QUIZ

Sports Environment

Answer Each Question 2, 1 or 0

2 = Yes, Often, or Usually   1 = Sometimes   0 = No or Never

_____ 1. Has your child participated on a sports team in the past six months?

_____ 2. Are members of your family active in sports, Little League, bowling, softball, etc.?

_____ 3. Do you participate actively in a sport?

_____ 4. Does your child participate in sports lessons (e.g., karate, gymnastics, etc.)?

_____ 5. Does your child exercise vigorously, outside of school, at least five times a week?

Scoring: Give yourself 2 points for "yes," "often," or "usually" answers, 1 point for "sometimes" answers, and 0 points for "no" and "never" answers. Total your points for questions 1 through 5 and write the answer below.

Your total score = _____ (0 to 10 points)

[1] Gallup Youth Survey. (February 19, 2002). *Teens and sports: "Let's play."* Washington, DC: The Gallup Organization.

[2] Zimmerman, J., & Reavill, G. (1998). *Raising our athletic daughters.* New York: Doubleday. p. 138.

[3] Weiss, M., & Ebbeck, V. (1996). Self-esteem and perceptions of competence in youth sports: Theory, research and enhancement strategies. In O. Bar-Or (Ed.), *The child and adolescent athlete. Encyclopedia of sports medicine, Vol. 6* (pp. 364-382). Champaign, IL: Human Kinetics Books.

[4] Jeziorski, R. (1994). *The importance of school sports in American education and socialization.* Lanham, MD: University Press of America.

[5] Scanlan, T., & Simmons, J. (1995). The construct of sports enjoyment. In G. Roberts (Ed.), *Motivation in sports and exercise* (pp. 199-215). Champaign, IL: Human Kinetics Books.

[6] Silby, C. (2000). *Games, girls, play: Understanding and guiding young female athletes.* New York: St. Martin's Press.

[7] *Ibid.*

[8] Sanders, S. (1999). *Champions are raised, not born: How my parents made me a success.* New York: Delacorte. p. 62.

[9] *Ibid.*

[10] Petitpas, A., & Champagne, D. (2000). Sports and social competence. In S. Danish & T. Gullotta (Eds.), *Developing competent youth and strong communities through after-school programming* (pp. 115-137). Washington, DC: CWLA Press.

[11] Ryan, Joan, & Ryan, Jean. (2000). *Little girls in pretty boxes: The making and breaking of elite gymnasts and figure skaters.* New York: Warner Books.

[12] Wilson, S. (2000). *Sports her way: Motivating girls to start and stay with sports.* New York: Fireside.

[13] American Academy of Pediatrics. Committee on Sports Medicine and Fitness. (2000). Intensive training and sports specialization in young athletes, *Pediatrics, 106,* 154-157.

[14] Larson, R., & Kleiber, D. (1993). Daily experience of adolescents. In P. Tolan & B. Coher (Eds.), *Handbook of clinical research and practice with adolescents* (pp. 125-145). p. 131.

[15] *Ibid.* p. 134.

[16] Larson, R. (2000). Toward a psychology of positive youth development. *American Psychologist, 55,* 170-183.

[17] Leff, S., & Hoyle, R. (1995). Young athletes' perceptions of parental support and pressure. *Journal of Youth and Adolescence, 24,* 187-203.

[18] Sanders, S. (1999). p. 37.

[19] Hoyle, R., & Leff, S. (1997). The role of parental involvement in youth sport participation and performance. *Adolescence, 32,* 233-243.

[20] Sanders, S. (1999). p. 52.

[21] Still, B. (2002). *Officials under assault.* Racine, WI: National Association of Sports Officials.

[22] Pollack, W. (1998). *Real boys.* New York: Random House.

[23] Wilson, S. (2000).

[24] *Ibid.* p. 18.

[25] Jeziorski, R. (1994).

[26] Wilson, S. (2000). p. 150.

[27] *Ibid.* p. 135.

[28] Bess, S. (1994). *Nobody don't love nobody: Lessons on love from the school with no name.* Carson City, NV: Old Leaf Press. p. 61.

[29] *Ibid.* p. 64.

[30] Burnette, E. (July, 1996). Involvement in athletics also boosts student athletes' motivation. *APA Monitor.*

[31] Silby, C. (2000).

[32] *Ibid.*

[33] President's Council on Physical Fitness and Sports. (1997). *Physical activity and sports in the lives of girls.* Washington, DC: U.S. Department of Health and Human Services.

[34] Title IX states: "No person in the United States shall, on the basis of sex, be excluded from participation in, be denied the benefits of, or be subject to discrimination under any education program or activity receiving federal financial assistance..."

[35] President's Council on Physical Fitness and Sports. (1997).

[36] Children's Nutrition Research Center. (Summer, 1998). *Nutrition & you.* Houston, TX: Baylor College of Medicine.

[37] Armstrong, K., & Drabman, R. (1994). The clinical use of sports skills tutoring with grade school boys referred for school behavioral problems. *Child & Family Behavior Therapy, 16,* 43-48.

[38] Cairns, R., & Cairns, B. (1994). *Lifelines and risks.* New York: Cambridge University Press.

[39] Hays, K. (1999). *Working it out: Using exercise in psychotherapy.* Washington, D.C.: American Psychological Association.

[40] Armstrong, K., & Drabman, R. (1994).

[41] Silby, C. (2000).

[42] Twemlow, S., & Sacco, F. (1998). Application of traditional martial arts practice and theory to the treatment of violent adolescents. *Adolescence, 33,* 505-518.

[43] Klint, K. (1990). New directions for inquiry into self-concept and adventure experiences. In J. Miles & S. Priest. (Eds.), *Adventure education* (pp. 163-172). State College, PA: Venture Publishing.

[44] Hattie, J., Marsh, H., Neill, J., & Richards, G. (1997). Adventure education and outward bound: Out-of-class experiences that make a lasting difference. *Review of Educational Research, 67,* 43-87.

[45] Larson, R. (2000). p. 176.

[46] Jackson, S., & Csikszentmihalyi, M. (2002). *Flow in sports: The key to optimal experiences and performances.* Champaign, IL: Human Kinetics.

[47] Conroy, P. (2002). *My losing season.* New York: Doubleday. p. 3.

CHAPTER 14

Creating a Lifetime of Enthusiasm for Sports

T HE LITERATURE ON YOUTH DEVELOPMENT IS FULL
of references to sports participation as a positive influence on
youth. Sports can teach valuable lessons about life, including the value
of hard work and perseverance. Unfortunately, sports involvement can
also get out of hand and teach detrimental lessons regarding winning at
all costs, breaking rules and using performance-enhancing drugs, and
disrespect of opponents and officials.

An example of the negative effects of sports is the increased use
of anabolic steroids. Boys are more likely than girls to want to gain
weight using drugs and may compromise their future health to gain a
competitive edge. Researchers have found that boys identified as jocks
in high school often engage in risky behavior, such as drug and alcohol
use, and promiscuous sex. Aggressiveness in sports has been shown to
correlate with lower scores on tests of moral reasoning. There is also a
positive correlation between sports involvement and obsessive weight
control in swimmers, gymnasts, and other athletes.[1]

In sports, the personal reward of meeting a challenge or mastering
one's environment is supplemented by a set of external rewards, including parental and peer-group recognition. Athletic prowess is highly
regarded among junior and senior high school students. Unfortunately,

"success" is often measured within a highly competitive system and is more narrowly defined. Much of organized sports is based on a "survival of the fittest" mentality.[2]

> One critic of organized sports participation in early childhood is the highly respected Harvard psychiatrist Eli Newberger. He bristles at the fact that 4 year olds can sign up for midget hockey and 6 year olds for Little League baseball. According to Newberger, 11 and 12 year olds often spend 40 percent of their free activity time engaged in organized sports.[3]

Newberger complains that organized sports are filled with too much aggressiveness and villainizing of the opponent, and often lead to risky behavior, and an overemphasis on winning. He says that while there are examples of good coaches who often help turn around the lives of troubled kids, he feels there are also many coaches who make things worse for children. Newberger relies heavily on anecdotes to support his criticisms: A high school football coach in Wisconsin gave a "Hit of the Week" award to the player who appeared, from analysis of game films, to have made the most vicious hit on an opposing player. Another coach from Iowa painted a fake chicken gold to represent the rival "Golden Eagles" and had his team kick it around the field to "get the Eagle."[4]

Newberger bemoans the fact that organized sports have taken the place of the informal network of neighborhood activities that youths a few decades ago organized themselves to occupy their time. In these various "pick-up games" there was little instruction, and the equipment was minimal; children created "playing fields" in yards and streets. There was no community recognition, no status – just plenty of fun. The relationship between playing sports in an organized setting versus an informal setting has been investigated. The results point to a mixture of advantages and disadvantages for both types. For example, one study compared the effects of informal sports (such as "pick-up" basketball games) with the effects of formal, adult-organized sports. The informal sports foster greater openness, freedom, joking, and positive feelings. The formal sports led to high concentration and a closer identification with group goals.[5]

Beverly Browne and Sally Francis at Oregon State University investigated whether adolescent participants in school-sponsored, organized sports (baseball, for example) experience greater feelings of social competence than their peers who choose to participate in more-independent, less-traditional sports, such as skateboarding. They found that positive outcomes (e.g., higher self-esteem, popularity among peers) can accompany participation in both traditional and nontraditional sports – even those often devalued by adults, such as skateboarding.[6] The point here is that good things can come from any sports participation.

> Newberger draws a sweeping conclusion: "An observer can't help but note the irony that the sports into which most boys are organized are not, by and large, the games they will play as adults. They are organized in largest numbers into baseball, football, soccer, hockey, and basketball. As adults they will watch these games in large numbers, but they won't play them. And not just because they've lost the physical skills to play them enjoyably. I suspect they don't play adult baseball and basketball because such games were ruined for them as kids. They remember them as tense and conflictual, so they trade them in for golf, hiking, jogging, swimming, fishing — trying to recover activities that might be playful to them."[7]

It is true that a declining number of adolescent boys are involved in team sports. Athletically talented youths tend to remain involved while often the less talented typically drop out. Newberger conjectures that the decline in numbers of boys committed to organized sports is partly because they have turned to activities that involve less work, fewer rules, and time with friends.[8] These activities mostly consist of "hanging out" together, watching television and videos, listening to music, going to parties. According to Newberger, pleasurable activities are not so much doing something with friends, but simply *being* together.[9] It is noteworthy, however, that there are consistent research findings reported in this book that adolescent involvement in less structured activity with peers is related to more at-risk behaviors.

Admittedly, however, it is accurate that 50 percent of youth sports participants drop out by middle adolescence. As already noted, those who are less skillful often discontinue sports participation rather than playing in less prestigious intramural or recreational leagues. Of concern also is the competitive nature of sports for younger children who have not reached cognitive maturity.[10] Too much emphasis on sports in early childhood, indeed, may be detrimental. For example, athletes who do not diversify their interests to include other activities besides sports do not fare well in the long run.[11] Participation in sports can be a way to learn important life skills, but there are no guarantees that this will occur. How youths experience sports is as important as the actual activity. Now, let's look at how we can make sure that sports participation works positively for youths.

Making Sports a Positive Experience

One of the things that sets sports apart from most leisure activities is the experience of challenge. According to the youths themselves, participating in sports provides a level of challenge, much like studying or taking a test. In their 1993 study, Reed Larson and Douglas Kleiber found that emotional involvement during sports activities was higher than during all other activities. Youth report feeling more motivated to be involved in sports than any other activities.[12]

Simply participating in sports does not guarantee that a person will derive such benefits.[13] The environment in which sports take place is a critical factor.[14] The coach's attitude and personality and the emotional environment that he creates within the team contribute heavily to making sports participation a positive experience. Let's look at the example of one famous coach, Ara Parseghian.

Parseghian, former head football coach at Notre Dame University, was one of the most successful coaches in collegiate history. How did he motivate his athletes to achieve both on the field and academically? His answer is surprisingly simple. The athletes in his program succeeded because he instilled pride, commitment to team effort, a strong work ethic (including study habits), and other important values.[15] Parseghian saw himself as a "people coach" because of his responsibility to help his players learn to master life from their athletic experience. He has noted three values in particular that each of his athletes took with him following graduation:

- "the ability to reach out and 'demand greater effort of himself,' achieving much more than he previously believed he could and increasingly self-confident as a result;

- the willingness to sacrifice, in which a student-athlete delays or gives up some other preferred action (or inaction, as the case may be) for the sake of another player or for the team;

- the ability to bounce back, to persist in times of difficulty and defeat, to keep trying in spite of pain, pressure or sorrow."[16]

In a 1997 study, psychologists Ronald Smith and Frank Smoll at the University of Washington found that boys in Little League baseball performed better and demonstrated greater effort when their coaches: 1) used a lot of positive reinforcement, 2) emphasized encouragement and technical instructions when mistakes occurred, and 3) promoted fun and personal improvement instead of winning. Based on their findings, Smith and Smoll developed a three-hour workshop for new coaches. Athletes who played for coaches who had attended this workshop reported more enjoyment, showed increased self-esteem and decreased performance anxiety, and were more likely to return to play the next season.[17]

Norwegian researcher Glyn Roberts and his colleagues found that some coaches create a performance-oriented climate that does not promote healthy youth development. These types of coaches put the focus on winning and performance in relation to others. Athletes who play for this type of coach generally think of talent as a personal endowment. They also tend to practice less and their motivation wanes when their abilities appear to be less than others. Another type of coach creates a mastery-oriented climate, with the focus on the development of the athletes' skills in relation to individualized standards. Athletes who play for this type of coach tend to view talent as the result of practice. They are more likely to persevere when confronted with difficulties and also tend to show more skill development during the season.[18] Roberts' findings coincide with what most sports psychologists advocate: emphasis on goal setting, personal effort, and individual improvement as keystones of coaching. Setting personal performance goals helps youths to invest in the activity itself rather than just the outcome of winning. If personal development is emphasized, athletes show enhanced motivation, performance, and overall quality of the sports experience.[19] Dave Scott, five-time Hawaii Ironman champion, says, "If you have set a goal for yourself and are able to achieve it, you have won your race. Your goal can be to come in first, to improve your performance, or just to finish the race – it's up to you."[20]

> **In sum, it is simplistic to say that by participating in sports, children and adolescents gain the skills to succeed in life. For many youths, however, participation in sports does promote healthy competition and teamwork, and it provides unique opportunities for achievement. Research has found consistently that high school students who participate in sports have higher academic achievement and greater personal aspirations.[21]**

To ensure that sports are safe and developmentally positive for America's youth, the National Alliance for Youth Sports spearheads a nationwide effort:

- To provide children with a positive introduction to youth sports.

- To have administrators, coaches, and game officials who are well-trained.

- To have parents complete an orientation session designed to help them understand the important impact sports can have on their child's development.

- To have youth sports implemented in accordance with the national Standards for Youth Sports. (The Standards are available on the Alliance's Web site.[22])

Another national organization, the Positive Coaching Alliance, works with youth leagues to incorporate a "double-goal" approach to sports. Winning is still a goal, but an even more important goal is to use sports to develop character and to teach life lessons.[23]

I believe that this country is on the threshold of a revolution in youth sports. Scott Lancaster, who is Director of the National Football League (NFL) Youth Football Development Program, agrees with Eli Newberger that organized youth sports have deteriorated. In his book *Fair Play,* he cites the pervasiveness of hyper-competitiveness, pressure on youths, and sheer boredom as the reasons so many youths quit sports. In his leadership role with the NFL, Lancaster has developed an antidote to address the problem: the Junior Player Development (JPD) program. JPD is being implemented in communities throughout the country and promises to change youth sports dramatically. The goal is to eliminate the negative aspects that have intruded on children's sports experiences, and quite simply, to provide an experience that makes all youths want to come back to every practice and game. JPD gives coaches and parents a blueprint of principles for change that can be applied to all sports:

- No scoreboards
- No coaches on the sidelines during games
- Boys and girls play together
- No tryouts or drafts
- Teaching of life skills is emphasized
- Always make it fun and keep it positive
- Limit "standing around" during practices
- Teach every position to every participant
- Emphasize the fundamentals
- Incorporate a progression of skill development for every participant
- Every participant gets equal playing and learning time[24]

In the JPD approach, coaches teach explicit life skills during on-field practices. They receive guidelines on how to incorporate these lessons as part of athletic situations, rather than as separate instruction, which could come across as preaching. Eight life skills are emphasized: 1) Self-control, 2) Responsibility, 3) Goal-setting, 4) Sportsmanship, 5) Smart Moves, 6) Teamwork, 7) Leadership, and

8) Perseverance. Coaches wear a wristband with a plastic pocket (the kind quarterbacks use in football to remember plays) to remind them of the skills. For example, the following table lists the coach's tips for teaching the skill of "responsibility":

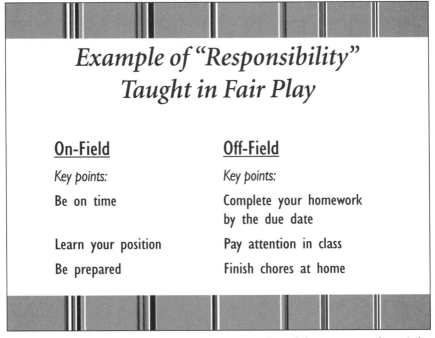

Example of "Responsibility" Taught in Fair Play

On-Field	Off-Field
Key points:	*Key points:*
Be on time	Complete your homework by the due date
Learn your position	Pay attention in class
Be prepared	Finish chores at home

Lancaster gives the following example of how a coach might incorporate a life skill into a practice:

"Remember that we learned the fundamentals of the linebacker position today, but we also learned about perseverance. Some of you may have made mistakes today, but is that any reason to get discouraged and lose your focus on what you should learn? No. The reason they put erasers on pencils is so that you can wipe out your mistakes and start over. When you make a mistake on your homework, you have the opportunity to erase it and correct it. Tomorrow is a new day. I want you to remember and feel good about what you did right today because everybody made progress and improved. But I also want you to think about what you might have done better and come back tomorrow ready to improve. This is perseverance."[25]

Lancaster makes an important point: most parents and coaches don't realize that children and teenagers approach sports from a very different viewpoint than adults. One doesn't have to win, or even do well, to enjoy sports. For example, he says that most athletes would rather play on a losing team than sit on the bench of a winning team. Winning a particular game has few long-term consequences for most youths. The relationships they have are more important than the scores. What's important is to have fun with friends and be challenged to improve their skills.[26]

Another factor that affects youth involvement in sports is having to be selected for teams. How many youths do we lose because of this singular issue? And it goes beyond athletics. To this day, I cannot play a musical instrument, partly because of the stressful experience of try-outs and ranking of "chairs" in the school band. I finally dropped out of band in junior high school.

Youths today experience growing up very differently than many of us did. We had fewer distractions. Now the majority of youths' time is devoted to such contemporary diversions as 150-channel television, videogames, the Web, cell phones, and many others. Teachers report that this generation of children must be continuously engaged. In this faster-paced world, sports must compete for children's attention. So the JPD approach encourages coaches to prepare well for each practice and to have fast-paced sessions in which children are constantly engaged in drills and are always moving. I hope that the JPD approach takes hold in this country. It appears to be the best chance we have to recapture what playing sports is all about: the love of the game!

Finally, it should be noted that the word *competition* is derived from two Latin words, *con petire*, meaning "to search together." Simply put, you discover your own skills best when you are matched against someone who is striving to do the same. Beating the other person or the other team is not the objective – rather, the goal is to discover your highest ability.[27]

The table below summarizes some simple parental do's and don'ts concerning your child's sports participation.

As I wrote about sports in the last two chapters, I was impressed with the importance of physical activity in children's lives. As I attempted to integrate information about exercise into the chapter, I concluded that it deserved its own chapter. So, while physical

Do's and Don'ts in Children's Sports Participation

- Don't insist that your child stick with a sport that provides little personal satisfaction.
- Do make sure that — first and foremost — your child has fun playing the sport.
- Don't pressure your child toward a particular sport.
- Do allow your child to try different sports until she finds the one(s) she likes.
- Don't define your child's sports success by winning.
- Do teach your child that "failure carries no penalty."
- Don't spend inordinate amounts of time attending your child's practices or competitions.
- Do support your child's sports involvement by showing interest, offering transportation to practices, and help with buying equipment.
- Don't fret if your child chooses another positive activity — such as an arts-based program — instead of sports.
- Do serve as a role model that regular physical activity is important, even if sports are not played.

activity is not technically an environment – it is associated with recreational pursuits – I devote the next chapter to the role of exercise
and physical education in lifestyles.

---

[1] Bloom, M. (2000). The uses of theory in primary prevention practice: Evolving thoughts on sports and after-school activities as influences of social competence. In S. Danish & T. Gullotta (Eds.), *Developing competent youth and strong communities through after-school programming* (pp. 17-66). Washington, DC: CWLA Press.

[2] Petitpas, A., & Champagne, D. (2000). Sports and social competence. In S. Danish & T. Gullotta (Eds.), *Developing competent youth and strong communities through after-school programming* (pp. 115-137). Washington, DC: CWLA Press.

[3] Newberger, E. (1999). *The men they will become.* Reading, MA: Perseus Books.

[4] *Ibid.*

[5] Larson, R., & Kleiber, D. (1993). Daily experience of adolescence. In P. Tolan & B. Coher (Eds.), *Handbook of clinical research and practice with adolescents.* (pp. 125-145). New York: Wiley.

[6] Browne, B., & Francis, S. (1993). Participants in school-sponsored and independent sports: Perceptions of self and family. *Adolescence, 28,* 383-391.

[7] *Ibid.* p. 313.

[8] *Ibid.*

[9] *Ibid.*

[10] Petitpas, A., & Champagne, D. (2000).

[11] *Ibid.*

[12] Larson, R., & Kleiber, D. (1993).

[13] Petitpas, A., & Champagne, D. (2000).

[14] Wilson, S. (2000). *Sports her way: Motivating girls to start and stay with sports.* New York: Fireside.

[15] Shannon cited in Jeziorski, R. (1994). *The importance of school sports in American education and socialization.* Lanham, MD: University Press of America.

[16] Parseghian, A., & Pagna, T. (1971). *Parseghian and Notre Dame football.* Notre Dame, ID: Men-In-Motion Press. p. 298.

[17] Smith, R., & Smoll, F. (1997). Self-esteem and children's reactions to youth sport coaching behaviors: A field study of self-enhancement processes. *Developmental Psychology, 26,* 987-993.

[18] Roberts, G., & Treasure, D. (1992). Children in sports. *Sport Science Review. 1* (2), 46-64. Roberts, G., Treasure, D., & Kavussanu, M. (1997). Motivation in physical activity contexts: An achievement goal perspective. *Advances in Motivation and Achievement, 10,* 413-447.

[19] *Ibid.*

[20] Jackson, S., & Csikszentmihalyi, M. (2002). *Flow in sports: The key to optimal experiences and performances.* Champaign, IL: Human Kinetics. p 94.

[21] Petitpas, A., & Champagne, D. (2000).

[22] www.nays.org

[23] Lancaster, S. (2001). *Fair play: Making organized sports a great experience for your kids.* New York: Prentice Hall Press.

[24] *Ibid.*

[25] *Ibid.* p. 176-177.

[26] *Ibid.*

[27] *Ibid.*

CHAPTER 15

Promoting a Lifestyle
of Vigorous Physical Activity

THROUGHOUT HISTORY, THE VIRTUES OF REGULAR
exercise have been extolled. Plato and Thomas Jefferson both
went on lengthy walks to ripen their ideas. In recent years, there has
been increased media attention on fitness and sports. Fitness clubs
have sprung up everywhere. Although this would appear to reflect a
greater awareness and acceptance of the benefits of physical activity
in our society, the rate of physical activity of the average individual
has not increased.

According to an article in the *New England Journal of Medicine*,
poor physical fitness is a better predictor of premature death
than a number of other factors, including smoking, hyperten-
sion, and heart disease.[1] Three in 10 adult Americans get no
exercise at all. Seven in 10 do not get enough exercise. Only 30
percent of adult Americans get regular exercise. As noted earlier
in this book, the amount of regular exercise girls get falls off
dramatically as they move through their adolescence. At age 16
or 17, more than half of the African-American girls and nearly
a third of European-American girls get no regular exercise at
all outside of school.[2] As Kate Hays, president of the sports

psychology division of the American Psychological Association notes, "Exercise has been more popularized than popular."[3]

According to the Institute of Medicine, people who want to stay healthy need to exercise at least an hour a day – double the U.S. Surgeon General's previous recommendations – with moderate physical activity, such as walking, slow swimming, or leisurely bicycle riding.[4] Parents will find the Kid's Activity Pyramid to be a useful guide to teaching children about regular exercise. Modeled after the food pyramid, the colorful visual display suggests activities appropriate for exercising with family or friends, or alone. Using the pyramid design, activities that should be done every day are at the bottom, forming the base of a healthy lifestyle; activities to be done several times a week are in the middle; and at the top of the pyramid are activities to be cut down on and held to a minimum, such as watching TV.[5]

There is some confusion about the terms exercise and physical activity, and how they relate to sports. First off, *sports* are recreational or competitive athletics. They typically involve rules, guidelines, and protocols. *Exercise* may or may not involve sports activities. Exercise is organized, focused physical activity that involves a certain amount of will power and exertion. It can be done alone and requires no equipment, although many people exercise with others and use elaborate equipment. *Physical activity* is synonymous with exercise, but some people consider it a preferable term because it does not carry some of the obligatory connotation attributed to exercise.[6]

As America has become less agrarian and more industrial and technological, physical activity has gradually disappeared from the typical American's daily life. Our jobs and occupations are increasingly sedentary. With little physical effort involved in our work lives, we have had to incorporate exercise into our leisure time. We have come to believe that activity is effortful. This belief conflicts with our image of leisure time as meaning inaction. This is an odd distortion of our genetic heritage. Regular movement is required to fulfill our genetic design if our bodies are to function trouble-free.[7]

Exercise serves as a buffer against stress and the health-destroying effects of stress. Consider this extraordinary experiment by

Hans Selye, the late professor at the University of Montreal and father of the stress research field: During the first phase of the experiment, Selye subjected 10 rats to a program of electric shocks, blinding lights, and loud noises for four weeks. All 10 rats were dead at the end of the month, apparently from the effects of the stressful environment. In the second phase of the experiment, Selye had 10 rats walk on treadmills daily until they were in prime physical health. He then subjected these physically fit rats to the same program as the first group of rats, and all 10 were alive and healthy at the end of the month-long study.[8]

Hard physical play can buffer stress. Sports can also help children through difficult times. In addition to the benefits of fitness, team members can become an extended support network. Take the example of 13-year-old Trina, whose parents divorced two years ago. Money has been tight, so she and her mother have moved from a house to two different apartments in the past year. Fortunately for Trina, the school district allowed her to remain in the same school. With the coach's "insistence" and support, she remained on the soccer team. The team was like family to her and the physical activity mediated her depression. In other circumstances, for example, if Trina had been forced to move to a new school and decided to drop out of sports, it could have led to deepening depression, anxiety, and perhaps self-destructive behaviors.

Physical activity not only stretches our bodily muscles but our mental muscles, that is, cognitive processing, as well. Exercise increases performance on cognitive tasks.[9] Also, when we exercise regularly, we tend to sleep better, eat more healthfully, and eliminate waste from our bodies more efficiently.[10] Exercise is effective in reducing a variety of disruptive behaviors, including hyperactivity.

Simply put, physical activity makes you feel good and feeling good increases self-esteem.[11] Exercise improves psychological mood state. Serotonin, the chief chemical ingredient in antidepressants, increases in the brain with exercise. Running programs have been found to be at least as effective as psychotherapy in mitigating moderate depression.[12] Exercise reduces LDL (bad cholesterol) and increases HDL (good cholesterol). As an added benefit for adolescents, high levels of exercise are associated with better relationships with parents.[13]

Physical Education

All parents are attuned to the fact they must help facilitate the learning process in their young children by teaching colors, numbers, and the alphabet. Most parents are less aware, however, of the importance of shooting a few hoops (for example) with their child. Intellectual education is widely recognized as a priority; too often, little value is placed on being physically educated. "A healthy mind in a healthy body" was the philosophy during the Golden Age of Greece, when vigorous physical activity was as much a part of life as intellectual studies. Unfortunately, while schools used to recognize the importance of providing physical education as a standard part of the core curriculum, that awareness is on the decline.

Beginning in the 1960s, most schools participated in the President's Physical Fitness Program, in which students could win fitness awards by passing rigorous tests at the end of each school year. Since then much of the emphasis placed on physical fitness has gradually fallen by the wayside. Some elementary schools now require PE only once a week and have reduced recess time, and some high schools have eliminated PE requirements altogether. Between 1991 and 1999, the percentage of students in grades K–12 who attended daily physical education classes declined from 42 percent to 29 percent, according to the Centers for Disease Control and Prevention.[14] A recent study reported in the journal *Pediatrics* says that one out of every five children is either obese or in danger of becoming obese. Rising levels of obesity among children will translate into higher levels of adult obesity.[15] Frank Booth, a professor in the Department of Physiology at the University of Missouri, has coined the term *Sedentary Death Syndrome* to describe the epidemic of physical inactivity and its relationship to chronic, preventable diseases. One-third of all youths between the ages of 12 and 21 do not regularly participate in vigorous physical activity.[16]

One reason for the change from the 1960s philosophy is that schools have turned their attention more toward academics, and each year it seems more class time has to be squeezed into the school day. Most parents today, when they hear that schools don't offer the same level of physical education that they once did, don't think it's a huge loss. Many people look at everything they have going on in their lives and they just can't find the time for exercise. So, when a high school student needs to decide whether to take an elective credit in physical education or a credit in physics, guess which one wins out?

> **Ironically, taking a physical education class or maintaining physical activity in some other way may help students with their academic performance. Recent research has begun to shed light on how movement directly benefits the nervous system. Muscular activities, and coordinated movements in particular, stimulate the production of neurotrophins, which are natural substances that stimulate the growth of nerve cells, resulting in an increase in the number of neural connections in the brain.[17] One study found that students who spend an additional hour in gym class each day performed better on exams compared to less-active students.[18]**

In one positive trend designed to teach children the skills they need to stay physically fit for the rest of their lives, some schools have developed new PE programs which are modeled after health clubs. Traditional PE programs have focused on general athletic skills like kickball and the 50-yard dash. Often, children who are not athletic and who don't play team sports do not learn to enjoy physical activity through these traditional PE experiences. In the "new" PE, gyms are designed like health clubs, with weight machines, exercise bikes, and treadmills. In-line skating is taught along with rock climbing and mountain biking. There is a real emphasis on kids finding at least one activity they enjoy.

Many schools assign students to academic classes based on their ability. Athletic programs should do the same so that youths at all skill levels can play. Children should be encouraged to try different sports until they find a favorite. Youths tend to stick with sports that mesh more with their natural abilities.

There are two types of school-based athletic programs: intramural programs, in which competition takes place between teams within the school, and interscholastic programs, with competition between teams from different schools. As youths get older, sports involvement in school or in the community may tend toward elitism. It's up to the school and community officials to ensure that there are programs for youths who just want to play for the fun of it. The intramural sports usually serve this function in schools. The more sports opportunities there are available, the better the chance for a child to find the best fit for him.

Exercise is sometimes perceived by adults as obligatory. If an activity is compulsory, it often doesn't feel fun or pleasurable. In helping a child find a good activity fit, the child's exercise history should be collected in order to help develop patterns of exercise the child will engage. Pertinent questions to ask include what kind of exercise has the child enjoyed in the past? What has the child wanted to try? What kind of exercise fits with the child's personality, such as the need to be socially engaged?[19] Also, some kinds of exercise are conducive to mood-enhancing effects, which in turn could serve as internal reinforcers to the maintenance of the exercise.[20]

One solution may lie in parents themselves. If parents are involved in regular physical activity, youth tend to follow in their footsteps. Emily, 12, and her 14-year-old brother, Arnie, are both involved in physical activities, as are their parents. Emily takes ballet classes and lifts weights, and Arnie plays hockey and works out on the stair machine. Their parents place a high priority on fitness, and it has influenced the way they set their priorities. Arnie says, "Exercise gives me more energy for things like going places with friends. It even helps me concentrate in class."

Researchers have found that 70 percent of girls who participate in sports have at least one parent who does also.[21] Parents who participate in sports can be important role models for their children and can share personal anecdotes about the many benefits of sports. Physical activity should be a part of family lifestyles. Families can go for group walks together or throw the Frisbee together. Exercise should become a routine part of every day. There is no ideal exercise; in fact, the ideal exercise is simply one that someone will do on a regular basis.

When we are young and first start a physical activity, what initially hooks us is the sheer fun and physical exhilaration. Later, we may continue the activity because we want to be with friends or want the challenge of playing at a higher level. Later in life, we may stick with a physical activity primarily for the health benefits it provides. Unfortunately, many people keep exercising only out of a sense of duty. It is difficult to keep doing something regularly if we don't like to do it, so enjoyment for its own sake is critical to sustaining any sport activity.[22]

Mihaly Csikszentmihalyi and sports psychologist Susan Jackson have identified some strategies to help people engage in routine physical activity.[23] Here are some of their suggestions:

- Build a ritual around your exercise time. Personalize your clothing and equipment, begin with a routine of stretching, and end by transitioning back to other activities with a ritual, such as taking a refreshing shower. When I lived in downtown Charleston, South Carolina, I used to end my daily jogs at Market Street, which bustled with vendors and the smells of the cafes. Walking through this area was always special, and I frequently bumped into friends.

- If an activity has become routine and is no longer challenging, liven it up by adding some kind of handicap. If you are shooting hoops, shoot only beyond the three-point line or work on your non-dominant hand. If you are running, try a hilly course. If you ensure that challenge is part of the activity, you are more likely to remain engaged in it and there's a greater chance you will extend yourself to a higher level of performance, which may trigger the flow experience. I have been jogging for 35 years, but I have recently reinvigorated my jogging by running on mountain trails. This small modification has brought a freshness to this entrenched activity that keeps me looking forward to my daily jog.

In the next chapter, you will collate the results of your quizzes from the ends of Chapters 4–13 and translate your responses into a specific action plan to help your child(ren) choose supportive environments and activities to engage in a positive life trajectory.

---

[1] Myers, J., Prakash, M., Froelicher, Do, D., Partington, S., & Atwood, E. (2002). Exercise capacity and mortality among men referred for exercise testing. *New England Journal of Medicine, 11*, 346, 793-801.

[2] Kim, S., Glynn, N., Kriska, A., Barton, B., Kronsberg, S., Daniels, S., Crawford, P., Sabry, Z., & Liu, K. (2002). Decline of physical activity in black girls and white girls during adolescence. *New England Journal of Medicine, 347*, 709-715.

[3] Hays, K. (1999). *Working it out: Using exercise in psychotherapy.* Washington, D.C.: American Psychological Association.

[4] Institute of Medicine (2002). *Dietary reference intakes for energy, carbohydrate, fiber, fat, fatty acids, cholesterol, protein, and amino acids.* Washington, DC: National Academies Press.

[5] Park Nicollet HealthSource. (1996). *Building your activity pyramid.* Minneapolis, MN: Park Nicollete Institute.

[6] Hays, K. (1999).

[7] *Ibid.*

[8] Nieman, D. (1998). *The exercise-health connection.* Champaign, IL: Human Kinetics.

[9] Field, T., Diego, M., & Sanders, C. (2001). Exercise is positively related to adolescents' relationships and academics. *Adolescence, 36*, 105-110.

[10] Hays, K. (1999).

[11] *Ibid.*

[12] Nieman, D. (1998).

[13] Field, T., Diego, M., & Sanders, C. (2001).

[14] National Center for Chronic Disease Prevention and Health Promotion. (2000). *Promoting better health for young people through physical activity and sports.* Atlanta: Centers for Disease Control and Prevention.

[15] Wang, G., & Dietz, W. (2002). Economic burden of obesity in youths aged 6 to 17 years: 1979 – 1999. *Pediatrics, 109*, 81.

[16] www.newswise.com/articles/2001/5/SEDS.TKC.html; accessed 3-12-03

[17] Hannaford, C. (1995). *Smart moves: Why learning is not all in your head.* Arlington, VA: Great Ocean Publishers.

[18] Olsen, E. (October, 1994). Fit kids smart kids: New research confirms that exercise boosts brain-power. *Parents Magazine*, pp. 33-35.

[19] Hays, K. (1999).

[20] *Ibid.*

[21] Zimmerman, J., & Reavill, G. (1998). *Raising our athletic daughters: How sports can build self-esteem and save girls' lives.* New York: Doubleday.

[22] Jackson, S., & Csikszentmihalyi, M. (2002). *Flow in sports: The key to optimal experiences and performances.* Champaign, IL: Human Kinetics.

[23] *Ibid.*

CHAPTER 16

Examining Children's Lifestyle Profiles

THIS CHAPTER IS DESIGNED TO ENABLE THE READER to begin putting the ideas in this book into practice. Before you can use behavior settings to improve the life of a child, you need a lot of data about how your child lives. Creating a time diary, such as the one discussed in Chapter 2, is a good way to begin. Such a diary will give you a rough approximation of how the child spends his time and the kinds of activities he is involved in. Time diaries can be extremely useful, but they do take a while to create.

Now you will create graphs on the following pages to give you a visual overview of your scores from the quizzes at the ends of Chapters 4–13. This profile will help you see how your child navigates his life space. Begin by transferring your scores from the quizzes to the list below:

_____ Home Setting (page 46)

_____ Neighborhood Setting (page 56)

_____ School, Co-Curricular and Service-Learning Settings (page 74)

_____ After-School Settings (page 85)

_____ Electronic Setting (page 103)

_____ Friends Setting (page 117)

_____ Faith Setting (page 133)

_____ Work Setting (page 145)

_____ Recreational and Leisure Settings (page 163)

_____ Sports Settings (page 183)

Each column on pages 212 and 213 represents one of the ten behavior settings. Draw a line across each column corresponding to your child's score for that setting, then lightly shade in the column area below your line.

You have just created a "big picture" view of time-use and activities in the major contexts of your child's life. Although this method is far from scientific, it presents a fairly clear picture of your child's environmental strengths and weaknesses.

Now, how do you translate this information into specific beneficial actions? At the end of each chapter about an environment, I summarized some specific actions you can take to help make an environment developmentally supportive for your child. Those actions are also summarized at the end of the book in the Appendix: "Creating Environmental Opportunities for Children." Scores in the 7–10 range for a setting indicate environmental strengths. For environments with scores in this range, go to the action tips in the Appendix to review the salient aspects of those environments. Usually, you will want to help your child maintain these strong environmental supports. A score in the low range (0–3) identifies that setting as a probable weak environment for your child. For a setting with a low score, you may want to choose at least one of the action steps from the table to help build that setting into a more supportive one for your child. Lastly, for scores in the middle range (between 4 and 6), you might want to consider some simple fine tuning to enable the environment to be a stronger support.

What constitutes a developmentally healthy home setting, school setting, neighborhood setting, or friendship group? For example, what is a "normal" quiz score which indicates a healthy lifestyle in each setting? Wouldn't it be helpful to have a specific number as a benchmark? I suppose most of you have had to endure a blood test to enable your doctor to check on how your body is functioning. Typically, the blood test comes back in a report that looks like the one below.

What's Healthy?

	Status	Reference Interval
Glucose	83	65 - 115
Calcium	9.8	8.5 - 10.6
Protein	7.3	6.0 - 8.5
Uric Acid	4.2	2.2 - 8.7

The key numbers in this report are the "reference intervals." These numbers let you see whether your individual values are within the normal range for a healthy person. Wouldn't it be helpful if we could do the same thing for a child's lifestyle? Impossible, you're probably saying, but sociologist Peter Benson at the Search Institute in Minneapolis has tried to do just that. He surveyed 273,000 youths nationwide and as a result of the analysis discovered that the difference between troubled teenagers and those leading healthy, productive, positive lives was strongly affected by the presence of "developmental assets." [1]

Lifestyle Profile

	Home	Neigh-borhood	School	After-School	Electronic	
10						
9						H
8						I
						G
						H
7						
6						M
						O
5						D
						E
4						R
						A
3						T
						E
2						
						L
1						O
						W
0						

for _____
(Your Child's Name)

	Friends	Faith	Work	Recreation	Sports

10 ——

9 ——

8 ——

7 ——

6 ——

5 ——

4 ——

3 ——

2 ——

1 ——

0 ——

H
I
G
H

M
O
D
E
R
A
T
E

L
O
W

Benson has identified 30 such critical assets. Fourteen of the assets are internal assets, that is, attitudes, values, and competencies that reside inside the child's personhood. The remaining 16 assets identified by Benson and his research team are external assets, that is, things in the child's environment that "support and nurture him or her, set boundaries, and involve the young person in structured time use with caring, principled adults."[2] Eleven of Benson's external assets closely resemble the contexts we have identified in this book. Benson provides what he has determined to be normal ranges – or suggested healthy doses – in these key areas, and I've summarized them in the table on page 215. He cautions, as I have in this book, that each child's needs should be examined on an individual basis, but guidelines such as these can help us get started.

Let's take a look at the last three assets on Benson's list. First, unstructured time. Youths do not need to spend every night at home. Benson simply advises that youths not be allowed to spend more than two nights out each week with friends *with nothing special to do.* Having something special to do, like going to the roller rink, is not unstructured time. It is a planned, pre-determined activity. The key thing is that the youth is not just hanging out; she is doing something positive. Other examples are playing soccer with friends, practicing for a school drama, going to a meeting in the community, attending a youth group, or participating in a service project.

Next is the area of homework. Generally, youths today do not do enough homework. Girls spend more time doing homework than boys. About a third of all students spend an hour a day, but another third say they spend only two hours a week on homework. Parents may want to encourage youths to do homework daily, even if none is assigned, when time can be set aside for reading or other school-related activities.[3]

A final example from Benson's list: It's important for parents to keep track of their children's whereabouts. When children go out, they should let you know where they'll be and how to reach them. Use a message board in the home or the telephone answering machine. Pagers and cell phones can also make it easier for everyone to say in touch.

Eleven of Peter Benson's External Developmental Assets [4]

External Asset	Guideline	Reference Interval
Nonparental relationships	Child receives support from nonparental adults.	3+ times/month
Caring neighborhood	Child experiences caring neighbors.	Yes
Parent involvement in schooling	Parent(s) are actively involved in helping the child succeed in school.	Yes
Positive peer influence	The child's best friends model responsible behavior.	Yes
Service to others	The child performs regular community service.	1+ hr./week
Creative activities	The child spends regular time in lessons or practice in music, theater, or other arts or hobbies.	3+ hrs./week
Youth programs	The child spends regular time in sports, clubs, or organizations at school or in community organizations.	3+ hrs./week
Religious community	The child spends time in activities in a religious institution.	1+ hr./week
Limited unstructured time	The child is out with friends, with "nothing special to do."	2 or fewer times/week
Homework	The child reports doing homework every school day, and reading for pleasure each week.	1+ hr./day homework 3+ hrs./week reading
Parental monitoring	Parents monitor their child's whereabouts.	Yes

Profiles of Involvement in Activities

Todd Bartko and Jacquelynne Eccles at the University of Michigan have specifically studied the profiles of adolescents' activity choices.[5] Eleven activities were assessed: sports, reading for pleasure, homework, chores, time with friends, watching television, school clubs, community clubs, volunteering, religion, and paid work. The six different clusters or profiles of involvement in activities that the researchers identified are outlined in the table on page 217.

Bartko and Eccles also measured the academic and psychological functioning of the youths, which allowed them to examine how behavior functioning is linked to activity settings. The findings are fascinating:

- The *School* and *High-Involved* adolescents had the highest grade point average (GPA) and *Uninvolved* teenagers had the lowest GPA.

- The fewest problem behaviors occurred in the *School* and *High-Involved* groups, and the most problem behaviors occurred in the *Sports*, *Uninvolved*, and *Work* clusters.

- *Uninvolved* adolescents had the most depressive symptoms.

- On a measure of psychological resilience (the ability to solve problems and overcome bad experiences), the *Sports*, *School*, and *High-Involved* groups all showed relatively high scores.

- Parents reported the highest level of internalizing problems (e.g., depression, anxiety) for the *Uninvolved* adolescents and the lowest for the *Sports* and *High-Involved* teenagers.

- Externalizing problems (e.g., acting out, aggression) as reported by parents were highest for the *Uninvolved* and the *Work* teenagers.

Bartko and Eccles concluded that the activities that youths participate in are connected to their overall functioning. Youths who engage in constructive activities that require effort and persistence do better than youths who engage in few constructive activities. However, it is the *pattern* of involvement across activity settings

Adolescent Activity Profiles [6]

Adolescent Activity Clusters	Characteristics
Sports	These teenagers were highly involved in sports activities; they also spent more time with friends.
School	These teenagers had high rates of involvement in school-based clubs, homework, and reading for pleasure.
Uninvolved	These teenagers showed low rates of involvement in all activities.
Volunteer	These teenagers had very high rates of involvement in volunteer activities.
High-Involved	These teenagers showed high rates of involvement in most activities, with high rates of involvement in constructive, organized activities and less involvement in passive, unstructured leisure.
Work	These teenagers had high rates of involvement in paid work and low rates of participation in other activities.

which is related to differences in functioning rather than any one activity. In a nutshell, there are multiple paths linking activity choices and psychosocial health.

A colleague of mine recently went to her daughter's high school graduation. Her daughter graduated among the top 100 students in the large school district, which published the accomplishments of these students. As I perused the booklet, I was astonished at the varied activities of the students. I've outlined a composite of one student's activities below.

School and Community Activities of a Graduating H.S. Senior

Rhoda Edwards, Senior

Honor Roll, 4 years

College to Attend: University of Nebraska

Activities: Class Secretary, Earthservice Corps Vice-President, SADD Club Treasurer, Buncombe County Youth Council, Junior Marshall, Prom Court, Rotary Club Student of the Month, Volleyball MVP award, Poetry published in Best Poets of 2002, Spanish Club, Math Team, Dance, Volunteer–Special Olympics, Kids Voting, Adopt-A-River volunteer, School-wide Blanket Drive Coordinator, One-Act Play Competition, Peer Mediator, Tutor, Church Soloist, Mission trips to Charleston, SC, Stage Crew, Ultimate Frisbee Club, Memorial Mission Hospital volunteer, Softball Team Co-Captain, Odyssey of the Mind, Dropout Patrol, Church Youth Group Secretary, Chorus, and Pep Club.

Whoa! This teenager would probably max out on Peter Benson's list of external assets. After I read about the activities of these students, my mind raced to thoughts of my own high school yearbook. In high school, I did not play a musical instrument. I did not participate in any school dramas. I did not contribute to the yearbook or literary magazine and I joined no clubs. I was not on the student council. Neither did I volunteer in the community or belong to any organizations. I did not attend church – I didn't have a hobby. Other than going to school and conscientiously doing my homework, I did mostly only one other thing . . . I ran. I ran cross country in the fall and track in the spring – and because our high school had an indoor running area in its dank basement, we ran in the winter. The summer was for training to be ready for the fall. Running consumed my life. It gave me a small peer group, regular goals, and wonderful adult guidance, in the form of my coaches. This example makes it clear why it may be impossible to generalize about the critical activities for children. The important thing is that youths get certain essential developmental elements within whatever activities they choose. So, rather than evaluating the range of activities in a child's life, the best approach may be to look at whether, given the types of activities a child participates in, he is being exposed to the critical experiences that will help develop essential character traits. In my case, one major activity provided most of the psychological tools – that is, essential traits of character – to successfully meet the challenges of life.

Consider the benefits of the cross-country and track teams I participated on in high school:

- Relationships with caring adults.
- A useful role and meaningful things to do.
- A safe place to be.
- Adult role models.
- Opportunities to make friends who model responsible behavior.
- The promotion of positive values, such as discouraging drug use and encouraging good nutrition.

- Opportunities to develop social competencies, such as sportsmanship.

That's a quick seven assets just off the top of my head, and many more could be listed. It's a good idea to seek out such asset-rich activities, especially as you try to include a balance of down time and family time in your child's busy schedule. Activities that provide opportunities for the child to acquire numerous life skills give more bang for your buck, so to speak.

Here's an analogy to explain what I mean: Most people are familiar with the new food pyramid. We all know that we are supposed to eat the largest percentage of our daily diet in whole grains, vegetables and fruits, followed by nuts, legumes and dairy products, then fish, poultry, eggs, and pasta, and finally red meat and sweets. However, many healthy people do not adhere to the food pyramid guidelines. For example, vegans do not eat meat, fish, poultry, eggs or milk, yet they can be very healthy, as long as they get the proper nutrients overall in their diet. There are 10 essential nutrients needed to maintain health. You can eat a lot of different kinds of foods to get these essential nutrients, or it is possible to eat a very limited number of foods, if they are carefully chosen, and still maintain health. These dietary guidelines correspond to the broad areas that Peter Benson has outlined. So, while Benson's guidelines are useful, just as the food pyramid is a helpful guide, what ultimately matters, regardless of the lifestyle a child is leading, is that she get the essential ingredients for healthy development.

What are the essential elements for developing and maintaining psychological and emotional health? Much has been written on the topic and many theorists identify similar elements. Dorothy Rich, popular author of *Megaskills*, has written about the attributes she feels youths need to make it in life. Her eleven "megaskills" are outlined on page 221.

This list of core life skills is as good as any. You'll recall that in Chapter 3 Reed Larson identified *initiative* as a critical attribute – a sort of root from which other critical attributes develop. Personally, I would add one critical skill to Dr. Rich's list. In my work with children, I have been impressed with the power of the ability to *delay gratification,* or

Dorothy Rich's Megaskills [7]

- **Confidence**: feeling able to do it

- **Motivation**: wanting to do it

- **Effort**: being willing to work hard to get it done

- **Responsibility**: doing what's right

- **Initiative**: moving into action

- **Perseverance**: completing what you start

- **Caring**: showing concern for others

- **Teamwork**: working with others

- **Common Sense**: using good judgment

- **Problem Solving**: putting what you know and what you can do into action

- **Focus**: concentrating with a goal in mind

what some researchers term "self-control." This has to do with resisting impulses and being patient. For example, psychologist Walter Mischel studied children's self-control by looking at whether preschoolers could delay the gratification of eating one marshmallow by waiting 15–20 minutes for two marshmallows. The same preschoolers were evaluated 14 years later. Those who were able to control their behavior when young scored an average of 210 points higher on the SAT! They also were judged more emotionally stable and were better liked by teachers and peers.[8] (Of course, correlational studies like this one do not prove causation by this one ability; however, it does show that such factors are associated with such positive outcomes.) I would certainly want my child to be involved in lifestyle activities where delay of gratification is part of the learning experience.

> **Because structured and unstructured activities run the gamut of diversity, Reed Larson points out, it is probably difficult to generalize about the overall effect of so many different activities.[9] We must look at each individual experience in the activity and how the child interprets and learns from participation in the activity. So, the best advice that can be offered, given that generalization is not possible, is for parents and professionals to seek out lifestyle activities that promote essential mental and psychological attributes. In addition, there is certainly room for customization. For example, if you feel strongly about nonviolence, you may wish to involve your child in activities that promote nonviolence. You may not allow your child to play with toy guns or to play videogames that involve violence. No football or karate! So while there may be a core set of attributes, such as those defined by Dorothy Rich, feel free to add attributes to the list, according to your own values.**

Goodness of Fit

Yet another variable that confounds all efforts to identify particular activities that promote healthy child development is the concept of person-environment fit. Goodness of fit is the match between a child's individual characteristics and an environment. One kind of context or setting may be positive for many children but not for a child with particular characteristics. Let's look at an example.

Suppose a child is quite hyperactive, finding it difficult to sustain attention for more than a minute or two. Let's look at two kinds of classrooms for this child. Suppose Teacher "A" is an elderly woman with many years of teaching experience. She runs a tight ship and she knows how she wants her class to be and she expects her students to do as she says. Teacher "B" is a young man, only two years out of college. He is full of energy and very enthusiastic. He runs more of an open classroom where the kids have lots of free time to work in learning centers. Though he does teach the whole class at once, it is only two or three times a day, for no more than 15–20 minutes. Here's the question: given a choice, which environment will this hyperactive child *fit* better into, Teacher "A's" or Teacher "B's"? The answer, in most but not all cases, is Teacher "B's". Many hyperactive children fit much better into more-open classroom arrangements than they do into more-traditional classrooms.

Here are a few more "test questions" for you: Given a choice, would you involve a hyperactive child in Girl Scouts or Sunday School? Piano lessons or karate lessons? The answers: Girl Scouts and karate lessons. These environments typically fit better with the behavioral style of most, but again not all, hyperactive children. Would you encourage a hyperactive child to learn golf or to run track? Run track, of course – if nothing else, he will burn off some energy.

> While particular activities and environments may appear inherently positive for all youths, it really depends on each youth's individual characteristics and whether or not there is a good match. Further, an overall lifestyle of many positive activities does not guarantee a healthy set of experiences. We must examine the specific ingredients in each child's experiences to determine if the proper psychological nutrients are there. For example, remember Rhoda, the graduating senior with an impressive list of activities? What if most of her experiences were superficial? Maybe she is intellectually gifted and needs to study very little to do well, and is participating in most activities to build a "resume" to gain admission to an elite college. If this were the case, another student with only a modest "resume" of activities that she was deeply involved in may be getting far better "nutrition" from her lifestyle.

Parents' Involvement in Arranging Activities

Parents have an important role in guiding their children toward activities with positive effects. Young children, in particular, depend almost solely on their parents to provide opportunities for social contacts. There are a myriad of choices: a neighborhood with other children for frequent informal contacts, the availability of child-centered activities like clubs or sports, and the accessibility of day-care or preschool facilities.

> **Although some parents get an opportunity to participate in their children's activities as coaches, den parents, and other such facilitators, most parents are relegated to the position of "signing agent" (registering the child for teams and lessons), taxi driver, and cheerleader. Research has shown that parent involvement and support, even at the most basic level, are important factors in a child's length of involvement and success in an activity or organization.**

There are marked economic class differences in children's utilization of community organizations. Children in lower-income families are only half as likely as their middle-income peers to participate in activities at all and are less likely to participate on a regular basis. Not surprisingly, middle-income mothers are also more likely than lower-income mothers to sign up their children for formal programs. It seems that by virtue of their ability to navigate the system and pay activity fees, middle-income mothers are better prepared to act as social agents and to introduce their children to the broader range of organized activities and resources beyond the boundaries of their homes and schools.[10]

There are also noticeable gender differences in the extent to which parents become involved in certain settings. For example, mothers communicate more regularly with child-care staff than fathers do, and mothers also tend to have more-regular contact with their children's teachers in elementary school. Likewise, mothers tend to be more involved in coordinating and communicating with other social institutions. Through activities in the PTA, Brownies, Cub Scouts, and the like, a mother helps both to maintain the communal social network and to integrate her child into it. Hence, middle-income American mothers today perform a disproportionate share of the mediation between the community and family; for the most part, they are the ones who help their families adapt to the external environment. They are the spiders who "weave the web," so to speak!

Generally, as a child gets older, the parents tend to play a decreasing role as active arrangers of the child's social contacts. Whereas direct tracking of a child's activities are often the norm in the preschool period, mere awareness of a child's social plans and activities is more common during adolescence.

Barriers to Arranging Available Activities

Although most parents feel that the way their children occupy their discretionary time is important, it is difficult for many parents to translate this belief into strategies that affect what their children actually do. According to Elliott Medrich and colleagues, "time use itself is not the singular responsibility of anyone – it is the product of relationships among parents, children, child-serving institutions, and the broader society."[11] But who is in charge? Perhaps this point highlights the very problem. No one has taken outright responsibility to ensure that a child's use of time, involvement in activities, and overall lifestyle is on the best possible path. As I have recommended in the chapter about schools, I believe that the schools must own some of this responsibility. If a child's academic success is determined in large measure by what a child does in the nonschool hours, this only makes sense. Parents, too, share responsibility and this is a primary reason that this book is written for both professionals and parents.

Joan Lipsitz has identified some of the primary obstacles to having youths participate in community activities; they are outlined on page 227. These and other barriers are important reasons that youths do not engage in positive activities. It doesn't have to be this way. The key to finding solutions to such obstacles is group problem solving. Too often, we fail to take advantage of the full power of teamwork – just when it is needed most. I find that when there is a barrier to involving a child in a particular activity, about 90 percent of the time it can be solved by brainstorming with a group of people who know the child – parents, teachers, clergy, relatives, etc.

Twelve-year-old Tika was nervous about the idea of joining an after-school soccer team. She liked to run and play, but what if she didn't like it or what if she was terrible at it? Would she have friends on the team? Tika wondered if it would just be easier to go home after school and watch TV, as she always did. It was safer to stick with what she was used to, even if it was boring. Her mother helped her weigh the pros and cons and arranged transportation through a church volunteer. Tika joined the middle school soccer team. The school principal encouraged Tika and talked to the soccer coach about trying to draw Tika and other "at-risk" girls into the team. The coach hit upon the idea of allowing the girls to wear their uniforms to school. After three months, Tika says, "My grades improved because I could not play if I made a grade below C. It helped me pay attention in school. I like being able to wear my soccer uniform to school on game days. I'm definitely going to keep playing soccer and maybe I'll try out for soccer in high school." Too often, we succumb to obstacles and by default, inaction. But if we really want to make something happen, we can usually find a way.

Finding Flow

Finally, you will recall from Chapter 3 that because flow is so productive, developmentally healthy, and enjoyable, adults and children both seek out activities where we can experience flow. Why, then, do youths spend so little time engaged in activities that make them happiest? The simple answer is that turning on the television or some such "instant entertainment" is a whole lot easier than all the tasks that are required to get ready for band rehearsal or baseball practice. Flow activities require an initial investment of energy before one is able to benefit. Many youths find it difficult to rally that investment of energy, so parents need to help boost their children over this initial hurdle.

In Chapter 3, we learned that adults may need to help by providing *scaffolding*, or extra supports, until the child can perform on his own. It also is useful to teach children the principles of flow – the payoff of working hard and focusing. Help children understand that they achieve the most and feel happiest when they develop their skills as fully as possible. Parents can help children understand this and can help them structure their lifestyles more according to flow principles.[12]

Obstacles to Youth Participation in Activities [13]

■ **Lack of Safety.** In some neighborhoods, it is not safe for children to walk to community activities.

■ **Lack of Transportation.** Lack of transportation can limit children's access to activities, particularly in rural and sub-urban areas.

■ **Lack of Financial Resources.** 47 percent of parents who leave their children alone at some time during out-of-school hours, say they do so because they cannot afford to do otherwise. The cost of supervision and enrichment takes its heaviest toll on low-income families.

■ **Lack of Information.** While it may seem obvious, it bears saying that one serious obstacle to engaging children in available activities is the lack of information. This, in addition to the lack of available activities in a community, is the ultimate limiting factor for parents and children seeking activities to fill out-of-school hours. According to a survey conducted by the Center for Early Adolescence, parents' primary source of information about possible activities is the messages their children bring home from school. Unfortunately, most schools don't seem to recognize that they are carrying the ball on this issue, and these messages often are unreliable and rarely inform parents about the complete range of options available in the community.

Summing Up

We have discovered that the effect of any given context on a child is influenced by multiple factors, including 1) the personality of the child, 2) the characteristics of the particular environment, 3) the peers in the setting, and 4) adult supervision. All of these factors interrelate to determine the outcome for a given child. There simply is no one-size-fits-all recipe of environmental activities. Understanding the lifestyle profiles of youths – that is, their use of time and involvement in activities – should help us provide ultimately more worthwhile and satisfying options for them. The goal is to help youths develop personality traits that enhance, rather than erode, the development of character. Children must experience a balance of activities that offer support from adults, on the one hand, and independent experiences that lead to self-confidence and the learning of important competencies on the other. You can't always hand-pick the experiences for your child that you think will nurture these competencies, but you can examine the lifestyle of your child and support participation in activities that are more likely to lead to healthy experiences.

As I noted earlier, I think that educators have the obligation to help ensure that their students are plugged into good activities. For professional counselors who work with youths who come to their attention because of behavior problems, likewise, there is an important place for assessing children's lifestyles. Paul Gump, a noted ecological psychologist, put it well in suggesting that a child with behavior problems is not "sick" so much as the child's lifestyle is.[14] In the next chapter, we'll look specifically at professionals' involvement in arranging lifestyle activities.

[1] Benson, P. (1997). *All kids are our kids.* San Francisco: Jossey-Bass.

[2] Benson, P., Galbraith, J., & Espeland, P. (1995). *What kids need to succeed.* Minneapolis, MN: Free Spirit Publishing. p. 3.

[3] *Ibid.*

[4] Gump, P. (1984). Ecological psychological psychology and clinical mental health. In W. O'Connor & B. Lubin (Eds.), *Ecological approaches to clinical and community psychology* (pp. 57-71). New York: Wiley.

[5] Bartko, W., & Eccles, J. (2003). Adolescent participation in structured and unstructured activities: A person-oriented analysis. *Journal of Youth and Adolescence, 32,* 233-241.

[6] *Ibid.*

[7] Rich, D. (1992). *Megaskills.* Boston: Houghton Mifflin.

[8] Kindlon, D. (2001). *Too much of a good thing: Raising children of character in an indulgent age.* New York: Hyperion.

[9] Larson, R. (2000). Toward a psychology of positive youth development. *American Psychologist, 55,* 170-183.

[10] Medrich, E., Roizen, J., Rubin, V., & Buckley, S. (1982). *The serious business of growing up: A study of children's lives outside school.* Berkeley, CA: University of California Press.

[11] *Ibid.* p. 54.

[12] Jackson, S., & Csikszentmihalyi, M. (2002). *Flow in sports: The key to optimal experiences and performances.* Champaign, IL: Human Kinetics.

[13] Lipsitz, J. (1986). *After school: Young adolescents on their own.* Carrboro, NC: Center for Early Adolescence.

[14] Gump, P. (1984).

CHAPTER 17

Professionals' Involvement in Arranging Lifestyle Activities

T O REITERATE MARY PIPHER'S QUOTE FROM EARLIER in this book, "Professionals should think less in terms of developing services for youths, and more along the lines of emphasizing activities."[1] Professional counselors seeking to introduce activity-oriented interventions for a child should first conduct a needs assessment. This is done by looking at the child's needs in comparison to a child of the same age, gender, and cultural setting whose lifestyle profile is *typical* for the 10 settings covered in this book. Next, the status of the "target" child should be inventoried, also across all 10 settings. See the "Sample Analysis" beginning on page 232.

The discrepancy between the "typical" child and the "target" child becomes the focus of intervention. It may not be necessary to overhaul all of the "target" child's environments. Modifying one or more settings may be sufficient to get the desired effect. Remember, a small modification in one environment sometimes will have a "ripple effect" on other environments. Of course such a ripple effect can be negative, so the situation must be monitored to ensure that only positive ripples are allowed to continue.

For example, in the sample analysis, suppose it is determined that the child has an interest in computers. The teacher who sponsors the

Sample Analysis
Typical Child Compared to Target Child

Age: 15   Gender: Male   Cultural Setting: rural Iowa

Environment	Guideline	Typical Child	Target Child
Home	Family shares some meals together; child has regular bedtime and enforced chore and homework responsibilities.	Yes	Family rarely eats together; no clear bedtime, or enforced chore or homework responsibilities.
Neighborhood	Neighborhood provides easy access to friends for spontaneous play/socializing.	Yes	Family lives on an isolated farm.
School	The child spends regular time in extracurricular sports, clubs, or organizations at school or in community organizations.	5 hours per week	None

Environment	Guideline	Typical Child	Target Child
After-School	The child is involved in an organized, supervised after-school program/activity.	Yes	Child cares for himself after school and often spends the time unsupervised hanging out with friends.
Electronic	The child spends only a moderate amount of time daily with electronic media (TV, computer, videogames, phone).	2 hours or less per day	Child spends 4–5 hours daily watching TV or playing videogames.
Friends	Child is involved with friends in organized and supervised activities.	Child is involved with friends mostly in organized activities, and when he is not, parents monitor via cell phone.	Child is out with friends, with "nothing special to do" 3 or more times a week.
Faith	The child spends time in activities in a religious institution.	Attends weekly service and participates in Sunday night youth group.	No involvement.

Environment	Guideline	Typical Child	Target Child
Work	If the child works, it is in a setting with positive supervision and exposure to good peers.	Works less than 20 hours a week in setting that has been screened by parents.	Child is working in a fast-food environment 25 hours a week, where he is exposed to friends who are involved in regular drinking.
Recreation	The child spends regular time in lessons or practice in music, theater, or other arts.	5+ hours per week.	No hobbies or special interests.
Sports	Child is engaged in daily physical activity, including weekly involvement in a sports activity.	Child participates on the intramural volleyball team weekly. Walks dog one mile every night.	Child hates sports because he isn't good at any. No interest in exercise.

school Computer Club lives near the child and offers transportation, making it possible for the child to stay after school and participate in the club. He becomes engaged in a productive activity, with good friends, which leads to participating in a Saturday PC-user group. He quits his fast-food job and gets small jobs networking computers, with the help of an adult mentor at the PC-user group. The child is asked to help with the computer network at school, increasing his status with his peers. He no longer just hangs out with friends, never watches TV, and his grades improve. He's making plans to travel with friends to Des Moines, Iowa, for a national computer conference. As you can see, a change in one environment ripples through numerous other environments. This child's entire friend, school, and work environments changed for the better with the improvement in the after-school setting.

In other cases, with seriously mentally ill youths, it may be necessary to facilitate change across most of the child's environments. Further, professional counselors may have to erect special "scaffolding" to enable the child to participate in some activities, such as getting a volunteer to help supervise the child in a recreational activity. In mental health parlance, these efforts are referred to as "wraparound" services and are typically combined with formal mental health services, such as psychotherapy and psychiatric medication. In the most extreme cases, when a professional counselor tries to avoid placing a child in an out-of-home residential treatment program, it is necessary to replicate the structure of such a treatment program by tightly planning the lifestyle activities of the child in each of the 10 environments. Since the best competence-building opportunities are in the child's ordinary environments, this offers the greatest chance to help such children. The scientific literature on out-of-home residential treatment indicates that while many youth improve during care, that improvement is not always maintained after discharge. Therefore, it is more preferable to arrange competence-building opportunities in the child's ordinary environments when possible than the more artificial life arrangements made in residential treatment.

It is important to identify interventions that will significantly affect the child's time use in positive ways. Various types of interventions that might be appropriate include 1) changing the pattern of use of existing activities, 2) identifying new activities, 3) strengthening existing activities, 4) expanding involvement to new areas within existing activities, and 5) developing well-planned mechanisms to make activities more accessible to the child and the child's family.[2]

Having a child join an already existing group (such as a sports team, club, or hobby group) can offer many advantages. Not only do such groups encourage social interaction through the sharing of common interests, but they also constitute ready-made social support systems. Professionals who help develop an out-of-school activity plan for a child must be sure to address the child's specific needs. A successful plan will build slowly on successive positive attachments, and it should eventually provide connections to a wide variety of activities.[3]

Of course, youths have their own ideas about what kinds of activities are best. According to the Carnegie Council on Adolescent Development, parents and youths routinely mention the following as elements of good community programs:

- Young teenagers consistently list "fun" and "friends" as the two major factors affecting their decisions about whether or not to participate in community programs. They want to be involved in activities that they perceive as being fun, and they don't want to be involved in groups in which they don't know anybody.

- In evaluating potential programs, both youths and their parents seek answers to these questions: Does the program offer interesting activities? Is the program in the proximity of the youth's home or school? If it is not nearby, is transportation offered? Is the program affordable?

- Safety is often a major concern, particularly in urban areas: Can youths get to and from the program safely? Are they assured of safe conditions at the program itself?

- Subtler issues of program philosophy and environment also come into play in the selection process: Does the program offer some measure of autonomy? Are the youths treated with respect? Are the staff members friendly, and do they care about children?[4]

Reed Larson and Douglas Kleiber add one more critical factor to the mix: challenge. They propose that enjoyment and challenge provide the first criterion for evaluating a free-time experience: "A child who has at least one activity that is absorbing enough to engage his or her interest will find it easier to get through the day."[5]

Although the research literature is sparse, it does appear that children with behavioral and emotional problems tend to be less involved in productive types of free-time activities – such as sports and involvement in community organizations – and they typically spend more time watching TV. Without meaningful uses of free time, these youths don't have the challenging experiences that help them get through the day. At the same time, they are missing out on experiences that are important to psychological development. In some cases, drug use or delinquent activities may be attempts to fill time and experience the same kind of enjoyment that most youths find in more positive activities.[6]

Mental health professionals historically have not given much attention to the ecology of behaviorally impaired children's daily lives. There is a need for more research on the daily activities of youths who are in distress. Dutch psychiatrist Marten deVries has suggested that professional counselors compile "thick" descriptions of the lives of children with behavior problems. How do they spend their free time? How do the activities and events in their lives affect their experiential states? What inhibits them from participating in the types of leisure activities that often play such constructive roles in the lives of other children?[7]

DeVries has edited a fascinating book, *The Experience of Psychopathology: Investigating Mental Disorders in Their Natural Setting.* Most of the contributors to the volume have used Mihaly Csikszentmihalyi's Experience Sampling Method (ESM) to study the lives of persons with mental illness. The belief is that disorder is situated within the contexts and rhythms of daily life. By using the ESM, the researchers develop a contextual analysis of the person's affect and behavior. As an example, there are significant differences in the time-budgets of depressed and non-depressed adolescents. Depressed adolescents tend to have limited contact with opposite-gender friends and spend more time at home in isolation in more passive leisure activities compared to the more productive and social activities of their non-depressed peers.

On this page is a sample analysis of a depressed 16 year old. When he was paged throughout the day, the teenager recorded what he was doing and his present mood-state. Typically, this data is collected mul-

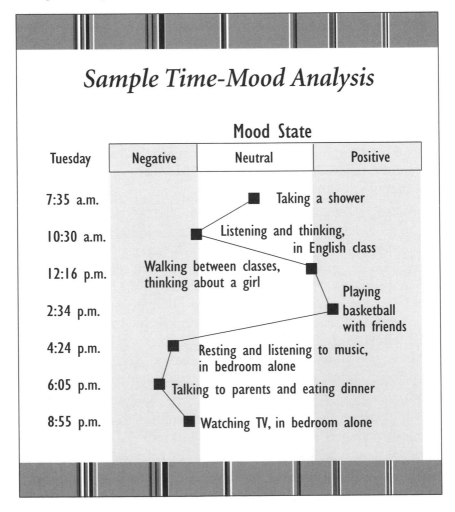

Sample Time-Mood Analysis

Mood State

Tuesday	Negative	Neutral	Positive
7:35 a.m.			Taking a shower
10:30 a.m.		Listening and thinking, in English class	
12:16 p.m.	Walking between classes, thinking about a girl		
2:34 p.m.			Playing basketball with friends
4:24 p.m.	Resting and listening to music, in bedroom alone		
6:05 p.m.	Talking to parents and eating dinner		
8:55 p.m.	Watching TV, in bedroom alone		

tiple times throughout the day for at least a week. A linear graph of the entire week's data provides clinically useful insights into the world of the depressed teenager. For example, while we would not conclude that this teenager's problem could be eliminated by persuading him to avoid time at home in isolated, passive leisure activities, it is clear that this one area of his life may be critical to the depression, and therefore, worthy of focus in his treatment. In this case, self-monitoring of his time use might provide a way to bring this experience to the attention and understanding of the teenager.[8]

Engineering an Activity Setting to Change a Specific Behavior

The discussion thus far has looked at children's time use in various contexts and involvement in activities as a general phenomenon, with the goal of getting youths into the types of activities that engender positive behavior. However, it's also possible to reverse the sequence – that is, to identify a specific positive behavior and then to facilitate the child's involvement in an activity that will likely encourage and shape that behavior. Imagine a child who is quiet and painfully shy who you would like to become more sociable and at ease in public. One way to achieve this transformation would be to have her take up an activity that will help her change from the way she is to the way you want her to be. Consider the following example: When 12-year-old Rodney's parents were divorced recently, he became depressed and also became a behavior problem at school. When school officials reacted by placing him in a special education classroom "for retards" (Rodney's words), Rodney's self-esteem plummeted. His school counselor, who saw him giving up and becoming passive, arranged for him to attend an activity after school twice-a-week, and not just any activity – bodybuilding. Rodney initially balked at bodybuilding class, claiming he felt like a klutz. To provide support and encouragement, the counselor arranged for a classmate of Rodney's to participate with him. After a few weeks, Rodney began to shape up and his confidence grew. His classmates began to treat him differently after he impressed everyone with his weightlifting ability in gym class.

Psychologist James Gavin, who has written about how to tailor fitness regimens to achieve lifestyle changes, cautions that in choosing a "mismatched" activity to help facilitate change, it is important to build in enough support to keep the child on track until the changes become self-rewarding. In Rodney's case, weightlifting was not a sport he was interested in. The school counselor and the weight trainer provided the critical support, working hard to ensure that Rodney attended the class. Once Rodney experienced success and new self-respect, self-motivation took over. Rodney's weightlifting offered an additional benefit not found in most activities in that it also helped to reduce tension.[9]

Gavin also cautions against making changes that are so extreme they are likely to fail. For example, in Rodney's case, a highly competitive activity would probably have been too drastic a change. A succession of gradual changes is more likely to help a child make the transition from an unsupportive situation to one that is psychologically healthier.

Finally, Gavin reminds us that introducing a new activity is not the only intervention option and may not be the best. In Rodney's case, for example, the counselor might have worked with the gym teacher to get Rodney more engaged in gym class, in which he rarely participated actively. If Rodney had been allowed to arrive at gym class early to help the teacher set up the equipment and prepare the activities, this leadership role might have enhanced his status among his classmates, increased his self-esteem, and diminished his depression. This intervention option of expanding one's involvement to new areas within existing activities is often highly effective.

In addition to changing behavior, an activity also may replace a less-desirable activity. For example, activities such as mountain biking and in-line skating can fulfill an important need for some people – the need for variety, challenge, thrills, and self-testing. Recent research on these "Type T" personalities by psychologist Frank Farley suggests that if individuals with high levels of such needs cannot meet them in appropriate and socially acceptable ways, they may seek thrills through dangerous and socially costly pursuits such as drug taking, reckless driving, gambling, and criminal behavior.[10]

To conclude this chapter about professionals' involvement in arranging lifestyle activities, it must be acknowledged that while for most children the home environment is a nurturing and supportive place, at the same time, some children live in families inundated with stressors. In this case, professional counselors must understand that the energy required to cope each day may overwhelm a child and result in little energy for investing in important activities in other environments.[11] While finding creative ways to involve children in stress-reducing activities outside the home is appropriate, professional counselors also must intervene to reduce family stressors and facilitate the achievement of a positive family environment.

Next, because some people argue that the hectic lifestyles of families are caused by *too many* activities, in the next (and last) chapter, I'll conclude with a look at how to find the balanced lifestyle.

---

[1] Pipher, M. (1997). *The shelter of each other: Rebuilding our families.* New York: Ballantine, 1997. p. 130.

[2] Maguire, L. (1991). *Social support systems in practice: A generalist approach.* Silver Springs, MD: National Association of Social Workers.

[3] Ibid.

[4] Carnegie Council on Adolescent Development. (1992). *A matter of time: Risk and opportunity in the nonschool hours.* New York: Carnegie Corporation. p. 77.

[5] Larson, R., & Keibler, D. (1993). Daily experience of adolescents. In P. Tolan & B. Cohler (Eds.), *Handbook of clinical research and practice with adolescents* (pp. 125-145). New York: Wiley. p. 132.

[6] Ibid. p. 141.

[7] deVries, M. (Ed.). (1992). *The experience of psychopathology: Investigating mental disorders in their natural setting.* New York: Cambridge University Press.

[8] Merrick, W. (1992). Dysphoric moods in depressed and non-depressed adolescents. In M. deVries (Ed.). *The experience of psychopathology: Investigating men-*

tal disorders in their natural setting (pp. 148-156.) New York: Cambridge University Press.

⁹ Gavin, J. (1992). *The exercise habit.* Champaign, IL: Leisure Press.

¹⁰ Roth, R., & Constantine, L. (July, 1995). A good PE class makes every student a winner. *APA Monitor, 26* (7), pp. 59-60.

¹¹ *Ibid.*

CHAPTER 18

Finding the
Balanced Lifestyle

SOME PEOPLE ARGUE THAT THE HECTIC LIFESTYLES of today's families are caused by too much going on – too many activities, including organized sports.[1] One person who takes this stance is family psychologist John Rosemond, whose nationally syndicated newspaper column on parenting and the family reaches millions of Americans every week. A reader once wrote a response to a column in which Rosemond advised parents to take their kids out of all after-school activities. The reader wondered if Rosemond's own children participated in anything except family activities.

Rosemond responded that his son dropped out of pee-wee football because he was afraid he might get hurt. Likewise, his son quit soccer in mid-season because the coach put too much emphasis on winning. In both instances, Rosemond supported the decisions but insisted that his son inform the coach personally. His daughter took private piano lessons in the home during her school years and acted in a few local theater productions. Rosemond explains:

"I witnessed what happened to families when children's after-school activities dominated a family's discretionary time . . . . everyone in the family always seemed to be in a constant state of hurry. . . . Our children, we decided, were going to look back, as adults, on family life that had been relaxed and relatively carefree. We were going to put family first, second, and third. As a consequence, we were marriage-centered, not child-centered. . . . The things we did together were active things, things that make for good childhood memories."[2] He concluded by saying that good citizenship begins at home, not on the soccer field.

I can't disagree with what John Rosemond chose for his family. However, as you've probably already guessed, I do disagree with his advice . . . to take children out of all after-school programs. I believe that much of his advice is solid, but he often comes across as suggesting that there is only one way to skin a cat. There are many families that are not stressed-out by involving their children in activities outside the home. For many of those children, the activities are a vital part of their lives. I don't doubt that there are negative outcomes for some families and children, such as Rosemond cites, but the lesson to be learned is to assess your particular situation and select children's after-school activities consciously and carefully.

The late author Rod Serling created the idyllic town of Willoughby, in the classic 1960s TV series *Twilight Zone*. In the Willoughby episode, a stressed-out businessman seeks refuge from his hectic life in the serene 19th-Century village, complete with barefoot boys carrying fishing poles, a band playing in the bandstand, and an organ grinder on the corner. John Rosemond too often sounds nostalgic for long-ago days, an observation that I think he would actually appreciate.

Rosemond's is not a lone voice crying in the wilderness. Family therapist William Doherty, whose work was discussed in Chapter 4, says that many parents have given over control of family time to school, community, sports, and church leaders. Although these people honestly desire to promote the healthy growth of children, the end result is often an intrusion on the lives of families.[3] Doherty feels the culprit is children's outside-the-home, outside-the-school activities: swim team, dance lessons, hockey practices, gymnastics, art, piano, soccer, karate – the list goes on. Juggling schedules and carpooling to games and rehearsals, families must work their schedules around ice time and pool time. Family dinner time together is frequently sacrificed.

Sandra Hofferth and John Sandberg, at the Institute for Social Research at the University of Michigan, have studied the pattern of family life and discovered two major changes in family life in recent years: 1) children have less free time, and 2) the free time they do have is increasingly structured. The study looked at a 16-year period, 1981–1997 and analyzed weekly hours that children ages 3–11 spent on major activities. Other findings:

- Playing time decreased 25 percent.

- Television viewing time decreased 13 percent.

- Church-going dropped 40 percent.

- Outdoor activities (walking, hiking, etc.) dropped 50 percent.

- Time in organized sports activities almost doubled.

- Household work, including accompanying parents on errands and shopping trips, more than doubled.

- Time in passive leisure activities (going to a movie, watching a sports event) increased five-fold.[4]

Out-of-school activities can balance academic life and offer youths unique opportunities for socialization. However, the recent phenomenon of "overbooking" children into too many activities at too young an age is a concern. When children begin structured activities too young, it can hurt development, according to David Elkind, author of the widely acclaimed book, *The Hurried Child*. Elkind used to advise parents to start extracurricular activities at about age 7 with three activities: 1) a social activity like Cub Scouts or a church youth group, 2) a creative activity such as a musical instrument or art, and 3) a physical activity like a sport or dance. Today, however, he feels that may be too much too soon. He advocates for more down time for children, that is, time to be in control and free of adult direction. He says when children are coerced into activities they don't like or into too many activities, it translates into pressure and, ultimately, stress.[5]

Of course, parents try their best to give their children the opportunities they need to succeed in today's world. Often, parents are driven by anxiety about not doing enough for their children. I think William

Doherty has pinpointed the key to how the problem has developed. He says:

> **"Over the last fifteen years or so, the word has gotten out to parents and community leaders that children and youth need to do something other than hang out. They need stimulating, structured activities that involve them with other young people and caring adults in the community. There is good research to support the wisdom of this idea. But the problem is that many of us have taken the message too far: if a moderate amount of structured activities is good for kids, then more must be better."[6]**

The phenomenon of overscheduled children is a new one. Professionals have rightly focused on the potential of activities to help children grow, but activities should not be a substitute for family time. Sometimes, too, activities can even contribute to family time. Many parents point to the time they spend driving their children to activities or attending games. Sharing music lessons or religious activities are ways to connect. Doherty also has noted that when a child gets involved in sports, school sports may be the way to go. For example, varsity athletics are highly regulated, specifying the length of the season and when teams can practice. Conversely, community sports leagues sometimes subscribe to the "more is better" philosophy.

In sum, it must be acknowledged that structured after-school programs, together with a full day of structured school experience, may infringe on a child's need for down time or independent time that is not directed by adults. In 2002, public television station WNET in New York produced a television show called *Frontier House* in which three families, for five months, lived as homesteading pioneers in Montana lived in the 1880s. The experience changed the way these parents raised their children. Mother Karen Glenn says it's difficult to replicate the experience, but she still tries. She advises: "Take a night to turn off the TV and unplug the phone, even if there's no conversation and everyone sits quietly or falls asleep. To bring the focus back to the family requires saying no to diversions."[7] Doherty makes the point that the psychological development of youths is based on needs that have evolved over millennia and may not be a good fit with this high-speed era of the Internet: "These slowed-down needs of children and families are out of sync with the fast-forward culture."[8] Doherty succinctly states the final case:

> "It's not because parents are enrolling their children in bad activities. We know from common sense and a lot of research that extracurricular involvement is good for kids. Sports, music, fine arts, and religious involvement — all of these contribute to a rich life for a child. The issue is one of balance."[9]

It is possible for whole communities to alter the environments of childhood in order to achieve greater balance. Parents in Wayzata, Minnesota, have taken action and formed an organization to address the way that childhood activities are changing family life. The organization, aptly named *Putting Family First*, asks coaches and instructors to cut back on practices, rehearsals, and meetings. They ask group leaders not to penalize children for missing practices because of a family event and to expect children to put family vacations ahead of practices. The group awards a seal (akin to the Good Housekeeping Seal of Approval) to groups which have shown a commitment to supporting family life.

If communities can regulate coaches and instructors to cut back on scheduled practices, rehearsals and meetings, surely it's worth looking at other ways to make changes community-wide. Reed Larson offers these suggestions:

> "Communities might make collective decisions — about the scheduling of events, store hours, limits on hours of youth employment, or curfews — that would provide more family time and homework time on weeknights. Employers of both youths and parents could be more attentive to rhythms — for example, by allowing them greater flexibility in work hours and the opportunity to "check in" with each other by phone after school. And certainly an important goal, already at the top of the agenda in some communities, is to provide more structured activities during free time that provide opportunities for positive development, such as after-school activities, internships, summer

recreational activities, and summer jobs. Much positive benefit can come from trying to do more to synchronize positive activities for youth with the rhythms of the community."[10]

Finding Balance

I have tried to avoid single-minded advice in this book. How you go about caring for your child depends on your individual family circumstances. Unlike many books, this one does not end with cut-and-dried recommendations but instead with some broad principles that parents and professionals may want to consider as they work to promote successful pathways through childhood, ensuring that our children become psychologically vigorous adults. Here are a few general guidelines:

- Limiting your children's involvement in electronic and digital media to balance it with other activities appears wise. For example, no more than two hours of TV, phone, Internet, or playing computer games per day.

- Modeling vigorous physical activity, and making exercise a routine part of life, can have a significant impact on your child. It is better to choose an activity that can be done every day. For example, kayaking is a fine activity, but if the lake is an hour away, and you can only realistically kayak on weekends, you should have another activity which can be done on weekdays, for example, power walking. Also, choose an activity that you enjoy. You won't stick with something that you don't enjoy. I am an avid runner, but a good friend of mine commented that "the best thing about running is when you stop." Obviously, he doesn't stick with it regularly.

- Protecting some key family rituals can provide a stable anchor for your child. A drastic family makeover is not necessary; there are lots of ways for families to live together successfully. But because our culture intrudes on many aspects of family nurturing, you should hard-wire a few rituals into your family life: shared meals (as many as possible), shared upkeep of the home, homework, bedtime, celebrations, and linkages with your children when they are away from home.

- Because of the solid grounding that faith organizations can provide, you should seek one out that is a good fit with your family. The personal and social capacities that youths can learn in many religious congregations may serve them well throughout their lives, in business, civic involvement, and other professional and non-professional activities. Religious activities may inculcate in your children abilities that increase their sense of competence, which may in turn enhance their positive life chances.

- The evidence points to the fact that playing sports helps our children grow into healthy, strong young adults. Sports participation and physical activity provides a golden opportunity for personal development. With appropriate adult guidance, sports participation can serve as a vehicle for developing social competence and for deterring destructive behaviors in youths.[11] Remember, not all sports require you to be a great athlete to participate. Help children find a sport that they can fall in love with, with good coaches, instructors, and peers . . . . an activity that will lead to a lifetime of "flow!" Whether it is through sports or an arts program, or some other activity, we need to find a way to keep our children "in the envelope" of intrinsically motivated challenge and learning.[12]

This book does not advocate that parents become entertainment directors for their children. Family life should not be centered around children's activities, rather activities should revolve around family life. In fact, children may often learn a great deal more about living by having the opportunity to observe adults in an adult world. The structures that organize contemporary American youths' lives limit much of their exposure to ideas of youth their own age. Thus, the pressures from peer groups become highly influential and narrow. We would do well to take a lesson from other contemporary cultures where adults are more involved in the lives of youth.

It has only been in the last century that the field of child development has emerged. During much of that century our lenses have focused on the internal landscape of the child and his interactions with parents. What we have explored together in this book is a different perspective of the lives of children. Putting on new lenses, we have looked at the external geography of childhood – the environments that children inhabit, hour-by-hour, and the activities that consume their time. There is now scientific support for the profound effects that environments have on children. Also, it is often easier to effect behavior modification by altering children's environments than by attempting psychological intervention.

> In past decades, children traversed along fairly well-marked trajectories in life. This is no longer the case. We may rely on life chances for children to find their way or, as I believe, we can nudge children onto positive life pathways by taking advantage of the potentials in particular environments. I hope that this book has empowered you and made you realize that you do have the knowledge to make a difference with your decisions. With the environmental onslaughts that this new millenium has brought, our children need all the help we can provide.

We parents are all imperfect. In raising our children, we will always fall short, so we must be satisfied with doing our best, especially when confronted with the many challenges that life throws in along the way.

I want to return to one point to conclude. For this book, I followed the scholarly and popular literature as much as a single individual can in this age of academic overflow. One statement stood out from the hundreds of thousands of sentences I read. It was the voice of Summer Sanders the Olympian, who you'll remember from Chapter 13, and who as a young swimmer experienced this:

"At the whistle, [I] dove off that block and swam as though sharks were lunging at my toes. And when I got out of the pool, having shaved maybe 10 seconds off my usual time, I was grinning like my face was going to split . . . What a revelation! I could place, even win, just by trying hard! When everybody was proud of me – when I'd even amazed myself – it felt so good I couldn't wait to try even harder next time. That's the whole secret of motivation. A little effort brings a little reward. A little reward sows a little confidence. A little confidence prompts a little more effort, an eagerness to take on a slightly greater challenge. Personal satisfaction brings confidence, and confidence inspires effort, until what started as a mere spark of interest has grown into a burning desire that can't be contained."[13]

I wish you well in helping to steer your children, or the children you serve, toward the activities in life that will ignite their fire!

---

[1] Rosenfeld, A., & Wise, N. (2001). *The over-scheduled child: Avoiding the hyper-parenting trap*. New York: St. Martin's Press.

[2] Rosemond, J. (2000, February 13). Values don't come from a soccer field. *Asheville Citizen-Times*, p. C-3.

[3] Doherty, W. (2000). *Take back your kids: Confident parenting in turbulent times*. South Bend, IN: Sorin Books.

[4] Hofferth, S., & Sandberg, J. (2001). How American children spend their time. *Journal of Marriage and the Family, 63*, 295-308.

[5] Elkind, D. (2001). *The hurried child: Growing up too fast too soon* (3rd ed.). Reading, MA: Perseus.

[6] Doherty, W., & Carlson, B. (2002). *Putting family first: Successful strategies for reclaiming family life in a hurry-up world*. New York: Henry Holt and Company. p. 62.

[7] Athineos, D. (June, 2002). Long journey home. *Better Homes and Garden*. p 150.

[8] Doherty, W., & Carlson, B. (2002). p. 164.

[9] *Ibid*. p. 5-6.

[10] Larson, R. (Winter, 1998). Implications for policy and practice: Getting adolescents, families, and communities in sync. In A. Crouter & R. Larson, R. (Eds.), Special Issue. Temporal rhythms in adolescence: Clocks, calendars, and the coordination of daily life. *New directions for child and adolescent development, 82*, 83-87. San Francisco: Jossey-Bass. p. 87.

[11] Petitpas, A., & Champagne, D. (2000). Sports and social competence. In S. Danish & T. Gullotta (Eds.), *Developing competent youth and strong communities through after-school programming* (pp. 115-137). Washington, DC: CWLA Press.

¹² Larson, R. (2000). Toward a psychology of positive youth development. *American Psychologist, 55,* 170-183. p. 180.

¹³ Sanders, S. (1999). *Champions are raised, not born: How my parents made me a success.* New York: Delacorte. p. 34.

Atogaki

A TOGAKI IS THE JAPANESE TERM FOR "AFTERWORD."
An Atogaki is the section at the end of a book where the author reviews main points and addresses loose ends. Japanese authors, however, often include an Atogaki for a quite different purpose: to point out any weaknesses in the book and to raise questions about what has been said. For someone who is eager to get at the truth, as opposed to just promoting his own ideas, it is important to identify shortcomings in his theories so that others might produce even better theories.[1] So, here is my Afterword, Japanese-style.

This book has been an attempt to map out systematically how environments influence the lives of American youths. There are numerous writings about the lives of contemporary American youths, including the discrete effects of particular environments. While these writings are very helpful, as a whole they present the average parent or professional counselor with a disjointed and fragmented account of the influences of all environments together. I have attempted to synthesize in this book some of what we know from both the scientific and popular literature into a more coherent, systematic account of the effects of environments inhabited by youths.

To restate the basic premise of this book, children grow up in various environments — in families, schools, peer groups, sports teams, religious organizations, and many others. Each of these settings, or environments, is a source of growth opportunities as well as risks. This book offers a set of lenses for looking at the contextual influences of these various settings on children's behavior. The viewpoint shows that places where people go to behave are the primary determinants of behavior and that these place-time-behavior units (what I've called "behavior settings") which are the best predictors of human behavior, also make up the fabric of daily life.

The first step to improving the quality of a child's life is to pay close attention to a child's daily experience. This means that both parents and professional counselors must look at the places, activities, and social contexts where children spend their time. Like Roger Barker, we must examine the child's life just as an observer would if she were able to follow the child around. How much time does the child spend in places that are supportive yet challenging? How much time does the child spend in "religious" activities versus media diversions? How much time does the child spend with adults versus friends? The answers to these questions can tell us much about the development of a youth.

By looking at the lifestyles of talented teenagers, we have been able to identify some of the best choices for all youths. Talented teenagers tend to use time more efficiently, and they are more often engaged in challenging activities. They are also generally more able to tolerate solitude. Being able to be alone with oneself appears to be necessary to develop talent. At least in the short run, youths must be able to tolerate some less positive experiences.[2] Because talented youths tend to use their skills to the fullest, they enjoy challenges and the difficulties that they sometimes must encounter. They develop the ability to persevere when others might succumb to obstacles. They often turn perceived hardships into enjoyable experiences and accomplishments.[3]

The development of talent requires a particular mind-set which depends largely on habits developed in a child's early environments. These habits become ingrained and take on the characteristics of a personality trait. The habit of "engaging life" can be developed early with the proper support from parents and others. Unfortunately, many youths today do not have meaningful goals. Often they have not found anything in life that they feel is worthwhile. Not surprisingly, people do not function well in such an idle "meaningless" state. Without goals, people lose motivation and concentration.[4] Activities like sports and artistic endeavors have clear goals. This is likely one of the reasons that such activities can produce flow experiences. Many athletes and music students report feeling "strong and active" compared to youths involved in other less-rewarding activities who report fewer feelings of potency.[5]

The best opportunities for youths to grow is in flow activities. In these challenging activities youths are able to test their limits, solve problems, and discover new things. Flow activities require a child to use increasingly complex skills.[6] We must help children invest energy in activities that produce flow, as opposed to nonessential activities that do not. We have many tough decisions to wrestle with. For example, is a part-time job really a good use of a teenager's time? The research shows mixed results but employment usually cannot be considered a "high-density" growth opportunity. How much time does a child spend watching TV? The list of questionable activities is large.

In facilitating the path to adulthood, how can we ensure that youths invest their time wisely? They can only concentrate on so many things, so how this precious commodity of attention is allocated is a critical factor. According to Mihaly Csikszentmihalyi and his colleagues, "one cannot accomplish any novel or difficult task without concentrating attention on it. Because it takes attention to make anything happen, it is useful to think of attention as psychic energy."[7]

How then do we get youths' attention focused on the challenging activities that will help them develop the skills needed in adulthood? Of course, sometimes their spontaneous interests can lead to such constructive purposes. At other times, however, adults must help guide them, while avoiding direct manipulation.

It's important for adults to remember that opportunities for children's personal growth occur in all settings – in schools, at home, at work, with peers. At home, a child may learn trust. In soccer, a child may learn personal discipline – in school, democratic ideals – in church, compassion – from friends, self-understanding – at work, patience – and so on. Through the accumulation of these lessons, youths develop the competencies that are necessary to succeed as an adult.

Succeeding in contemporary American society requires the ability to function effectively in many different settings. A critical question to ask then is: Are we providing youths with the kinds of experiences which will enable them to thrive in adulthood? Both parents and professionals need to steer children toward environments and activities that offer the best opportunities for growth toward competent adulthood. Generally, we're talking about contexts in which youths experience both enjoyment and challenge. It is in these settings that they encounter the positive experiences that help them maintain clear vision and a sense of optimism about life.

Nature Versus Nurture Debate

Seventeen-year-old Suzanne says innate ability is probably responsible for her success in school: "I think I was kind of born a perfectionist and just being highly motivated. I've always wanted to do my best just for myself. I like to go the extra mile. That's just the way I was born." Here Suzanne has succinctly expressed the "nature" point of view in the nature versus nurture debate. "Nature" means you are born with certain skills; in other words, traits and abilities are to a great degree inherited.

The "nurture" position, on the other hand, holds that it is the environment in which youths are raised and all the external influencing factors that surround them that mostly determine their performance.

Obviously, in this book, I have argued that children's behavior is greatly dependent on their surroundings. But what about the nature viewpoint? Surely it must have some validity. Take, for example, Albert Einstein. His brain, which was preserved when he died, was analyzed and found to have 400 percent more glial cells per neuron (nerve cell) than the brain of the average person. Glial cells bind neurons together and provide a medium for the transfer of electrochemical messages between them. Obviously, Einstein's neurological switching station – his "thinking" mechanism – was super-developed.

In his book, *The Blank Slate: The Modern Denial of Human Nature*, Massachusetts Institute of Technology psychologist Steven Pinker argues that the brain is hard-wired with genetic instructions which govern our responses to events. Although he forcefully challenges the theory that parents can mold their children like clay, in the end he too concedes that human behavior is the product of both innate influences and the environment.[8]

By using MRI imaging, scientists recently have come to better understand teenagers' brains. The sometimes baffling behavior of adolescents, once blamed on hormones, is now thought to be more dependent on neurobiological factors. For example, adolescent preoccupations with risk-taking may be explained by incomplete development of the frontal lobes, the part of the brain behind the forehead. The frontal lobes enable us to comprehend the consequences of our behavior. Teenagers also have a high level of the neurotransmitter dopamine, which may make them desire more stimulation, which, in turn, may lead them toward more risky behavior.[9] But experts like neuropsychiatrist Richard Restak contend that activities like music, math, and sports still help structure the brain faster and better than watching TV or hanging out with friends. He claims that in the end, the choices adolescents make regarding how they spend their time can actually affect the quality of their brains.[10]

Mihaly Csikszentmihalyi's research reveals a compelling and optimistic fact: Successful youths are not born high achievers, but they are able to work harder because they have developed more self-discipline through their lifestyle of activities. Genes are not destiny. About two-thirds of youths' time is taken up by things that they have to do. It is how they spend that precious remaining one-third of their lives – their discretionary time – that makes the difference. Do children fill their time with developmentally empty activities because there isn't anything they feel like doing, or do they improve their lives by taking ownership of their activities?

A number of years ago, Csikszentmihalyi and Reed Larson conducted a retrospective study with colleague Olga Beattie Emory. The sample consisted of 30 adult men, half of whom were successful professionals: doctors, lawyers, and professors, while the other half were blue collar workers. The childhood backgrounds of all 30 men were similar: poor immigrant families, characterized by parental alcoholism and illiteracy. Half of the men rose above these roots to a life of achievement, while half did not. What was the difference? Why were some men able to overcome their depressed upbringing?

The researchers concede that there may have been a number of influential variables, but one resounding theme emerged. The men who rose above their backgrounds developed goals in adolescence that focused their lives. They embraced a set of challenges that motivated them to overcome obstacles and develop important skills. The men who failed to overcome their roots did not create such life-themes to shape their psychic energy.[11]

> It is acknowledged that our genes play a robust role in determining our behavior. Nonetheless, if we understand better the environmental factors of the equation over which we have some control, we can foster youths' achievement of their full potentials.[12]

Limitations of Research Studies

Compared with their non-participating peers, youths who participate in school co-curricular activities and community youth organizations generally have higher self-esteem, more internal locus of control (feelings of control over one's life), lower rates of delinquency, and higher educational aspirations and achievement. Naysayers note that the claims are without evidence. The basic problem with the correlational relationships found in some research studies is that participation in these activities is selective. Youths from higher socioeconomic backgrounds and youths who are tracked into advanced academics tend to participate more in these activities and, hence, are the ones questioned in these studies. They also tend to have more parental support for participating in these types of activities. These factors in themselves predict positive outcomes for children, so the old chicken-or-the-egg quandary muddies the interpretation of correlational findings. When these factors are controlled (i.e., negated) in research studies, the correlation between participation in activities and positive consequences is usually reduced or disappears – but not always. For example, one study that factored in controls for parents' socioeconomic status and high school grades found that participation in extracurricular activities is associated with advanced occupational attainment 24 years later.[13]

One researcher, who was able to sort out effects, showed that the characteristics of a teenager are more likely to be the cause, rather than the result, of excessive use of the media. He found that excessive music listening generally does not precede a teenager's doing poorly in school. Instead, teenagers who do poorly in school tend to turn to music as a coping measure or perhaps to reinforce an identity different from mainstream culture.[14] The point is that we must be careful about jumping to conclusions when using correlational data.

So I concede that correlational studies – which constitute much of the research cited in this book – have their limitations. Another problem is that to present a balanced view, researchers also must assess all possible negative effects of participation in youth activities. For example, research on competitive sports suggests that they are associated with increased competition anxiety and more self-centered moral reasoning. Do such negative outcomes also occur in other demanding activities, such as in music competition?[15]

I have inferred throughout this book that there may be environments and activities that alone are superlative in nature and capable of putting youths on a positive trajectory. Some studies are beginning to look at this claim. For example, sociologist Thomas Cook at Northwestern University's Institute for Policy Research and his colleagues looked at the ways in which several environments – schools, neighborhoods, families, and friendship groups – jointly contribute to positive change during early adolescence. Success was measured by academic performance, mental health, and social behavior. The researchers found that the individual context effects were only modest in size, while the *joint* influences of all four environments was cumulatively large. They point out that "many theorists and program developers have made strong claims about the especially positive consequences of extreme values of a given context, or about magical combinations of two or more important contexts, or about one social context being more important than others at a particular age."[16] But their results indicate that no behavior setting can be considered as a silver bullet. Yes, environments do matter in determining how children's lives develop, but they do so cumulatively more than singly, according to the researchers. To make improvements in any one context helps, but it may not be sufficient. Clearly, parents and professional counselors should look at changes across multiple environments.

Media

Many teachers today claim that children are hooked on the total media culture. They say electronic diversions have become habit-forming for many youths. Can this flood of images and sounds be good for them? Are we, in the words of media critic Neil Postman, "amusing ourselves to death?"

Such dire conclusions, though important as warnings, are probably premature. Many studies show a mixture of both positive and negative effects. For example, Ulric Neisser, a professor of psychology at Cornell University, has studied the phenomenon of rising IQ in our culture. The average person's IQ scores have been rising at the rate of about 3 points per decade. Neisser attributes this to our new culture of visual literacy: "Kids aren't necessarily wiser; they are quicker. There is so much visual stimulation, it increases visual analysis." On the other hand, college entrance exam scores have been falling in recent years. Why? How do we reconcile these seemingly contradictory facts? Perhaps part of the answer is because the SAT measures knowledge of particular subject matter, whereas IQ tests measure one's ability to reason. "IQ is up because reasoning is rising," Neisser says, "but vocabulary and general knowledge is going down."[17]

You will recall that the American Academy of Pediatrics recommends no TV viewing for children younger than 2 years of age and a maximum of two hours a day of "screen time" (TV, computers, or videogames) for older children. However, child psychiatrist Elizabeth Berger cautions against extreme measures such as a complete ban on television. She is concerned that such an approach may make a child into a social outcast. She argues that preparing a child for life means preparing him or her to be one of the boys or girls. She makes a good point that it can be awful for a child to feel too different from other children.[18]

Further, it can be argued that we are not certain that some of the negative effects of television are causal. For example, it appears that teenagers who view an excessive amount of TV do less well in school. However, these teenagers may turn to TV because they do less well in school.[19] Further, television may help adolescents cope with the intensity of their lives by providing a needed respite or by providing a distraction from family conflict.[20]

So the general theme is that the pervasive electronic environment appears to have some benefits as well as some negative repercussions. It has taken some 40 years to begin to understand the effects of television on children, and it will likely take at least as long to begin to comprehend the full implication of computers and other new technologies in the lives of youth. When it was invented, the automobile was decried as an invention that would destroy family life. Nevertheless, each generation adapts to the evolving technologies of the day. Change is certain, and much of it can be for the good.

Sports Versus the Arts

I devoted Chapter 14 to some of the controversies surrounding youth sports. Here, I again want to acknowledge early evidence from some research that indicates that arts-based activities may be the most potent and positive choices for youths. Psychiatrist Eli Newberger, who is so critical of our society's overemphasis on sports activities, says that in his own childhood, he played far more music than sports. Youths' evolving sense of identity and competence call for activities suitable to them, and not all youths are athletically inclined.[21]

Stanford researchers Shirley Brice Heath and Milbrey McLaughlin studied 120 after-school programs and the at-risk children who attended them over a 10-year period. They observed theater groups, sports programs, academic programs, and others. They

found that arts programs were generally more effective in changing youths' lives, as evidenced by significant results on an array of measures. They found that the arts programs tended to involve the youths in more-complicated collaborations, requiring more verbal skills, than the other types of activities.[22]

Heath and McLaughlin's study is to be commended because it has attempted the difficult task of gaining a qualitative understanding of after-school activities. Study findings support the hypothesis that arts experiences can positively influence psychosocial development. Further, the study provides clues as to how this influence is developed. The study has numerous limitations, including a research group that was more "at-risk" compared to the rest of the study sample, and further, arts experiences which appeared to be much more intensive and comprehensive than most after-school arts programs. However, Heath and McLaughlin readily admit that the conclusions of their research are limited to learning within highly specific contexts and conditions. Nevertheless, this data does support Eli Newberger's view that arts programs may be best for youths. Obviously, further research on this topic is needed. For example, it would be useful to identify youths who progress well in an activity, and retrospectively to analyze how they differ from individuals who show less progress.[23] Another possible issue to explore: How often do youths in gymnastics versus drama clubs versus service-learning activities have the experience of setting goals, developing plans, or interacting with people from different backgrounds?[24]

Though the reasons for positive developmental experiences may be diverse, certain commonalties may nonetheless be recognized across the various environments. For example, University of North Carolina developmental psychologists Robert and Beverly Cairns found that the development of a distinctive skill or talent was a common way to gain social acceptance by both peers and adults. While athletic ability is not necessary for gaining status in high school, it is helpful. Other status-heavy skills and activities include participation in the performing arts, cheerleading, involvement in student government, and exemplary scholarship. The presence of a socially desirable personal attribute or skill, for which an adolescent has a sense of achievement and feels recognition, positively influences adaptation in multiple areas of the youth's life.[25] This is what we need to aim for – the experience of some success – not necessarily any specific target activity.

Final Thoughts

I have tried not to be overly prescriptive in this book. The emphasis has been on raising *awareness* of an arena of a child's life which often is not closely examined: the child's environments. Some of the environmental modifications described in this book are common sense; others are less so. Often, children will get into rewarding, successful activities with minimal or no help. Others may not be so self-directed and will need more adult guidance to make it happen. Hopefully, I have run some red flags up the pole, pointing out possible signs that a child may be vulnerable to various negative effects in particular environments. Whether it is being without adult supervision after school or viewing excessive amounts of television, it is worth examining a child's circumstances. Likewise, the protective effects of certain environments, like faith-based youth groups or service-learning activities, may be strengths that can be added to a child's already successful lifestyle.

Even guidelines that seem straightforward are not always applicable, however, due to individual characteristics. Take the example of the 20-hour maximum work week for teenagers. Recall that after 20 hours, most of the negative effects of employment appear to be triggered. This is generally the case, but each circumstance is unique. Some youths may be able to work only 10 hours-a-week without suffering, while others may be able to work more than 20 hours-a-week without negative repercussions. The trick is to know your child and how she spends her time. As I discussed, a time diary can help in this respect and can be enlightening! Then the challenge becomes to support a child adequately to engage in healthy activities that engender success. Obviously, we do not always have carte-blanche options – barriers may hinder or prevent your child's participation in particular activities. Transportation, cost, and supervision are common barriers, as well as the motivation of the child. It is always wise to take a close look at barriers to see if they are surmountable, because overcoming obstacles can lead to getting children into good environmental situations.

The ultimate goal of the approach described in this book is to create personal environments that nurture and support the healthy growth of children into adulthood. The life paths of children are sometimes set early and may be difficult to alter. It is therefore essential that we ensure that children's environments provide the opportunities for developing the habits and personal characteristics that will make for success later in life. I hope that this book will be a launching pad for that ideal.

---

[1] I was exposed to this concept in T.R. Reid's delightful book, *Confucius Lives Next Door*. Atogaki is pronounced "AH-TOH-GAH-KEE."

[2] Csikszentmihalyi, M., Rathunde, K., & Whalen, S. (1993). *Talented teenagers: The roots of success and failure.* New York: Cambridge University Press.

[3] *Ibid.*

[4] Csikszentmihalyi, M., & Larson, R. (1984). *Being adolescent: Conflict and growth in the teenage years.* New York: Basic Books.

[5] Csikszentmihalyi, M., Rathunde, K., & Whalen, S. (1993). p. 143.

[6] Csikszentmihalyi, M., Larson, R. (1984).

[7] Csikszentmihalyi, M., Rathunde, K., & Whalen, S. (1993). p. 11.

[8] Pinker, S. (2002). *The blank slate: The modern denial of human nature.* New York: Viking Penguin.

[9] Strauch, B. (2003). *The primal teen: What the new discoveries about the teenage brain tell us about our kids.* New York: Doubleday.

[10] Restak, R. (2001). *The secret life of the brain.* Washington, DC: Joseph Henry Press.

[11] Csikszentmihalyi, M., & Larson, R. (1984).

[12] Csikszentmihalyi, M., Rathunde, K., & Whalen, S. (1993).

[13] Larson, R. (2000). Toward a psychology of positive youth development. *American Psychologist, 55,* 170-183.

[14] Roe, K. (1983). *Mass media and adolescent schooling: Conflict or co-existence.* Stockholm: Almqvist & Wiksell.

[15] *Ibid.*

[16] Cook, T., Herman, M., Phillips, M., & Settersten, R. (2002). Some ways in which neighborhoods, nuclear families, friendship groups, and schools jointly affect changes in early adolescent development. *Child Development, 73*, 1283-1309. p. 1306.

[17] Phalen, K., & Reid, R. (May 17-19, 2001). Why rising IQs don't tell the whole story. *USA Weekend.* p. 25.

[18] Berger, E. (1999). *Raising children with character: Parents, trust, and the development of personal integrity.* New York: Aronson.

[19] Roe, K. (1983).

[20] Larson, R., & Kleiber, D. (1993). Daily experience of adolescents. In P. Tolan & B. Coher (Eds.), *Handbook of clinical research and practice with adolescents* (pp. 125-145). New York: Wiley.

[21] McLaughlin, M. (2000). *Community counts: How youth organizations matter for youth development.* Washington, DC: Public Education Network. p. 19.

[22] *Ibid.* The study compared the attitudes, behaviors, and outcomes of youth participating in community-based organizations with those of a representative sample of American youth, based on the National Educational Longitudinal Survey (NELS). The NELS is a study of 8th graders whom the National Center for Educational Statistics followed from 1988 through 1994. The survey looks at the role of schools, teachers, community, and family in promoting positive outcomes. The researchers administered a questionnaire containing a subset of NELS items to youth involved in the community-based organizations they studied. They then compared the responses from these youth with those from the youth participating in the 1992 NELS second follow-up. These comparisons allowed the researchers to make statements about the circumstances, attitudes, and outcomes of youth involved in their research compared to "typical" American youth.

[23] Larson, R. (2000).

[24] *Ibid.*

[25] Cairns, R., & Cairns, B. (1995). Social ecology over time and space. In P. Moen, G. Elder & K. Luscher (Eds.), *Examining lives in context: Perspectives on the ecology of human development* (pp. 397-422). Washington, DC: American Psychological Association.

Creating Environmental Opportunities for Children

Setting	Guiding Principle & Action Steps
1. Home	*Principle*: Keeping some key family rituals in the home setting will create a nurturing sanctuary that can help counteract some of the negative influences that can creep into the other environments of childhood.

Action Steps:

- Limit the amount of time that the TV is on in the home.

- Have *at least* two slow-paced family meals together each week (and make sure the TV is off).

- Make bedtime a predictable, special time, especially for younger children.

- Give children a regular chore responsibility, starting at about

Setting	Guiding Principle & Action Steps
(Home)	age 6, increasing the complexity and time commitment as they grow older. ■ Create a regular homework time and place. ■ Celebrate family with special rituals: holidays, birthdays, annual vacation.
2. Neighborhood	*Principle*: For young children especially, the neighborhood is their social universe. If you can choose your neighborhood: *Action Steps:* ■ Select a neighborhood with shorter distances between houses and less automobile traffic. Such an atmosphere usually results in more friends and more spontaneous play for children (with the fringe benefit of less time spent with "canned entertainment" such as television). ■ Select a neighborhood with close availability of libraries, community centers, parks, and child care – these places can enhance family life and activities. ■ Select a neighborhood with "nearby nature" for access to unique play areas and connections to the restorative and imaginative quality of natural settings.

Setting	Guiding Principle & Action Steps
3. School, Co-Curricular and Service Learning	*Principle*: An essential element for school success is for a child to feel connected to the school. Some ways to facilitate connectedness include: *Action Steps:* ■ Do some research (perhaps talk to a school counselor) to identify the best teachers in your child's school and try to see that your child benefits from these teachers. Students are more connected to school when they have a caring teacher who teaches with enthusiasm and responds to their special needs. ■ If your child has a unique learning style that is not being accommodated, look for other educational environments that promise to provide a better fit for your child – alternative schools, charter schools, or even special learning tracks within a school. An alternative is to steer your child toward classes and teachers that better fit the child's learning style. ■ Get involved in your child's schooling. Involvement may take many forms: helping your child with homework, calling the school with questions or when there are problems, attending school meetings, and even volunteering at the school. There is a strong relationship between par-

Setting	Guiding Principle & Action Steps
(School, Co-Curricular and Service Learning)	ent involvement and a child's school behaviors, including academic performance, attitudes, and motivation.

■ Encourage your child to be regularly involved in a co-curricular activity, such as a varsity or intramural sport, choir, orchestra, theater group, debating team, student government, student yearbook or newspaper, or various school clubs. Co-curricular activities include relationships with one or more adults. These adults often become mentors who have an ongoing presence in the child's life, so get to know the coaches and teachers who lead your child's co-curricular activities. Co-curricular activities also are the best way to engender strong peer relationships in school. Peer relations in school must be positive for a child to feel connected.

■ Help remove barriers to your child's participation in co-curricular activities: advocating for schools to offer flexible bus schedules or forming a carpool with other parents are two ways you can help.

■ Talk to the school about available service-learning activities. Community service and service-learning activities enable youths

Setting	Guiding Principle & Action Steps
	to assume meaningful roles and feel needed.
4. After-School	*Principle*: There are numerous options for children's after-school care and participation. No one approach is optimal; each child's circumstances should be looked at individually. However, the time from 3 p.m. to 6 p.m. is the risky time in which adolescents can become involved in activities that threaten their health and safety. Unsupervised time spent with peers after school is related to increased antisocial behavior. *Action Steps:* ■ Involve elementary-age children in a structured after-school program. A guiding principle is that youths who participate in structured after-school activities show better behavioral adjustment than youths who are in unstructured after-school situations. By involving children in a structured after-school program, you enable them to form meaningful and enduring relationships with adult activity leaders. Such adults often become important mentors to children. ■ Make sure children who need it have a chance for some "down time" during after-school programs. Highly-structured after-school programs juxtaposed with a

Setting	Guiding Principle & Action Steps
(After-School)	day of structured classroom experience can be a bit too much for some children.
	■ If your teenager must be unsupervised after school, remain in touch, for example, by having cell phone contact.
	■ Minimize "risky time" for adolescents. This is the time from 3–6 p.m. when teenagers are most likely to encounter negative developmental experiences, such as suffering accidents or exposure to peer pressure to engage in risky behavior (drug use, dangerous sexual practice, criminal activity). Know where teenagers are and what they are doing!
5. Electronic	*Principle*: Research has clearly demonstrated that media play a significant role in the socialization of youth, and they can and do influence children's attitudes and behaviors across a wide range of areas. Youths today spend more time participating in media-related activities than in any other activity other than sleeping. Our culture conditions children to develop the need for constant entertainment. Giving electronic and digital media a moderate place in the life of families can free up important time for

Setting	Guiding Principle & Action Steps
(Electronic)	more-meaningful activities. *Action Steps:*

Action Steps:

- Set some clear rules about when children can watch television, such as no TV before homework is completed.

- Set limits for the maximum time allowed with media, especially on school nights. The American Academy of Pediatrics recommends no TV for children younger than 2 years old and a maximum of two hours a day of "screen time" (TV, computer, videogames) for older children.

- Keep TVs out of children's bedrooms.

- During "National TV-Turnoff Week" (the last week in April) turn off your TV for a week. You do not need to become an anti-TV zealot, however, banning TV forever from your children.

- Watch movies and TV shows with your child and have discussions about what you watch.

- Monitor your child's viewing – make sure the material is age appropriate.

- Regulate computer and electronic game use. Computers may be even

Setting	Guiding Principle & Action Steps
(Electronic)	more addictive than TV. Long hours in front of the computer may displace other important activities such as recreational and social activities.
	■ Each day make sure your child is given the maximum opportunity to talk. The use of language is critical for healthy brain development. Anything that limits a child's verbalizations, such as solitary computer use, may be detrimental.
6. Friends	*Principle:* What children experience outside the home, in the company of their peers, has a profound effect on their development. Assessing how the environment impacts a child's peer relationships is an important step to improving the lives of children. Friendships are in large measure driven by their environment, so the neighborhood you live in and the activity settings where your child lives are especially important.
	Action Steps:
	■ Encourage school friendships by helping with transportation. Adolescents place a premium on friendships with school friends that extend to nonschool settings.
	■ Steer children toward activity settings where wholesome

Setting	Guiding Principle & Action Steps
(Friends)	children can befriend your child. Peer pressure is more likely to support a teenager doing well.

- Keep track of your children's whereabouts, their friends, and the types of activities they engage in. This is critical for helping your children to find supportive activity settings and to avoid non-supportive ones.

- Insist on – and support – your child spending time in productive pursuits. During the teenage years, a conflict may arise between investing time in friends of the opposite gender and investing time in more-productive pursuits. This is natural, but don't let it get out of hand.

7. Faith

Principle:
In seeking healthy developmental activities and supportive environments for children, parents would do well to consider the potential benefits offered by religious organizations. The faith environment may well have as powerful an impact on the lives of some children as any environment.

Action Steps:

- Encourage religious activities such as attendance at religious services and involvement in church youth groups. Research indicates that belief

Setting	Guiding Principle & Action Steps
(Faith)	in religion and participation in religious activities tend to divert youths away from high-risk behaviors, more toward participation in sports and exercise, and toward more positive relationships with their parents.

- Choose a faith setting where your family feels comfortable and get involved in its activities. Faith experiences can assume considerable significance in the psychological and social development of children.

- Do some research before you choose a faith setting. Not all denominations and churches offer the same degree of support, and some affiliations can be potentially destructive. If a church that you have chosen proves to be unsupportive, find another one.

8. Work

Principle:
Employment during the teenage years has become a norm in American society. By their senior year, 80 percent of adolescents will be employed part-time. Working while in school may contribute to students' academic development. Jobs often help adolescents become personally, interpersonally, and socially more mature.

Action Steps:

- Insist that some of your teenager's

Setting	Guiding Principle & Action Steps
(Work)	earnings be saved.
	■ Monitor your child's work time. Working over 20 hours-per-week can be detrimental, probably because long work hours can lead to an increase in unstructured time.
	■ Do not allow work to displace time for important developmental activities, such as schoolwork, co-curricular activities, and hobbies.
	■ Do not allow long work hours to diminish time spent on important health maintenance activities (nutrition, sleep, exercise, stress-reducing down time).
	■ Visit your child's work setting to know first-hand its attributes and get to know your child's supervisor. Work-related adults can be influential mentors for a child. Many employers are quite attuned to the challenges that working students confront and do show concern and support for their youthful employees' success in school.
9. Recreation and Leisure	*Principle*: With the absence of formal apprenticeship structures during adolescence, recreational and leisure activities can provide experiences that help adolescents transition to adulthood, that is, from full-time education to

Setting	Guiding Principle & Action Steps
(Recreation and Leisure)	employment. Some benefits of these types of activities can be fairly subtle – parents must be perceptive.

Action Steps:

- Involve your child in a youth organization which provides substantial learning and practice opportunities with adults and older youths who serve as teachers and models.

- Specifically, you might want to involve your child in an arts activity. Studies show that youths who participate in arts-based organizations have opportunities to practice thinking and talking as adults. When students worked in arts activities at least three hours-a-day, three days-a-week, for one full year, they demonstrated improved academics and ability to plan for the future for themselves. Also, during free time, adolescents who are involved in arts tend to find ways to use time for specific learning goals.

- Limit the time that teenagers spend in unstructured activities with peers on weekend evenings. Unstructured time is associated with higher substance abuse.

- Provide safe, supervised opportunities for teenagers to have the

Setting	Guiding Principle & Action Steps
(Recreation and Leisure)	excitement and emotional climax of weekend evenings. For teenagers, there must be a balance between adult supervision and independence.
10. Sports	***Principle:*** Participation in sports presents opportunities to learn lessons that shape character traits, such as perseverance, fortitude, dedication, a strong work ethic, commitment, and responsibility. ***Action Steps:*** ■ Encourage children to try different sports until they find a favorite. Youths will naturally tend to stick with sports that mesh more with their natural abilities. ■ Provide plenty of support and encouragement for young athletes. Positive parental support is directly associated with the child's greater enjoyment. ■ If possible, encourage youths to get engaged in sports before adolescence; it may help teenagers avoid some of the normal distractions of adolescence. Sometimes "normal" adolescence leads to preoccupations with music, cars, spending money, and opposite-gender relationships.

Setting	Guiding Principle & Action Steps
(Sports)	■ Encourage other kinds of activities, if your child is not athletic. When students succeed in an activity, they are more likely to be integrated into a positive social network. The development of an admired skill seems to be important in adolescence. Sports is one way to gain this status, but involvement in other activities, such as the performing arts, also provides successful avenues to acceptance in school.

About the Author

RICHARD L. MUNGER HAS SPENT 25 YEARS AS AN administrator in public community mental health. He is a practicing child psychologist in Asheville, North Carolina, and formerly Associate Professor of Psychiatry, John A. Burns School of Medicine, University of Hawaii. He received his Ph.D in Educational Psychology from the University of Michigan.

INDEX

A

abuse, 6-7

  drug/alcohol, 77, 79, 84, 111-112, 122-124, 127, 141-142, 153, 156, 162, 174, 219, 234, 237, 240, 272

achievement, 26-27, 262-263

activation energy, 26, 29

activities, x, 34, 37, 44, 115

  after-school, 78, 233, 243-244, 247, 271-272

  arranging, 223-225

    barriers to, 73, 225-227, 270

    professional involvement in, 231-242

      changing specific behaviors, 239-241

  community, 17, 28, 31, 218

  daily, 8, 237-238, 254

  co-curricular/extracurricular, 20, 27, 31-32, 64-68, 72, 80, 83, 141

  family, 21, 37, 39

  flow, 26, 33-34, 255

  leisure/recreational, 28, 68, 102, 114, 125, 239, 245

  skill-building, 90

  structured, 14-15, 16, 79

  mismatched, 239-240

  over-scheduling, x, 245, 246

  monitoring, 151-154, 233, 272

  physical, xii, 53, 78, 90, 100, 199-207

    modeling, 248

    routine, 205

    starting a, 205

  profiles of, 216-222

    adolescent, 217

  religious, 8, 20, 254

  service-learning, 68-71, 73, 125, 214, 263, 270-271

  structured/supervised, 31-32, 152, 153, 162, 189, 214, 217, 222, 228, 243-244, 246, 255

  unstructured/unsupervised, 112, 141, 152, 217, 222

  voluntary, 31-32

adventure experiences

  Outward Bound, 180

affection, 108, 124

after-school, 77-86

activities, 78, 233, 243-244, 247, 271-272

settings, xi, 20, 34, 77-86, 209, 212, 271-272

   unsupervised, 6-7

supervised, 77, 79, 80, 81, 83, 246, 271, 272

unsupervised/self-care, 77, 81-82, 112, 271

   consequences of, 79

   location of, 82

American Academy of Pediatrics, 91, 101, 102, 171, 260, 273

American Psychological Association, 200

American Psychologist, 3

Anderson, Craig, 97

apprenticeships, 138, 149, 161, 277-278

Armstrong, Kevin, 179

arts, 15, 16, 27, 114, 150, 153, 182, 196, 215, 234, 245, 249, 261-263, 278

   youth groups, 157-161

Attention Deficit Hyperactivity Disorder (ADHD), 52, 62-63, 111, 179, 222-223

   effect of nature on, 52

Awakening to Nature, 53

B

Bandura, Albert, 30, 174-175

Barker, Roger, 1-2, 5, 17, 63, 254

Bartko, Todd, 216

bedtime routines, 39, 42, 45, 232, 248, 267

behavior

   agentic, 154

   antisocial, 79-80, 83, 153

   prosocial, 93, 127

behavioral activation system (BAS), 30

Belle, Deborah, 79

Benson, Peter, 211, 214-215, 219-220

Berger, Elizabeth, 260-261

Bess, Stacey, 175-176

Biophilia Hypothesis, 52

(The) Blank Slate: The Modern Denial of Human Nature, 257

books/reading, 90-92, 113-114, 150, 161, 216-217, 238

Booth, Frank, 202

Boston University, 79

brain

   development, 89, 91, 100-101, 203, 274

   glial cells, 256

   teenagers, 257

Browne, Beverly, 189

C

Cairns, Robert and Beverly, 178-179, 262

Calvert, Sandra, 99

Carnegie Council on Adolescent Development, 236

Carver, Craig, 128

celebrations, 39, 44-45, 248

Center for Early Adolescence, 227

Center for Online and Internet Addiction, 95

Centers for Disease Control and Prevention, 202

Children's Digital Media Center, 99

Children's Domain, 51

Children's Nutrition Research Center, 178

Claremont Graduate University, 8

Clark, Reginald, 13, 67-68

clubs, 14, 21, 150, 152-155, 215-217, 219, 223-224, 232, 235-236

    Adolescent Creative Theater (ACT), 152

    Boys/Girls Scouts, 44, 79, 152, 154-155, 223, 245

        benefits of, 154

        stance on homosexuality, 155

    Little League, 129, 155, 174, 188, 191

    New Scenes, 152

    Odyssey of the Mind, 152

commitment, 26, 108, 168, 181

community

    activities, 17-28, 31, 218

    organizations, 71, 157, 160, 224, 232, 236-237

    service, 68-71, 73, 161, 215, 270-271

    setting, 130

competence, ix, 3, 27, 79, 81, 143, 214, 235, 249

    development of, 8, 177

    personal, 110

    social, 160, 220

        promoting, 153-155

computers, 14, 88-89, 93-96, 102, 155, 260, 273-274

    chat rooms, 79, 95

        Multi-User Domains (MUDs), 99

    e-mail, 101

    instruction, 93-94

    Internet activity, 79, 87-88, 93-96, 101-102, 155, 248

        monitoring, 95-96, 102

    instant messaging, 87-88, 102

Conroy, Pat, 181

Cook, Charles, 53

Cooper, Harris, 80

Corey, Julie, 53-55

Cornell University, 260

Cronkite, Walter, 6

Csikszentmihalyi, Mihaly, x, 8, 15-17, 25-26, 29-30, 33-34, 109-111, 114-115, 180-181, 205, 237-238, 257-258

D

Department of Labor, 137-138

depression, 80, 122, 142, 177, 216, 238-239

developmental assets, 211-215, 219, 220

deVries, Marten, 237-238

discipline, 26, 65

    self-, 140, 155, 161, 175-176, 255-256

Dr. Dave's Cyberhood, 96

Doherty, William, 39, 43, 244, 246

Doll, Beth, 108

Dornbusch, Stanford, 141

Drabman, Ronald, 179

E

Einstein, Albert, 256

Elkind, David, 91, 245

Emory, Olga Beattie, 257-258

employment, 5, 21, 80, 127, 139, 149, 216-217, 235, 248, 255

    effect on school performance, 140-143

    effects on teenagers, 142-144, 263

    monitoring, 144, 162, 277

    reasons for, 139-140

    schedules, 140-142, 144, 263

    setting, ix, 35, 137-147, 210, 213, 234, 276-277

environmental press, 5-6

Evert, Chris, 170

exercise, xii, 123, 132, 197, 199-207, 234, 248, 276, 277

    benefits of, 201-202

    girls and, 199, 204-205

(The) Experience of Psychopathology: Investigating Mental Disorders in their Natural Setting, 237-238

Experience Sampling Method (ESM), 25-26, 237-238

F

Fair Play, 193

family, 5, 253

    activities, 21, 37, 39

    interactions, 11, 37, 39

    meals, 21, 39, 39-41, 45, 232, 238, 244, 249, 267

    re-entry to, 43

    rituals, 39, 41, 248, 248, 267

    time, 243-244

Faris, Robert, 112-123

Farley, Frank, 240

feedback, 25, 81, 115

Fegley, Suzanne, 141

flow, xi, 17, 22, 150

    activities, 26, 33-34, 255

    biological basis for, 29-30

    finding, 226-228

    importance of, 25-36

    in hobbies, 26

    in music, 25

    in sports, 25, 26-27, 158-159, 161, 180-181

    in television watching, 26

    triggering, 205, 255

Francis, Sally, 189

Frazer, Mark, 5

French, Davina, 150

Fritsch, Melissa, 125

Frontier House, 246

G

Gallagher, Winifred, 29

Gallup Youth Survey, 121-22, 167

Garbarino, James, 6

Gardner, Howard, 60

Gavin, James, 240

Georgetown University, 99

Giamatti, Bart, 14-15

Giordano, Peggy, 110

Gitlin, Todd, 87-88

Glen, Karen, 246

goals, 15, 81, 255, 264

    developing, 115, 128, 154, 175, 191-193, 258, 262

    group, 188

    skill-building, 79

Godby, Geoffrey, 20

gratification, 91

    delaying, 33, 52, 220-222

Greenberger, Ellen, 139

Grossman, David, 96

Gump, Paul, 63

Gurian, Michael, 154

H

habits, 11, 21, 175

Hahn, Kurt, 180

Hanger, Howard, 154, 158-159

Harris, Judith Rich, 108-109

Harvard University, 174, 188

Hattie, John, 180

Hays, Kate, 199-200

Healy, Jean, 100-101

Heath, Shirley Brice, 157, 160, 261-262

Henggeler, Scott, 43

hobbies, 13-14, 16-17, 91-92, 114, 142, 144, 150, 153, 215, 234, 236, 277

    flow experienced from, 26

Hofferth, Sandra, 245

homework, 14, 16-17, 39, 41-42, 45, 80, 82, 91, 112, 140, 142, 144, 194, 214-215, 217, 232, 273, 277

honesty, 4, 176

Huesmann, L. Rowell, 97

Hummer, Robert, 129-132

(The) Hurried Child, 245

I

independence, 44, 162, 236-237

initiative, 14-15, 30-32, 220-221

(The) Intentional Family, 39

intervention, 231, 250

    effective, 43, 236, 240

    for mentally-ill children, 235

Institute of Medicine, 200

Iowa State University, 97

J

Jackson, Susan, 30, 33-34, 180-181, 205

Jeziorski, Ronald, 168

Johnson, Magic, 169

Jones, Gerald, 97

Junior Player Development (JPD) Program, 193-195

K

Kaiser Family Foundation, 40, 98-99

Kaplan, Rachel and Stephen, 51, 52-53

Kid's Activity Pyramid, 200

(The) Kid's Guide to Service Projects, 71

Killing Monsters, 97

Kindlon, Dan, 25, 33

Kleiber, Douglas, 42, 171, 190, 237

Kulik, James, 93-94

L

La Greca, Annette, 111

Lancaster, Scott, 193-195

language

    competence, 160-161

    development, 89, 91, 262, 274

    of book, xii-xiii

Larson, Reed, x, 31-32, 42, 98, 109, 114-115, 153-154, 171, 180, 190, 220, 222, 237, 247-248, 257-258

Lewis, Barbara, 71

Lipsitz, Joan, 225

Little Girls in Pretty Boxes, 170

M

Mahoney, Joseph, 79

Massachusetts Institute of Technology, 257

materialism, 69, 88, 92, 139-140, 143, 169, 182, 279

McHale, Susan, 113

McLaughlin, Milbrey, 157, 261-262

Meals on Wheels Program, 71

media (electronic), x, 87-106, 149, 248

   activities, 17, 150

   and children, 88-89, 100-101, 260-261

      diary, 101

   nature of, 89, 154

   setting, xi, 34, 87-106, 107, 210, 212, 233, 273-274

Media Unlimited, 87-88

Medical University of South Carolina, 43

Medrich, Elliot, 49-50, 225

Megaskills, 220, 221

mentors, 7, 72, 81, 130, 144, 154, 235, 270-271

Minow, Newton, 93

Mischel, Walter, 221

monitoring, 8, 239

   activities, 151-154, 233, 272

   children's whereabouts, 39, 43, 82, 83, 215, 275

      low, 82

   computer use, 95-96, 144, 162, 277

peers, 112

television watching, 96, 102, 273

Moore, Robin, 51

morality, 155

   development, 128, 154

   directives, 130

   tradition, 128

Morgan, Jack, 138

Mortimer, Jeyland, 142

motivation, ix, 3, 63, 168, 180, 190, 221, 249, 250-251, 255, 270

   process of, 30

   self-, 15

multi-tasking, 100

multiple intelligences, 60

music, 4, 13, 28, 29, 60, 78-79, 114, 125, 157, 219, 223, 243, 245-246, 257, 279

   flow experienced in, 25

   organizations, 151, 270

   teenagers and, 97-98, 101, 150, 169, 182, 238, 259

   videos, 98

My Losing Season, 181

N

National Alliance for Youth Sports, 192

National Association of Sports Officials, 174

National Football League (NFL) Youth Football Development Program, 193-195

National Girls and Women in Sports Day, 176

National Longitudinal Study of Adolescent Health, 11

National Science Foundation, 99

National Study of Youth and Religion, 8, 127-129

National TV-Turnoff Week, 102, 273

nature, 52, 245

  and ADHD, 52

  nearby, 52-53

  versus nurture, 256-258

neighborhood

  new, 5

  settings, xi, 3, 34, 49-57, 209, 211-212, 268

    quality of, 49-50, 215, 232

Neisser, Ulric, 260

New England Journal of Medicine, 199

Newberger, Eli, 188, 189, 193, 261, 262

Northwestern University, 259

(The) Nurture Assumption: Why Children Turn Out the Way They Do; Parents Matter Less Than You Think and Peers Matter More, 108-109

O

One Boy's Day, 2

Oregon State University, 189

The Other Parent, 88-89

P

Parseghian, Ara, 190-191

passion, 15-17

Passmore, Anne, 150

Pediatrics, 202

Peebles, Cynthia, 138

peer(s), 37, 107, 249, 253, 255-256, 258, 274

  fitting in with, 110, 169, 179, 187, 280

  groups, 64, 109-111, 150, 262

  influence, 111

    negative, 111-113

  interaction, 42, 79-80

  monitoring, 112

  networks, 110

  pressure, 6, 116, 275

  relationships, 50, 72, 130, 151, 169-170, 216, 232, 270

    formal, 50

    supportive, 110

Pennsylvania State University, 113

perseverance, 193-195, 221, 279

Pettit, Gregory, 82

physical education, xii, 197, 202-206

Pierce, Kim, 80

Ping, Wu, 92

Pinker, Steven, 257

Pipher, Mary, 5

play, 50-51, 245

  group, 50, 108

  in a natural setting, 52 , 245

  spontaneous, 50, 53, 100, 232

Pollack, William, 174

Positive Coaching Alliance, 192

Postman, Neil, 260

praise, 81

President's Council on Physical Fitness and Sports, 178

President's Physical Fitness Program, 202

principle of progressive conformity, 2

priorities, 92, 204

private speech, 91

Protecting Adolescents from Harm, 59

Putting Family First, 247

R

radio, 88, 91

Raymore, Leslie, 149-150

Reavill, 168

reciprocity, 108

recreation/leisure, 14-15, 21, 78, 150-151

  achievement leisure, 150, 151

  activities, 28, 68, 102, 114, 125, 239, 245

    skill-building, 90

    structured, 14-15, 16, 79

  setting, xi, 20, 35, 149-165, 197, 210, 213, 234, 277-279

  social leisure, 151, 245

  structured, 151-152

  time-out leisure, 150, 151

Regnerus, Mark, 125

relationships

  intimate, 108

  online, 94-96

  opposite-gender, 108, 110-111, 116, 156-157, 169, 182, 275, 279

  peer, 50, 72, 130, 151, 169-170, 216, 232, 270

    -student, 61, 215

  same-gender, 108

  social, 63, 65, 94, 107-108, 113, 128

  teacher-student, 59-60

  with adults, 72, 80-81, 83, 130, 131, 144, 215, 219, 270-271

  with parents, 132, 142, 276

religion, 8, 13, 121-134, 215, 216, 245, 253, 255

benefits of, 121-124, 128-132

experiences, 130

parents and, 8, 127-128

setting, xi, 4, 121-135, 210, 213, 233, 275-276

youth groups, 124-126, 132, 151, 154, 245, 249, 263, 275-276

respect, 41, 70, 170

responsibility, 4, 28, 39, 41, 45, 82, 108, 168, 221, 225, 279

promoting, 140, 181, 193-194

Restak, Richard, 257

Rich, Dorothy, 220-222

Roberts, Glyn, 191-192

Robinson, John, 20

role models, 110, 130, 174-175, 178, 204, 219

Rosemond, John, 92, 243, 244

Ruscoe, Gordon, 138, 140-150

S

sacrifice, 168, 191

safety, 50, 79, 83, 123, 162, 219, 227, 236

Sandberg, John, 245

Sanders, Summer, 169, 172-173, 250-251

scaffolding, 29, 226, 235

Scanlan, Tara, 168

school

alternative, 62, 72, 223, 269

attendance, 81

charter, 62, 72, 269

college preparatory, 62

community, 62

connectedness, 59, 64, 72, 127, 217

curriculum, 21, 69, 72, 269

open classroom, 223

physical education, 197, 202-206

free, 62, 225

-home linkage, 59, 61, 215, 269-270

instructional methods, 60-61

gender-specific, 60-61

new, 5

overmanned, 63

pluralistic, 61

private, 62

setting, xi, 3, 34, 59-76, 209, 212, 253, 269-271

sizing, 63

-student match, 61-63

success, 67-68

-to-work transition, 138-139

traditional, 222-223

vocational training, 62

work-study programs, 140

Scott, Dave, 192

Search Institute in Minneapolis, 211

Sedentary Death Syndrome, 202

selection effects, 141

self-confidence, 67, 177, 180, 191, 221, 239, 250-251

self-control, 179-180, 193, 221

self-esteem, 30, 109-110, 128, 168, 177, 191, 201, 239

self-image, 110, 124, 157, 169, 177, 178, 187

self-reflection, 81, 115, 150, 160

self-reporting, 26, 114, 124

self-worth, 168, 173

Selye, Hans, 201

Serling, Rod, 244

service learning
  activities, 68-71, 73, 125, 214, 263, 270-271
  settings, xi, 34, 59-76, 209, 262, 269-271

setting/environment, 2, 29
  after-school, xi, 20, 34, 77-86, 209, 212, 271-272
    unsupervised, 6-7
  children, 2
  co-curricular, xi, 34, 59-76, 142, 144, 149, 209, 258, 269-271
    and school success, 67-68, 160
  electronic, xi, 34, 87-107, 210, 212, 233, 273-274

faith, xi, 4, 121-135, 210, 213, 233, 275-276

friends, xi, 34-35, 107-119, 210, 211, 213, 233, 275

home, xi, 3, 34, 37-48, 209, 211-212, 241, 253, 267-268

modification, x, 5, 231, 250, 263

natural, 51-52

neighborhood, xi, 3, 34, 49-57, 209, 211, 212, 268

pathways, 1-10
  negative, 7
  positive, 7

recreational/leisure, xi, 20, 35, 149-165, 197, 210, 213, 234, 277-279

restorative, 51-52

school, xi, 3, 34, 59-76, 209, 212, 253, 269-271

service-learning, xi, 34, 59-76, 209, 262, 269-271

sports, xi, 35, 167-186, 210, 213, 234, 253, 279-280

supportive, 4-6, 132

work, xi, 35, 137-147, 210, 213, 234, 276-277

sex, 77, 79, 84, 88, 90, 110, 112, 122, 127, 169, 174, 177

sibling care-taking, 83

skills,
  attentional, 52

developing, 33-34, 81, 193-195

leadership, 70-71, 130, 193, 240

literary, 91

social, 80, 94, 111

sleep, 42, 90, 100, 101, 144, 277

Smith, Christian, 112-123, 125, 128, 129

Smith, Ronald, 191

Smoll, Frank, 191

socialization, 21, 101, 108-109, 176, 272

sports, 3-4, 7, 13, 14, 17, 21, 28, 33, 40, 50, 64, 68, 78, 79, 92, 113, 114, 123, 132, 141, 149, 199, 200, 216, 232, 238, 243, 257, 276

aggressiveness in, 187-188

benefits of, 168-169, 178-182, 187-188, 190-196, 201-202, 204-205, 217, 219, 224, 239-240, 249, 261-263

coaches, 175-176, 224

competitive nature of, 190, 193, 195, 240, 259

enthusiasm for, promoting, 187-198

flow experienced from, 25-27, 158-159, 161, 180-181

girls and, 167, 176-178

informal, 188-189

martial arts, 179-180, 222-223, 244

negative effects of, xii, 187-

190, 259, 261-263

organized, 151, 155, 169-170, 189, 222, 236, 244-246, 270

parental involvement in, 171-175, 196-197

setting, xi, 35, 167-186, 210, 213, 234, 253, 279-280

specialization, 170-171

winning in, 188, 192, 195

sportsmanship, 193, 221

Standards for Youth Sports, 192

Stanford University, 157, 174-175

Stattin, Hakan, 79

Steinberg, Laurence, 139, 141

stereotyping, 176-177

Steyer, James, 88-89

stress, 40, 51, 130, 143, 200-201, 245

emotional, 171

reduction, 100, 144, 200-201, 241, 277

work, 141, 142

suicide, 122, 177

T

talented youths, 15-17, 31, 110-111, 115

developing, 31, 254-255

lifestyles of, 16

Teen Research Unlimited, 139

telephones, 41, 88, 214, 248

television, 13, 20-21, 34, 37-39, 41, 45, 53, 78-80, 87-88, 102, 113-114, 152, 180, 200, 216, 226, 234, 238, 245, 248, 255, 273

  educational, 94

  effect on children's development, 89-93, 260

  flow experienced from, 26

  monitoring, 96, 102, 273

  removing, 92, 260-261

  teenagers and, 98-99, 150

  total television homes, 91

Thomas, Darwin, 128

time, 37

  diary, 17-19, 20

  down, 80, 83, 89, 142, 144, 215, 246, 271, 277

  free, 13, 20, 33, 43, 113, 156, 247

    family, 243-244

  managing, 140, 169, 238, 245

  use, 9, 25, 210, 225, 232, 239

    adolescents, 37, 43, 156-157, 238, 257

    Americans, 20, 21

    balance, 13, 243-251

      finding, 248-251

    chores, 13, 17, 38-39, 41, 45, 78, 82, 114, 194, 245,

    health-maintenance, 13, 17, 90, 100, 114, 142, 144, 219,

    220, 277

    implication of, 21-22

    Japanese, 21, 43

    Korea, 21, 43

    monitoring, 14-15, 17-21

    patterns of, 11-23

    rhythms, 37-39

Time for Life: The Surprising Ways Americans Use Their Time, 20

Title IX, 178

transportation, 73, 116, 227, 235, 236, 270, 274

Twilight Zone, 244

Type T personalities, 240

U

United States Department of Education, 157

United States Surgeon General, 200

University of California, 49

  UCLA, 168

University of Kansas, 1, 63

University of Louisville, 138

University of Miami, 111

University of Michigan, 51, 92-94, 97, 216, 245

University of Minnesota, 142

University of Missouri, 80, 202

University of Montreal, 201

University of Nebraska, 108

University of North Carolina, 4-5, 51, 125, 128, 178-179, 262

University of Oregon, 168

University of Texas, 129, 132

University of Washington, 191

V

videogames, 79, 88, 91

   educational, 97

   monitoring, 96, 97

   violence in, 89, 93, 96-97

volunteering, 70, 125-127, 129, 216-217

W

WNET, 246

Walsh, David, 91, 96

Wasserstein, Shari, 111

Weiss, Maureen, 168

Wilson, Susan, 174, 175

Woods, Tiger, 170

Y

youth groups, 278

   arts-based, 157-161

   community-based, 157, 258

   religious, 124-126, 132, 151, 154, 245, 249, 263, 275-276

Youth Safety Survey, 95

Youth Service America, 71

Z

Zimmerman, Jean, 168